9/17⟩
2/2⟩ I X 3/21/16 C201
6/23

Duncan J. D. Smith

ONLY IN
HAMBURG

A Guide to Unique Locations,
Hidden Corners and Unusual Objects

Photographs by
Duncan J. D. Smith

The
Urban
Explorer

I dedicate this book with love and thanks to Roswitha,
without whom the following pages could not have been written,
also to the people of Hamburg, who without exception
were friendly and helpful during my research in the city

ABOVE: The statue of Charlemagne, the founder of Hamburg, stands on Michaelisstrasse
(see no. 1)

Page 2: A traditional fishing boat at the Museumshafen Övelgönne with the Waltershof container
terminal beyond (see no. 50)

Contents

Southern Suburbs:

Bergedorf (inc. Bergedorf, Billwerder, Kirchwerder, Lohbrügge)
Harburg (inc. Altenwerder, Cranz, Neuenfelde, Neugraben-Fischbek)

Northwest Suburbs:

Altona (inc. Altona-Altstadt, Altona-Nord, Bahrenfeld, Blankenese,
Gross Flottbek, Nienstedten, Othmarschen, Ottensen, Sternschanze)
Eimsbüttel (inc. Harvestehude, Rotherbaum, Stellingen)

Northeast Suburbs:

Hamburg-Nord (inc. Barmbek-Nord, Eppendorf, Hoheluft-Ost, Ohlsdorf, Uhlenhorst, Winterhude)

Wandsbeck (inc. Jenfeld, Poppenbüttel, Volksdorf, Wellingsbüttel)

Appendices

Introduction

> "There is a great contrast between the silent town of Hannover, the quiet and almost deserted sands of Lüneburg, and the crowds, the activity, and the bustle of Hamburg … they appear extraordinary to an inhabitant of Hannover, when he visits Hamburg for the first time."
>
> Travels in the North of Germany, Thomas Hodgskin (1820)

Straddling the mighty River Elbe, and its tributaries the Alster and the Bille, Hamburg is Germany's greenest and second-largest city. It is also the most populous non-capital city in the European Union – and one of its best kept secrets. Hamburg's official name is the Free and Hanseatic City of Hamburg *(Freie und Hansestadt Hamburg)*, which makes reference to it having been a Free Imperial City under the Holy Roman Empire of Barbarossa (1155–1190)*, and a member of the Hanseatic League during the Late Middle Ages. Both helped transform Hamburg into one of the most important ports in northern Europe, a designation it retains to this day despite having been damaged severely by flood, fire and war.

Hamburg's riverine geography and maritime history is all pervading, prompting many of the recommendations proffered by today's mainstream guidebooks. The undemanding visitor thus gains easy access to a broad array of museums, galleries, restaurants, and noteworthy buildings, reflecting the history of the city from the time of its founding under Charlemagne (Charles the Great), King of the Franks (742–814), up to the present day as one of the sixteen member states *(Bundesländer)* of the Federal Republic of Germany. However, there is far more to Hamburg than meets the eye, and this guidebook has been written for independent travellers wishing to discover something more of the place for themselves. It only takes a few minutes of planning, and a glance at a good street map**, to escape the crowds and discover a very different Hamburg.

Based on personal experience walking through the city's seven boroughs *(Stadtbezirke)* the author points the explorer in a new and unusual direction. This is the Hamburg of prehistoric remains and little-known gardens; abandoned ice cellars and converted factories; quirky museums and intriguing places of worship; Oriental tea houses and unusual shops; hidden lighthouses and strange ships; not to mention a Cold War-era civilian shelter and the remains of an abandoned pneumatic postal system, both of which can now be visited. Hamburg is also a city with a turbulent past, its poignant Jewish history and numerous memorials to the victims of Nazi aggression still bearing grim witness to terrible times.

As might be expected, many of these unusual historic locations are located in Hamburg's former walled town (Altstadt and Neustadt), which lies either side of the Alster Canal, at the heart of Hamburg-Mitte; it was here, where the Alster joins the Elbe, that the history of Hamburg began. This central borough stretches the full width of the city and includes leafy St. Georg, notorious St. Pauli, and the rapidly developing HafenCity. South of the Elbe, Hamburg-Mitte incorporates fascinating dockland areas such as Finkenwerder, Rothenburgsort, and Wilhelmsburg.

A similar number of locations, however, lie *outside* these well-trodden areas, especially north of the Elbe, in the affluent boroughs of Altona and Eimsbüttel to the northwest, and the working class boroughs of Hamburg-Nord and Wandsbek to the northeast. Further hidden corners await discovery in the predominantly rural southern boroughs of Harburg and Bergedorf.

Using Hamburg's extensive transport network of regional trains *(Regionalbahn)*, underground and elevated trains *(U-Bahn/Hochbahn)*, suburban trains *(S-Bahn)*, buses *(MetroBus/Autobus)*, and harbour and river ferries *(Hafen- und Elbefähre)*, the explorer can quickly reach all the locations described – and that's without detracting whatsoever from the sense of personal discovery that each of these places has to offer. Indeed, directions have been kept to a minimum so as to leave the visitor free to find their own particular path. Whether searching for remnants of Charlemagne's Hammaburg, tracking down what's left of Hitler's U-Boat bases, visiting a Hindu temple in the suburbs, marvelling at how a ship can be put inside a bottle, or exploring Hamburg's North Sea outpost of Neuwerk, it is hoped that the explorer will experience a sense of having made the discovery for themselves.

Duncan J. D. Smith, Hamburg & Vienna

* The dates given after the names of Germany's various monarchs are the actual years they reigned for, whereas those given after important non-royal personalities relate to their birth and death.

** Most street maps of Hamburg cover the city centre and surroundings; the excellent Falk Stadtplan Extra covers all seven boroughs and shows rail, S-Bahn, U-Bahn and bus routes.

(Borough names are given beneath each chapter title, with district names in brackets. At the end of each chapter there is a selection of other locations within walking distance. An alphabetical list of opening times appears at the back of the book.)

Do these angular forms in Domplatz recall the embankments surrounding Charlemagne's Hammaburg?

1 The Mystery of the Hammaburg

Hamburg-Mitte (Altstadt), the archaeological remains in Domplatz
U1 Messberg, U3 Rathaus, Mönckebergstrasse; Bus 3, 4, 6
Rathausmarkt (Petrikirche)

In 1982 the mysterious remains of a ring-shaped earth embankment with an outer ditch were uncovered in Domplatz. Inexplicably both embankment and ditch were breached in two places rendering the site difficult to defend. Historians suggested that these enigmatic remains might be those of the Hammaburg, the fortress commissioned by Charlemagne (Charles the Great), King of the Franks (742–814) in 808 to prevent unwanted Slavic and Viking incursions into the region after his expulsion of the Saxons. Subsequent archaeological excavations, however, have failed to positively identify the site as such, and the location of the Hammaburg remains a mystery. (The word 'burg' means castle but the derivation of 'Hamma' is obscure, meaning perhaps 'forest' or 'water meadow'.)

So what exactly was found in Domplatz? The answer may lie in the history books. The story of Hamburg proper begins in 804AD, when Slavic Obotrites were awarded the marshy area between the Elbe and the Alster by Charlemagne for their assistance in expelling the Saxons, who had occupied the area since the fourth century. After forging a new alliance with pagan Denmark in 817 the Obotrites were themselves chased out of the area by the Franks. It was against this tumultuous backdrop that Archbishop Ansgar of Bremen (801–865) received the Hamburg region as his seat in 831, from Charlemagne's son and successor Louis the Pious (778–840). On the debris of the Obotrite settlement in Domplatz Ansgar constructed a monastery fort, from where he set about converting Saxony (present day Northern Germany) to Christianity. For his efforts he was dubbed the 'Apostle of the North', and in 847 Hamburg was united with Bremen as the bishopric of Hamburg-Bremen.

To discover how these early settlements might have appeared visit the Hamburg Museum (Museum für Hamburgische Geschichte) at Holstenwall 24 (Neustadt). A pair of fascinating scale models on the first floor suggest that the most likely reconstruction of the remains is as a so-called Saxon Ring Embankment, rising 3–4 metres high using material excavated from an outer trench. The embankment probably had a wooden palisade running around the top of it and it is calculated that the space inside would have measured around 35 metres across. Ceramic finds and remains of Late Saxon-style houses suggest an original construction date of the late eighth century AD. Large angular steel forms have recently been installed in Domplatz to give an impression of the former location and dimensions of these structures.

Despite being ransacked by Vikings in 845, by Slavic and Danish forces in 880, and by the Obotrites once again in 983, the missionary settlement in Domplatz was always rebuilt by the Christians. Increasingly important by virtue of its strategic location by the mid eleventh century the monastery fort had been joined by several other equally intriguing structures, each of which is depicted in the museum models. Most important was the stone-built Cathedral of St. Mary (Mariendom) of Archbishop Bezelin of Cologne (1035–1043), which can be seen rising above the remains of Ansgar's abandoned monastery fort. Although nothing remains on the ground to permit a reconstruction, the columns of the cathedral are recalled by a grid of illuminated white plastic squares installed today in the grass of Domplatz.

Bezelin was also responsible for a sturdy circular tower located immediately north of the cathedral, the foundations of which were unearthed in 1962 at Kreuslerstrasse 4, during the construction of a vicarage for the Church of St. Petri (St. Petri Kirche). Known as the Bischofsturm (Bishop's Tower) it has been suggested that the tower was the first element of a new stone circuit wall planned for the defence of the cathedral, the completion of which was halted by Bezelin's death. Considered the oldest surviving remains of a building in Hamburg, the shadowy 12th century ruins are visible from the street outside the St. Petri-Hof.

Before Bezelin's time the monastery fort was only protected by the timbered ramparts of Archbishop Unwan (1013–1029). His tenure was coloured by a longstanding power struggle with Bernard II, Duke of Saxony (1011–1059), the remains of whose own castle were identified in the south west corner of Rathausmarkt during the construction of the new town hall. Known as the Alsterburg the castle is clearly depicted on the riverbank in one of the museum models. Unwan eventually sued for peace in Northern Germany and in 1021 secured obedience to the archdiocese from the Obotrites as opposed to the Duke of Saxony.

One final structure is the so-called Neue Burg, a circular rampart discovered in the 1950s on a spit of land projecting into the Nikolai Fleet, which still carries the name today (it is now occupied by the ruined Nikolaikirche). It has been identified as a castle erected in 1061 by Bernard II's son, Duke Ordulf (1059–1072), and again it is depicted in the museum models.

This model in the Hamburg Museum (Museum für Hamburgische Geschichte) shows how Hamburg might have looked in the eighth century

In 1189, in return for supporting his Third Crusade, Holy Roman Emperor Frederick I (Barbarossa) (1155–1190) granted the town the status of an Imperial Free City, with customs-free access along the Lower Elbe into the North Sea. The new harbour town of Hamburg resulted, taking its name from the shadowy Hammaburg, which was eventually consigned to history.

Other places of interest nearby: 2, 11, 12, 14, 34

2 Controversy at the Afrika House

Hamburg-Mitte (Altstadt), the Afrikahaus at Grosse
Reichenstrasse 27
U1 Meßberg; Bus 4, 6 Brandstwiete

"The greatest, bravest and most self-sacrificing shipowner the cities of
the Hanseatic League have ever seen" is how Albert Ballin (1857–1918)
described fellow shipping magnate Adolph Woermann (1847–1910), on
the occasion of his death in 1910. Certainly Woermann was one of the
most powerful ship owners of his day but the term "self-sacrificing"
sits less easily with him in the light of modern public opinion over Germany's colonial past.

Adolph Woermann inherited the trading company of C. Woermann
from his father Carl in 1880. From 1882 Woermann's ships began sailing regularly from Hamburg to Nigeria and from 1884 to Cameroon,
where they exchanged gunpowder, weapons and Schnapps for palm
oil, rubber, cocoa and cotton. The trade became increasingly lucrative
despite the morality of supplying alcohol to West Africa being raised
several times in the Reichstag. Initially German business in Africa was
conducted through intermediaries but increasing competition from
England and France, and falling prices for African-grown products,
encouraged German businessmen to push inland and establish their
own plantations and depots. It was Woermann who convinced German
Chancellor Otto von Bismarck (1815–1898) of the necessity to protect
German interests by force, thereby establishing the first German colo-
nies on African soil (see no. 79).

In 1890 Woermann allowed his ships to be used to transport slaves
drafted for the construction of a railway from Togo to the Congo Free
State in Central Africa, where the colonial powers had been allowed to
trade freely since the Berlin Conference of 1884. Further controversy
followed in 1904, when the Herero people in German Southwest Africa
(today Namibia) rose up against their colonial rulers over the issue of
land ownership and slavery (see no. 79). At the time the Woermann
Line (Woermann-Linie) was the only shipping company providing a
regular troop transport service to the area. These troops, under their
commander Adrian Dietrich Lothar von Trotha (1848–1920), suppressed
the uprising killing approximately 65 000 Herero men, women and

children in the process. As if this were not bad enough, it was later discovered that Woermann had deliberately overcharged for the freight his ships carried during the conflict, thereby making him an illegal profit of millions of Reichsmarks at the expense of the German Empire.

It should be with such facts in mind that today's enlightened visitor approaches the Afrikahaus at Grosse Reichenstrasse 27 (Altstadt). The building was commissioned in 1899 by Adolph Woermann and his half-brother Eduard, to serve as headquarters for their increasingly successful company, which during the 1890s had also taken over control of the German East Africa Line (Deutsche Ost-Afrika Linie). It was built to a

A proud African warrior guards the entrance to the Afrikahaus on Grosse Reichenstrasse

design by the architect Martin Haller and is certainly one of the more impressive shipping line offices in Hamburg's so-called *Kontorhausviertel* (Office Quarter).

The façade of the Afrikahaus can easily be recognised by the diamond-shaped Woermann company flags rendered in coloured ceramic wall tiles. The arched main entrance contains a pair of ornate iron gates adorned with metal palm trees and the name 'Woermann', to one side of which stands the life-sized bronze sculpture of an African warrior (the so-called *Togo Negro*), cast in Dresden in 1901. Beyond is a courtyard, with a further entrance flanked this time by the sculptures of two huge elephants emerging from the bush. Above them are further African echoes in the form of a fragmentary mosaic depicting an ostrich and a monkey.

After both world wars the entire Woermann fleet was handed over to the Allies as reparations. Despite this the trading company of C. Woermann managed to survive, and still exists today as an import and ex-

A pair of elephants flank the portal leading to the offices of C. Woermann

port business dealing mainly in machine parts and steel. The offices of the company, together with those of several other unrelated businesses, lie beyond the elephant portal. Although out of bounds to the public it is possible to catch a glimpse of the stairwell, which is adorned with nostalgic photographs of old Woermann Line ships.

Central Hamburg contains numerous other shipping line offices, with architecture as imposing as the Afrikahaus but without the controversy. The Laeiszhof, for example, at Trostbrücke 1 was also designed by Martin Haller, this time for the shipping company of Ferdinand Laeisz. Their five-masted vessels traded in the lucrative nitrate and guano business with Chile. On the roof of the building can be seen the small sculpture of a poodle, placed there in honour of the curly-haired wife of Carl Laeisz, whose nickname was Poodle! The roof of the nearby Globushof is adorned rather more seriously with sculptures of sailing ships. Haller, who was partly responsible for Hamburg's Town Hall (Rathaus), also designed the Sloman House at Steinhöft 11, Germany's oldest shipping company still in operation (1791) (it boasts Hamburg's oldest paternoster elevator), as well as the Hapag-Lloyd headquarters at Ballindamm 25 (see no. 33).

Other places of interest nearby: 1, 3, 4, 11, 12, 14

3 The Red Brick King

Hamburg-Mitte (Altstadt), the Chilehaus at Fischertwiete 2
U1 Meßberg; Bus 4, 6 Brandstwiete

The term Brick Expressionism *(Backsteinexpressionismus)* is used to describe a specific variant of Expressionist architecture popular in the larger cities of Northern Germany and the Ruhr in the 1920s. Used in the main for large-scale public and industrial structures, brick is the main visible building material. Although the style developed contemporaneously with the pared-down New Objectivity *(Neuen Bauens)* of Bauhaus architecture, Expressionist architects did not entirely forego ornamentation. Conversely they used the rough surfaces, angular profiles and earthy hues of clinker bricks to enliven large, otherwise monotonous, façades and in doing so reflected the industrial dynamism of the period in which they worked.

One of the undisputed stars of Brick Expressionism was Johann Friedrich 'Fritz' Höger (1877–1949), an architect from Schleswig-Holstein, who was responsible for some outstanding examples of the style in Hamburg. An early work is the Klöpperhaus at Mönckebergstrasse 3 (Altstadt), which Höger designed as an office building *(Kontorhaus)* for the wool merchant Heinrich Adolf Klöpper (hence the sculptures of sheep worked into the façade). Built in 1912–1913 it is worth noting that Höger's original design for the building was neo-Baroque but that this was dramatically streamlined by Fritz Schumacher (1869–1947), the director of public works for Hamburg, who would himself become a strong proponent of Brick Expressionism (see nos. 20, 21, 23, 28 & 76).

Höger's greatest triumph in brick is undoubtedly his Chilehaus at Fischertwiete 2 (Altstadt), designed for Henry B. Sloman, a shipping magnate who made his fortune importing nitrates from Chile for use in the gunpowder industry. Unveiled in 1924 it was the first building to be erected in the so-called *Kontorhausviertel*, a quarter consisting of large company office buildings ranged around Burchardplatz (see no. 2). Ten storeys high with 2800 identical windows, the Chilehaus has one flat façade and another gently curving, the two culminating in an angular profile that resembles the prow of a huge ship. The 4.8 million bricks needed to construct the Chilehaus earned Höger the epithet of "Red Brick King". Although the building is not open to the public it is possible to peek inside the entrance portals, which contain stone tablets

on which are inscribed the names of the many companies subsequently based here.

Another of Höger's brick buildings stands alongside the Chilehaus. The Sprinkenhof at Burchardstrasse 6 is the largest office building in the *Kontorhausviertel* and was built in three phases between 1927 and 1943. Unlike the tapering footprint of the Chilehaus, the Sprinkenhof consists of a series of massive blocks, the façades of which are broken up by windows separated by terracotta motifs of commerce and industry, the whole resembling a gigantic fisherman's net.

A third example of Höger's Brick Expressionism is the Broschek-Haus on Grosse Bleichen (Neustadt),

Fritz Hoeger's magnificent Chilehaus resembles the prow of a ship

named after the printing firm that commissioned the building in 1927 (it now serves as a hotel). The façade of the building is marked by the intricate use of decorative brickwork in which are embedded hundreds of golden triangles, which shimmer in the sunlight. Unfortunately Höger's intention of creating the illusion of a ship at sea is lost on most passers-by because the building's sail-like steeple was never built.

There are many other less well known *Kontorhäuser* in Hamburg including one at Stubbenhuk 10 (Neustadt), built for the Getreideheber-Gesellschaft (Grain Elevator Association). As well as an ornate Expressionist brick façade the building (which is not open to the public) has a wonderful stained glass window over the main doorway, depicting a busy dockland scene including several grain elevators in action.

Other places of interest nearby: 1, 2, 4, 6, 7

Sheltering from the Cold war

Hamburg-Mitte (St. Georg), the Cold War civilian shelter beneath Steintorwall
S1, S3, S21 Hauptbahnhof; U1, U2, U3, U4 Hauptbahnhof

The use of the term 'Cold War' to describe post-war tensions between the United States and the Soviet Union was first coined by the American financier and presidential economic advisor Bernard Baruch (1870–1965), during a congressional debate in April 1947. The phrase is now widely used to describe the period of conflict, tension and competition between the two superpowers and their allies from the mid-1940s until the early 1990s.

The origins of the conflict and the reasons for the rapid unravelling of wartime alliances against Nazi Germany have long been a matter for discussion. The most likely cause was a plethora of conflicting political and commercial interests over how a post-war Europe should look, compounded by paranoia and misunderstandings on both sides. Fortunately, the Cold War never escalated into a global conflict: in reality it was played out by means of proxy wars, military coalitions, espionage, propaganda, and a nuclear arms race. The stockpiling of deliverable weapons on both sides ultimately proved enough to deter direct military engagement between the two superpowers.

Whilst the tensions and paranoias of the times were reflected most acutely in Berlin, especially after the city was abruptly divided in 1961, other German cities were also made ready for a possible nuclear conflict. The most tangible manifestation of this was the construction of radiation-proof civilian protection shelters *(Atomschutzbunker)*, although the fact that they could only ever hold a small percentage of the population suggests that their provision was as much for propaganda as for practical reasons.

For a glimpse into this rarely-seen world it is highly recommended to take a tour with the Hamburg Underworlds Association (Hamburger Unterwelten e.V.), on one of their occasional visits to a Cold War-era shelter (Tiefbunker Steintorwall) that lies hidden beneath Steintorwall, alongside Hamburg's main railway station (Hamburger Hauptbahnhof). Like contemporary shelters elsewhere in Hamburg (for example beneath Hachmannplatz on the opposite side of the railway station, which can be visited on tours made by the Under Hamburg Association (unter-hamburg e.V.)) it was originally constructed during

The Steintorwall civilian shelter beneath the main railway station is protected by hydraulically-operated steel doors

the Second World War, and then modified later for use as a radiation-proof shelter (see no. 5).

Completed in 1944 the Steintorwall shelter was one of the biggest Second World War shelters in Hamburg, stretching down three storeys and with space for 2460 people. The steel-reinforced concrete walls are 3.75 metres thick. Whilst the railway station above was very badly damaged during the war and later re-built, the shelter remained intact. To destroy it was deemed too difficult because of its proximity to the station, and instead it was secured and forgotten about.

Not until 1965, with the deepening of the Cold War, was the shelter opened up again and modernised. Radiation-proof doors were installed, as was a new diesel engine to power the ventilation system, and bunk beds for 2702 persons. In 1969 the new shelter was ready and handed over to the local authorities for use in an emergency. Such shelters were provisioned so as to keep their occupants alive for a maximum of fourteen days after which it was every man for himself. Despite being mothballed following the end of the Cold War the Steintorwall shelter has been maintained in full-working order ever since.

Roughly contemporary with the Steintorwall Cold War shelter is the former Wedel Auxiliary Hospital (Hilfskrankenhaus Wedel) in Schleswig-Holstein, seventeen kilometres west of Hamburg. The construction of auxiliary hospitals throughout West Germany specifically to treat victims of nuclear war began in the 1950s, and accelerated following the erection of the Berlin Wall and the Cuban Missile Crisis in the early 1960s. Whilst most contained only basic facilities and medical stores, some of these hospitals, such as the one in Wedel, incorporated their own subterranean shelter, too. The former hospital can be visited today courtesy of the Hamburg Underworlds Association.

Other places of interest nearby: 1, 2, 3

5   Bunkerworld

Hamburg-Mitte (Hamm), a tour of Second World War
civilian air raid shelters finishing at the Bunkermuseum
at Wichernsweg 16
U2, U4 Rauhes Haus; Bus 116 Rauhes Haus

The first Allied air raid on Hamburg during the Second World War took
place on the evening of 10th September 1939, when ten aircraft of the
Royal Air Force dropped propaganda leaflets over the city. It was a very
different scenario just over a year later when in November 1940 British
Bomber Command sent two hundred aircraft to target the city's important shipyards. The commencement of the aerial war on Nazi Germany
– over 180 air raids would be made on Hamburg alone – prompted a
crash air raid shelter-building programme in an effort to protect the
civilian population. Requiring an estimated 200 million cubic metres of
steel-reinforced concrete it would be the largest building project in history. By the end of the war, with much of Hamburg lying in ruins, many
of these shelters remained intact and can still be seen today.

   Hamburg's air raid shelters take several different forms. The most
capacious were those occupying the lower storeys of the city's colossal
anti-aircraft towers *(Flaktürme)*. Two of them, which could each hold up
to 30 000 people when necessary, are still standing (see no. 30). Much
smaller and of a uniform rectangular plan were the *Hochbunker* (high
bunkers), built exclusively for use by civilians. A pair of such shelters in
Altona-Altstadt can be explored as part of a fascinating tour given by
the Hamburg Underworlds Association (Hamburger Unterwelten e.V.).
The largest at Schomburgstrasse 6–8 had room for about 1800 people,
whilst the smaller one at Holstenstrasse 14a could hold 450 persons.
Like other shelters in Hamburg both were modernised in the 1960s and
70s for use during the Cold War (see no. 4). The association also visits
a unique *Hochbunker* in the grounds of the University Clinic in Eppendorf (Universitätsklinikum Eppendorf), which served as a specialist
hospital shelter.

   A style of air raid shelter unique to Hamburg was the Zombek Bunker. Designed by Paul Zombek they consisted of a concrete cylinder
containing a continuous ramp, which enabled the shelter to be utilised
as efficiently and quickly as possible. Each could hold between 600
and 1800 people. The shelters were made more appealing to the civilian population by the addition of decorative brick façades (sometimes

Hamburg's only air raid shelter museum can be found in the district of Hamm

finished off with a sculptured martial eagle) and tiled roofs. A dozen or so Zombek Bunkers were constructed, of which several have subsequently been reused, including a Portuguese restaurant at Vorsetzen 70, a bar at Rothenbaumchaussee 2, and a branch of MacDonalds on Steintorplatz.

Air raid shelters were constructed beneath the ground, too. Of Hamburg's several so-called *Tiefbunker* (deep bunkers) the one beneath Steintorwall (St. Georg) next to the main railway station is another location that is visited by the Hamburg Underworlds Association. With walls 3.75 metres thick the shelter could hold almost 2500 people. Together with a smaller counterpart on nearby Hachmannplatz (which together with a similar shelter beneath Berlinertordamm (Borgfelde) is visited by the Under Hamburg Association) it was re-fitted for use during the Cold War.

The most common type of subterranean air raid shelter was the *Röhrenbunker* (tube bunker), and Hamburg's only air raid shelter museum, the Bunkermuseum built at Wichernsweg 16 (Hamm) in 1940–41, is housed in one of them. Like the city's five hundred other *Röhrenbunker* it is reached by means of a steep staircase. At the bottom there is a gas-proof door beyond which lie four elongated chambers, each 17 metres long, 2 metres wide, and 2.25 metres high. At the far end are chemical toilets and an emergency exit. One of the chambers has been restored to its original appearance, with a wooden bench down one side, on which fifty people could sit, and shelves opposite for personal possessions such as gas masks, suitcases, flash lamps, and helmets. Nearby there is a hand-cranked ventilator to provide fresh air. Another chamber contains vivid written testimonies from those who lived through the air raids, whilst another contains a collection of charred and rusted artefacts excavated in the surrounding area. Most affecting are the two glass bottles warped during the fire storm created by Operation Gomorrah in July 1943 (see no. 70).

6 The Last of the Workers' Canteens

Hamburg-Mitte (HafenCity), the Oberhafen-Kantine at
Stockmeyerstrasse 39
U1 Steinstrasse or Bus 34, 112, 120 Spaldingstrasse
then walk

At the point where the nineteenth century Customs Canal (Zollkanal), which separates Altstadt from the Speicherstadt, meets the Oberhafen, in the former district of Klostertor (now Hammerbrook), can be found the Oberhafenbrücke. This historic road and rail bridge was built between 1902 and 1904 as a swing bridge *(Drehbrücke)*, so that tall-masted sailing boats carrying freight could pass safely between the harbour and the canal. The bridge remained in service for just over a century until it was rebuilt in its present form in 2008.

Although the old bridge has gone, there is still a small reminder of how the area appeared during the nineteenth century in the form of the Oberhafen-Kantine, located alongside the modern Oberhafenbrücke at Stockmeyerstrasse 39. Such workers' canteens, or 'coffee hatches' *(Kaffeeklappen)*, were once as much a part of the dockland scene as the cranes and the railways and the warehouses: today, unfortunately, the Oberhafen-Kantine is the very last of its type.

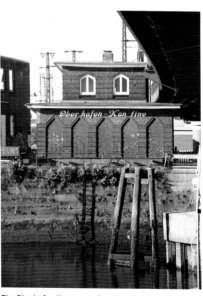

The Oberhafen-Kantine was opened in 1925, around the same time as the building of Hamburg's famous Chilehaus (see no. 3). Both were executed in the same architectural idiom, namely North German Brick Expressionism, indeed it is often said that a few of the millions of bricks required for the Chilehaus, which were transported by barge across the Oberhafen, were used to build the canteen.

For just over seventy years

The Oberhafen-Kantine on Stockmeyerstrasse is the last of Hamburg's traditional workers' canteens

The canteen preserves its original fixtures and fittings

the Oberhafen-Kantine remained in the hands of the same family, from its first proprieter, Hermann Sparr, whose initials still appear over the doorway, to the last, his daughter Anita Haendel, whose death in 1997 aged 83 marked the end of an era. During this period the canteen never closed, despite war and economic crises. By the late 1990s, however, the building was in desperate need of restoration and it was cordoned off having been deemed unsafe by the authorities. Fortunately, in 2000 the historical importance of the café was realised, and it was placed under protection. Plans to dismantle the building brick-by-brick and to re-build it nearer the city centre did not come to fruition. Instead, in 2005 the battered fabric of the canteen was restored, its characteristic tilt stabilised, and in 2006 it was reopened. Today, a part of the canteen actually stands *beneath* the upper deck of the Oberhafenbrücke, which was widened during its rebuilding.

The original interior of the café was refurbished, too, including the simple studded leather seats, hanging lights, and the pulley-operated food elevator used to haul food up from the kitchen in the cellar. Once again old workers' favourites such as homemade *Frikadelle* (Danish-style pan-fried patties made from seasoned ground beef, onion, egg and bread), Bockwurst, potato salad, and unique herring sausages (known as *Hamburger Weißwurst*) are available. Whilst enjoying the unique ambience it is worth reflecting on the origin of the world-conquering American hamburger, which seems to have developed out of the humble Hamburg *Frikadelle* after it found its way across the Atlantic several centuries ago. Unlike the hamburger, however, a *Frikadelle* is never served on a bun.

The Oberhafen-Kantine occupies one of the quieter corners of the HafenCity district. Conceived in 1997 and scheduled to take 20 years to complete, HafenCity is a mixture of apartments and offices, cultural and leisure attractions, parks, shops and restaurants. It is perceived as one of the most daring and unusual urban development ventures in Europe, and encompasses a massive 160 hectares of land and water.

Other places of interest nearby: 3, 7

7 Speicherstadt Revisited

Hamburg-Mitte (Altstadt), the Speicherstadtmuseum at
St. Annenufer 2
U1 Meßberg, U3 Baumwall; Bus 6 Bei St. Annen

The origin of the Free Port of Hamburg is to be found in a charter of
1189, granted by Holy Roman Emperor Frederick I (Barbarossa) (1155–
1190) in recognition of support given for his participation in the Third
Crusade. Hamburg merchants were given the privilege of imposing
custom duties on ships using the Lower Elbe, whilst their own ships
were exempted from such burdensome duties all the way to the North
Sea. In 1241, as an Imperial Free City, Hamburg joined the Hanseatic
League and became one of the most important trading centres and
ports in Northern Europe.

At the unwinding of the Holy Roman Empire in 1806 Hamburg became a sovereign state (Free and Hanseatic City of Hamburg) within
the German Confederation. With the establishment of the German
Empire in 1871, however, and the country's subsequent move towards

A classic view of the Speicherstadt from the courtyard of the Sandthorquai-Hof

protectionism, Hamburg could not be both a customs free zone and a part of the empire. Consequently Hamburg was required to join the German Customs Union *(Zollverein)*, in return for which it received the right to construct a free port within which the old merchants' privileges remained effective, notably the duty-free storage and processing of imported goods.

Hamburg's integration into the union took effect on 15th October 1888, and Emperor William II (1888–1918) was on hand to unveil a plaque (which can still be seen set into the flood barrier at Brooksbrücke). Beyond the bridge, where once stood the densely populated residential districts of Kehrwieder and Wandrahm, the new free port took the form of a series of huge canalside warehouses, constructed in three phases between 1885 and 1927. Known as the Speicherstadt the self-contained area was cordoned off from the rest of the city, and physically separated by the Zollkanal (Customs Canal), which allowed barges and inland ships to avoid the free port.

Although half of the Speicherstadt was ruined during the Second World War much of it was restored. By the 1970s, however, it was gradually abandoned in favour of the container terminals of Waltershof and Altenwerder (see no. 43). With the decreased economic importance of free ports in an era of European Union free trade the Speicherstadt was removed from the free port in 2003, and many of its old warehouses have subsequently been converted for use as offices, cafés and museums, the latter including the German Customs Museum (Deutsches Zollmuseum) at Alter Wandrahm 16.

Today there is much of interest in the Speicherstadt to attract visitors, and they flock here by the boatload to take in the endlessly photogenic red-brick façades and green copper roofs of the old warehouses. To escape the crowds three locations can be singled out. Firstly, to get a sense of an old warehouse in action take a stroll along Am Sandtorkai, where some of Hamburg's three hundred Asian carpet salesmen ply their colourful trade (see no. 8). Secondly, for a classic view of the Speicherstadt enter the courtyard of the Sandthorquai-Hof (1881) at Neuer Wandrahm 2/Pickhuben 6, where a former loading bay provides a simultaneous view of three canals, three bridges, and at least five rows of warehouses. Thirdly, visit the privately-administered Speicherstadtmuseum at St. Annenufer 2, which is housed inside a typical Speicherstadt warehouse. Founded on timber piles it has a red-brick façade (broken up by loading bays serviced by a mechanical hoist) and a fireproofed wood interior. Adjacent to the museum entrance hangs a rusting nameplate inscribed *Quartiersmann. Quartiersleute*, or ware-

Another classic scene in the Speicherstadt

house people, once accounted for the majority of the workforce in Speicherstadt, and were responsible for the storage, inspection and refinement of bulk raw cargoes from overseas *(Colonialwaren)* (such as coffee, tea, cocoa, nuts and spices) on behalf of the city's merchants. The Speicherstadtmuseum recalls their duties with objects such as gripping claws, tea chests, and sample takers.

The transition from traditional warehousing to containerisation is illustrated at the Hamburg Harbour Museum (Hafenmuseum Hamburg), which is housed in one of the so-called *50er Schuppen* warehouses at Australiastrasse 50a (Kleiner Grasbrook). They were erected between 1906 and 1912, when the growing preference was to warehouse goods for shorter periods, and instead to forward them as quickly as possible. The museum's barges, cranes, sack barrows, and harbour railway were a vital part of this process.

The maritime theme is continued at the 25hours Hotel HafenCity at Überseeallee 5, which features bunk-bed berths, toilets resembling a ship's engine room, and a sauna installed inside a freight container! HafenCity itself is regenerating so fast that it even warrants its own railway line, namely the U4.

Other places of interest nearby: 1, 2, 3, 8, 9, 11, 12, 24

8   Of Carpets and Spices

Hamburg-Mitte (Altstadt), Spicy's Gewürzmuseum at
Am Sandtorkai 34
U1 Meßberg; Bus 4, 6 Auf dem Sande (Speicherstadt);
Harbour Ferry 72 Elbphilharmonie

With the advent of containerisation during the 1970s Hamburg's famous Speicherstadt gradually relinquished its one hundred-year role as the city's warehouse district (see no. 7). It would be wrong, however, to think that the old warehouses lost their traditional function entirely, since almost half the complex is now occupied by import-export companies dealing in the transhipment of oriental carpets. There are almost three hundred of them, trading an estimated 3.6 million square metres of carpets each year. This makes Hamburg the largest carpet warehouse in the world.

A good selection of carpet warehouses can be found on Am Sandtorkai, which acts as the border between the Speicherstadt and the

Visitor sampling at Spicy's Gewürzmuseum on Am Sandtorkai

Old fashioned spice counter at Spicy's Gewürzmuseum

HafenCity immediately to the south. Am Sandtorkai can be reached by crossing the Niederbaumbrücke, itself suitably adorned with a 27.5 metre-long stone mosaic carpet created by the artist Frank Raendchen (b. 1962). The carpet warehouses begin beyond the bridge, their ground floor loading bays often left wide open in an attempt to lure passers-by. Typical is the Rahimi Handel warehouse at Am Sandtorkai 32, its numerous rooms piled high with glorious hand-woven wool and silk carpets from Turkey, Iran, Pakistan, China, and Afghanistan.

Amongst the many other exotic wares that were once common-place in the Speicherstadt were spices, and so it seems fitting that Am Sandtorkai 34 is today also home to the world's only spice museum. Spicy's Gewürzmuseum was founded in 1991 in nearby Mundsburg, and moved into the Speicherstadt in 1993. The rooms now occupied by the museum were themselves used to store spices a hundred years ago (although today trans-shipment takes place in the modern part of the harbour).

Across an area of around three hundred and fifty square metres the spice museum illustrates all aspects of the cultivation, harvesting, processing, and transporting of spices, as well as relating the historical role of the spice trade in the colonial and maritime history of Hamburg. This is done with reference to more than nine hundred objects repre-senting the last five hundred years of spice production.

Probably the most memorable part of a visit to Spicy's is the row of fifty samples of raw spices from around the world, which visitors can

Rahimi Handel on Am Sandtorkai is just one of many carpet warehouses in the Speicherstadt

touch, smell, and taste. The spices are either displayed partly exposed in their original transit materials (usually sacks or chests), exactly as they appear upon arrival from their point of origin, or else displayed in small bowls.

Dominating the museum space are several large pieces of machinery, which were once used for the processing and refining of spices. Made predominantly of wood, it is interesting to note that today the use of such machines is banned because of the danger of wooden splinters breaking off and entering the spice flow.

In amongst the machines are numerous showcases giving detailed information about the various spices, their uses, and their countries of origin. The central area of the spice museum is reserved for the four special exhibitions hosted annually by the museum, details of which can be found on the museum's website (www.spicys.de).

Other places of interest nearby: 7, 9, 10, 11, 24

9 The Floating Church

Hamburg-Mitte (Altstadt), the Floating Church (Flussschifferkirche) moored at Kehrwiedersteig, near the junction of Kajen and Hohe Brücke
U3 Baumwall; Bus 6 Auf dem Sande (Speicherstadt)

A real curiosity amongst Hamburg's many churches is the so-called Floating Church (Flussschifferkirche) moored at a pontoon off Kehrwiedersteig, near the junction of Kajen and Hohe Brücke. Before being converted into a Protestant church in 1952 this 26 metre-long vessel plied the River Weser as a lighter *(Kastenschuten)*, that is a flat-bottomed barge used to transfer goods from ship to shore (the name is thought to be derived from the German *lichten*, meaning to lighten or unload). In 1970 it was re-fitted and into the former seven metre-wide cargo hold was inserted an altar, a pulpit, an organ, and a font, as well as wooden pews for a congregation of one hundred and thirty. There is even a tiny belfry on the roof, the bell of which can often be heard ringing out across the harbour. Particularly charming are the nautical

The Flussschifferkirche is a floating church moored at Kehrwiedersteig

Inside the Flussschifferkirche with an altar painting by Ludger Trautmann

themes etched onto the windows down either side of the nave.

As such Hamburg's Floating Church provides an unforgettable experience, whether it be for mass, which is celebrated most Sundays at 3pm (sometimes with a specifically maritime theme), or special occasions such as baptisms and weddings. The Floating Church can also transfer to different berths if needed, indeed until 2006 it was moored in the Billwerder Bucht, a bay at Ausschläger Elbdeich on the southern shore of Rothenburgsort.

Hamburg boasts several other unusual Christian places of worship, including a beautiful church on Niendorfer Marktplatz (Niendorf), unusual because it is a rare example of the Baroque style in Northern Germany. Commissioned by King Christian VII of Denmark (1749–1808) it was erected in 1769. Directly to the rear of the church is the Niendorfer Gehege deer reserve. Equally attractive is the Bergstedter Kirche at Bergstedter Kirchenstrasse 7 (Bergstedt), which is illuminated only by candlelight and is situated close to the beautiful Rodenbeker Quellental, a valley on the Alster.

One of Hamburg's oldest churches is the Sinstorfer Kirche at Sinstorfer Kirchenweg 21 (Sinstorf), the history of which can be traced back to the ninth century. It is distinguished by having some fine wall paintings and a separate wooden belfry. Rather more recent but no less interesting is the English Church of St. Thomas à Beckett at Zeughausmarkt 22 (Neustadt), built in the early nineteenth century by the Company of Merchant Adventurers of London. It was financed using compensation paid to the company by the City of Hamburg after their fabric merchants' guild (which had been active in the city since 1611) was expropriated during the Napoleonic blockade known as the Continental System.

Other places of interest nearby: 8, 9, 10, 11, 12, 17, 24

10 On the Banks of the Nikolaifleet

Hamburg-Mitte (Altstadt), the Nikolaifleet at
Deichstrasse 21–23
U3 Rödingsmarkt; Bus 3, 6 Rödingsmarkt

A canal in North German dialect is 'fleet' and the Nikolaifleet is where the Port of Hamburg had its origins in 1189, after the town had been granted the status of an Imperial Free City by Holy Roman Emperor Frederick I (Barbarossa) (1155–1190). Unlike a real canal, however, the Nikolaifleet was not artificial but rather once the main arm of the Alster River, indeed as late as the nineteenth century it was referred to as the Lower Alster.

Between the thirteenth and fifteenth centuries the Nikolaifleet formed a part of the defensive moat of the walled Altstadt. When in the sixteenth century a new city wall was built farther to the west (recalled in the street name Neuer Wall), and large ships began docking where the Alster joined the Elbe, the Nikolaifleet was developed as an inland port. By the early nineteenth century it was lined with timber-framed brick-built warehouses to which goods were ferried from the docks by barge. Only as a result of the Great Fire of 1842, and the subsequent reorganisation of the city centre, was the Alster made to flow along the Alsterfleet, and with the opening of the Speicherstadt in 1888 the warehouses along the Nikolaifleet gradually lost their importance.

Although the hustle and bustle of the old Nikolaifleet is now long gone it is still worth experiencing what remains of the area, notably between Holzbrücke and Hohebrücke, which is one of the very few parts of the city centre to have survived both the Great Fire of 1842 and the Second World War. The waterway itself is best viewed from the Holzbrücke, and then more closely from a pontoon that can be reached down a narrow passageway at Deichstrasse 21–23 (such a passageway is known in Hamburg as a *Fleetgang*). From here a series of characterful waterfront warehouses can be observed, their footings sinking gently into the green-brown mud made visible at low tide due to the abandonment of water regulation here. Several warehouses still retain the winches once used to haul goods up from the barges below, as well as the loading bays through which the goods were passed.

On the opposite bank of the Nikolaifleet is Cremon, a thirteenth

Timber-framed buildings on the Nikolaifleet appear much as they did in the early nineteenth century

century merchants' route running between the Nikolaifleet and the now infilled Katharinenfleet. The old buildings on this side, many of which are seventeenth and eighteenth century office buildings *(Kontorhäuser)*, are among some of the finest examples of North European Baroque architecture to be found anywhere.

Returning to the Deichstrasse side of the Nikolaifleet, the purely functional riverside frontages could not be more different from the ornate façades facing Deichstrasse itself. They are connected by wide sloping corridors, enabling goods to be passed from boats on the river via ground floor storage areas to carts waiting on the street higher up. Merchants' living quarters were located on the floors above, which sometimes rise as high as seven storeys.

Although half the buildings on Deichstrasse were destroyed during the Great Fire, which incidentally broke out here at number 44, many others survived and their street façades remain excellent examples of the varying styles of old Hamburg architecture: a Venetian-style façade at number 19; a pair of post-fire façades at 21–23; a Baroque portal of 1659 at 25; a warehouse dating from 1780 at 27 (said to be the oldest warehouse in Hamburg); a Baroque Burgher house *(Bürgerhaus)* (1680)

A baroque sculptural detail on a door at Deichstrasse 25

at 37, of a type once commonplace in Hamburg between the sixteenth and eighteenth centuries; another Burgher house (1700) at 39; and lastly Hamburg's finest Baroque portal at 47.

In addition to the Nikolaifleet several entirely artificial waterways were created to enable more goods to be brought from the Elbe docks into the city for warehousing and onward distribution. Subsequently abandoned and infilled these canals were replaced by roads, their old warehouses now marooned and either abandoned or else reused. The Katharinenfleet, for example, is remembered in a street name and a row of fine late eighteenth century warehouses at Reimerstwiete 17–21. Similarly, the lost Deichstrassenfleet is recalled on Steintwietenhof by a further handful of former warehouses.

Other places of interest nearby: 7, 8, 9, 11, 12, 17, 24

11 All Aboard!

Hamburg-Mitte (Altstadt), a tour of historic ships finishing
with Das Schiff at Holzbrücke 2
U3 Rödingsmarkt; Bus 3, 6 Rödingsmarkt

The waterways of Hamburg are plied by every type of sailing vessel, from container ships, tug boats, barges, and dredgers to ferries, pleasure cruisers, speed boats, and yachts. In amongst them are numerous historic craft, many of which are moored permanently in Hamburg, which can usually be boarded by the public. Adding much to the maritime feel of Hamburg, some of these vessels are well known, whilst others take a little more finding.

Hamburg's three best known museum ships are moored in a row between Bei den St.-Pauli-Landungsbrücken and Vorsetzen (Neustadt). They are the merchant sailing ship *Rickmer Rickmers* (1896), once used on the Hamburg-Chile nitrate route, the freighter *Cap San Diego* (1961), formerly used to transport meat and textiles from South America to Germany, and the red-painted *Das Feuerschiff* (1952), an English-built lightship now used as a floating café, bar and restaurant.

Less frequented but some would say more interesting are the vessels moored in Hamburg's museum harbours. The Traditionsschiffhafen on Am Sandtor Kai (HafenCity), for example, was opened in 2008 and consists of a rotating roster of approximately twenty historic ships, moored to a zig-zag series of pontoons (note that some of the ships are absent between June and September working the Kiel Canal and the Baltic). Most celebrated is the elegant coal-fired river steamer *(Dampfschiff) Schaarhörn* built in Hamburg in 1908 for the purposes of surveying the Elbe, and still in full running order. Other noteworthy craft include the following: the sailing barge *(Fracht-Ewer) Johanna* (1903), used to transport salt along the Elbe to Hamburg; the steam-powered icebreaker *Elbe* (1911); the flat-bottomed fishing boat *(Fischer-Ewer) Catarina* (1890), the last of a type once common on the Elbe during the nineteenth century and used to catch smelt, eels and sturgeon; the fireboat *(Feuerlöschboot) Repsold* (1941); the single-screw tug *(See Schlepper) Fairplay VIII* (1962); and the fully-rigged *Grönland* (1867), used on the First German North Pole Expedition.

Hamburg's other museum harbours are smaller but no less interesting, including a selection of old Elbe and North Sea fishing boats at Övelgönne and Finkenwerder (see nos. 28 & 50). The Hamburg

Hamburg-Mitte

Formerly a grain barge the HoheLuftschiff in Harvestehude now serves as a floating children's theatre

Harbour Museum (Hafenmuseum Hamburg) at Australiastrasse 50a (Kleiner Grasbrook) incorporates the Bremer Kai on which is moored the steam-powered dredger *(Schutensauger) Sauger IV* (1909) and floating crane *(Schwimmkran) Saatsee* (1917), as well as the bulk freighter *(Stückgutfrachter) Bleichen* (1958), and several lighters *(Kastenschuten)*, which are flat-bottomed barges once used to shuttle goods from ship to shore.

Other unusual vessels are moored in isolation and include a Russian submarine and a floating church (see nos. 9 & 27). To these can be added the customs ship *(Zollboot) Oldenburg* outside the German Customs Museum (Deutsches Zollmuseum) at Alter Wandrahm 16 (Altstadt), the colourfully-painted *HoheLuftschiff* at Kaiser-Friedrich-Ufer 27 (Harvestehude), which is a former grain barge now serving as a floating children's theatre, and the fireboat *(Feuerlöschboot) Feuerwehr IV*, constructed in 1930 and moored at Kehrwiederspitze (Altstadt).

Particularly interesting is the story of *Das Schiff*, Europe's only seaworthy theatre ship, which is moored at Holzbrücke 2 (Altstadt). Built in Holland in 1912 as the 20 metre-long sailing barge *Seemöve* the steel-hulled vessel carried grain and fertiliser between Hamburg and

Denmark. The vessel was motorised in the 1920s, sunk during the war, raised, lengthened to 34.5 metres, and transformed into the coastal motor vessel *MS Rita Funck*. After finally being decommissioned in 1975 the vessel came into the hands of Christa and Eberhard Möbius, who converted it into a theatre capable of holding a capacity audience of 120 people (no seat is further than seven metres from the stage). Many renowned actors have subsequently trodden the boards here including Peter Ustinov and Gert Fröbe, who played the villain in the James Bond film *Goldfinger* (1964). The vessel has also been taken to venues as far away as Oslo and Mallorca, and is serviced at Hamburg's Blohm & Voss shipyards every two years. In 2000 Anke and Gerd Schlesselmann took over and together with the actor Michael Frowin they continue to offer the finest onboard theatre in Europe.

To learn more about the history of shipping and seafaring in Hamburg visit the Hamburg Museum (Museum für Hamburgische Geschichte) at Holstenwall 24 (Neustadt), which contains some magnificent model ships as well as the atmospherically reconstructed bridge of the steamship *Werner*. Also visit the International Maritime Museum Hamburg (Internationales Maritimes Museum Hamburg) at Korea Strasse 1 (HafenCity), which is housed in Kaispecher B, one of the oldest remaining warehouses in Hamburg (1878) (Kaispecher A is now the site of the Elbe Philharmonic Hall (Elbphilharmonie Hamburg)). The museum illustrates more than 3000 years of international maritime history across its nine "exhibition decks".

Other places of interest nearby: 2, 7, 9, 10, 12, 24

A Forgotten Pneumatic Postal System

Hamburg-Mitte (Altstadt), remains of the *Großrohrpost* at Altenwallbrücke
S1, S3 Stadthausbrücke; U3 Rödingsmarkt

It was the ancient Greek scientist, Hero of Alexandria (c. 70–10 BC), who first described machines worked by air pressure in his book *Pneumatica*. One of the many applications of such technology over the following two millennia was pneumatic post, that is a system of delivering letters in capsules through pressurized air tubes. The pneumatic postal system was invented by the Scottish engineer William Murdoch in the early nineteenth century and was developed by the London Pneumatic Dispatch Company, the first system being installed in 1853 to convey telegrams between the London Stock Exchange and the city's main telegraph office.

Throughout the second half of the nineteenth century, pneumatic postal systems were constructed in many large cities, the most extensive of which were in Paris and Berlin. Others included Vienna, Prague, Marseille, Munich, Rome, Algiers, Chicago, New York, Rio de Janeiro, and, of course, Hamburg. Such networks were punctuated regularly by pneumatic post stations, and were used to link post offices, banks, stock exchanges, and ministries. In Germany, France, Italy and Austria special postal stationery was issued especially for pneumatic use.

During the second half of the twentieth century, however, with the dislocation brought about by war and the advent of fax machines and computers, the pneumatic systems were gradually abandoned, the last to go being Prague, following the city's extensive flooding in 2002.

Hamburg's own pneumatic postal system (called *Rohrpost* in German) was inaugurated on 24th

A pipe running beneath the Altenwallbrücke bridge once carried Hamburg's pneumatic post

A section of Hamburg's pneumatic post

October 1864. What made it ultimately unique, however, was that when eventually pneumatic postal systems were being closed down elsewhere, the one in Hamburg was actually replaced in the 1960s by an upgraded system called the *Großrohrpost*. This extensive new network was made up of pairs of pipes (each with an increased diameter of 45 centimetres) through which travelled capsules 1.6 metres in length travelling simultaneously in both directions, each containing up to a thousand letters at a time.

Work on the first line of the new network, which connected the centre of Hamburg with the airport, began in October 1960, although the extensive flooding of the city in 1962 halted work (the height reached by the flood waters is recorded on a building at Rödingsmarkt 27). Despite this setback, by 1967 a network of five lines had been created, stretching five kilometres across the city from Wandsbek to Altona. Post that was now taking more than half an hour on Hamburg's increasingly busy roads took only a couple of minutes by means of the new *Großrohrpost*.

Hamburg's *Großrohrpost* was intended to be a pilot scheme for similar pneumatic postal systems elsewhere in Germany – but this was not to be. The relentless vibrations caused by the city's traffic repeatedly damaged the pipework, and in 1976 the system was once again abandoned. Although the post stations of the network have subsequently been dismantled, much of the pipework remains, and can still occasionally be spotted where it runs above ground. A good example is suspended beneath the Altenwallbrücke in Altstadt, alongside similar gauge pipes for water and power. For a glimpse into this rarely-seen world it is highly recommended to join the Hamburg Underworlds Association (Hamburger Unterwelten e.V.) on one of their occasional walks beginning at Steintorwall in search of further remains of the *Großrohrpost*.

Other places of interest nearby: 2, 9, 10, 11, 13, 14

13 Some Not So Innocent Addresses

Hamburg-Mitte (Neustadt), the former Gestapo Headquarters
at Stadthausbrücke 8
S1, S3 Stadthausbrücke; U3 Rödingsmarkt; Bus 3, 31, 35, 37
Rödingsmarkt

The outbreak of war in 1939 meant that grandiose plans for the architectural reinvention of Hamburg as a *Führerstadt* (City of the Führer of the Reich) never came to fruition (see no. 51). No significant buildings other than those connected directly with the war effort were constructed in the city during the period of National Socialism (see nos. 5 & 30). Instead, the Nazi administration commandeered existing buildings for their governmental needs, "Aryanised" business premises considered to be of economic use, and converted or destroyed buildings perceived as representing a threat (notably the city's synagogues) (see no. 53). These locations, most of which have been reused and which today appear innocuous alongside Hamburg's former anti-aircraft towers, air raid shelters, bunkers and concentration camps, serve as unsettling reminders of how Nazism once pervaded the city.

Law and order in Hamburg during the Third Reich was maintained by the Gestapo *(Geheime Staatspolizei)* (state secret police) and the SS *(Schutzstaffel)*, an elite police and military organisation responsible for many crimes against humanity. The Gestapo made their headquarters in the imposing Stadthaus at Stadthausbrücke 8 (Neustadt), which prior to Hitler becoming chancellor had been used by the Hamburg police force. Anyone deemed an opponent of the Nazi Party could be detained here without recourse to the law courts, and the building soon gained a reputation as a place of torture. Embedded in the pavement in front of the building are several bronze cobblestones *(Stolpersteine)* recording how two people jumped to their death from the windows above rather than face interrogation by the Gestapo. Now home to the Department for City Development and Environment (Behörde für Stadtentwicklung und Umwelt – BSU) there is a further memorial inside the entrance portico.

The SS in Hamburg were housed in specially constructed barracks comprising parade grounds and accommodation blocks. The SS barracks at Tangstedter Landstrasse 465 (Langenhorn), for example, which were erected in 1937 and used by the 'Germania' regiment now serve as a hospital. Another SS barracks, the Lettow-Vorbek Barracks (Lettow-

Stolpersteine in the pavement outside the former Gestapo Headquarters on Stadthausbrücke

Vorbeck-Kaserne) at Wilsonstrasse 49 (Jenfeld), were opened in 1939 (see no. 79). Germany's regular armed forces, the Wehrmacht, had their headquarters at Sophienterrasse 14 (Harvestehude), today a peaceful residential street quite at odds with the imposing building erected in 1936 that features crossed swords and martial eagles on its façade.

Many Jewish business across Germany were "Aryanised" during the 1930s and their owners forced to resign. One of the most famous examples was that of Beiersdorf, the company responsible for both the world's first water-in-oil skin cream (Nivea) and self-adhesive plaster. Perhaps less well known to today's busy shoppers are the Jewish origins of two of Hamburg's premier shopping addresses. The department store of Oskar Tietz at Jungfernstieg 16–20 (Neustadt) was renamed the Alsterhaus after its expropriation in 1935, and the owner of the Hirschfeld & Robinson clothing store at Neuer Wall 19 was murdered after his shop was ransacked during Reichskristallnacht, an anti-Jewish pogrom of 1938.

Hamburg's synagogues suffered a similar fate, with some destroyed and others left standing. The Bornplatz Synagogue on Joseph-Cerlebach-Platz (Rotherbaum) was demolished in 1939 and replaced by an air raid shelter, which is now used by Hamburg University. The synagogue of the New Israelite Temple Association (Synagoge des Neuen Israelitisches Tempelvereins), which opened in 1931 at Oberstrasse 120 (Harvestehude), fared a little better and is now used by the North German Broadcasting Service (Norddeutcher Rundfunk). The building's predecessor constructed in 1844 lies in ruins at Poolstrasse 12–13 (Neustadt), where it is used as a car repair workshop.

Other places of interest nearby: 12, 14, 16, 17, 18

14 A Little Piece of Venice

Hamburg-Mitte (Neustadt), the Alsterarkaden on the Kleine
Alster between Reesendammbrücke and Schleusenbrücke
S1, S3 Jungfernstieg; U1, U2, U4 Jungfernstieg, U3 Rathaus

Those who enjoy shopping arcades will not be disappointed by Hamburg: the city centre is graced with several to suit most tastes. The majority are modern and purpose-built, for example the Bleichenhof at the corner of Grosse Bleichen and Bleichenbrücke. By comparison the Kaufmannshaus directly opposite is older, having been erected as a shopping arcade in the late nineteenth century. Similarly, the neo-Renaissance arcade on Colonnaden was built as part of a private residential street in the 1870s and has long contained shopping facilities. Other arcades occupy buildings that once had different functions, for example the Levantehaus on Mönckebergstrasse, which once contained the offices of the Levante Shipping Company, and the Alte Post at Poststrasse 11, which not surprisingly began life as a post office (the crests carved on the building's façade represent the various postal services once handled here, including the Princely House of Thurn and Taxis, and the Royal Postal Agency of Sweden).

Undoubtedly Hamburg's most attractive arcades face across the Kleine Alster towards Rathausmarkt. Called the Alsterarkaden they were erected to a design by Alexis de Chateauneuf (1799–1853) in the immediate wake of the Great Fire of 1842, which destroyed so much of the old centre of Hamburg. Taking Venetian architecture as his inspiration the architect located the Alsterarkaden directly at the water's edge, thereby imbuing the ensemble with a deliberately Mediterranean feel. The effect is enhanced by the old-fashioned wrought iron lanterns and ornate balustrades, as well as the curving stone staircase of the Friesen Keller restaurant, winding down into the water next to the Reesendammbrücke.

The Alsterarkaden are justifiably popular with locals and tourists alike, especially on a warm summer's day when the dazzling white arches entice visitors to explore the stylish cafés and shops they contain, including Hamburg's oldest outfitters Ladage & Oelke (in actual fact these premises occupy the ground floor of the elegant five-storey town houses erected *behind* the arcades in 1846). It is advisable if possible to visit the Alsterarkaden before 9am, when the only living things to disturb the delightful view across the water towards the Town Hall

(Rathaus) are the Alster's famous snowy-white swans (they spend the winter months on the Mühlenteich in Eppendorf).

At the west end of the Alsterarkaden is the Schleusenbrücke, a combined bridge and sluice that enables small sailing craft to pass northwards from the Elbe and Alsterfleet into the Kleine Alster, and thence onwards into the Binnenalster and Außenalster. The line of the Alsterarkaden is continued westwards beyond this point by means of a series of modern arcades (the so-called New Alster Arcades), which date from the late 1990s. They echo the repeated arches of the old arcades by means of an undulating glass portico, which stretches for eighty metres along the Alsterfleet.

Early morning is the best time to visit the Alsterarkaden

Returning to the Alsterarkaden it is easy to miss the Mellin-Passage, a small separate arcade in its own right that connects the old arcades with Neuer Wall. Named after a former shopkeeper who once had premises here the passage was created at the same time as the town houses, and can therefore lay claim to being Hamburg's oldest shopping arcade. The ceiling is decorated with some splendid *Jugendstil* frescoes added in the early years of the twentieth century. If anything the selection of shops in the Mellin-Passage is more varied than those of the Alsterarkaden, including the old established bookseller Felix Jud, the Royal Porcelain Manufacturer KPM (Konigliche Porzellan Manufaktur), the Arka Tee-Pavillon, and the Saliba Syrian and Lebanese restaurant.

The Mellin-Passage lays claim to being Hamburg's oldest shopping arcade

Unlike the Alsterarkaden, which were designed by a single architect, Hamburg's Rathaus was the work of seven. Following the destruction of the old town hall during the Great Fire the new one was built between 1886 and 1897 on a foundation of 4000 oak piles, and rendered in the neo-Renaissance style. Viewed together with the Kleine Alster and the Alsterarkaden, the ensemble has echoes of St. Mark's Square in Venice. The new town hall was built to reflect the wealth and independence of the State of Hamburg and officially boasts 647 rooms, although the accidental discovery of another in the tower in 1971, during a search for a document fallen behind a filing cabinet, suggests there could still be more.

Other places of interest nearby: 1, 2, 12, 13, 16

15 Peace in a Japanese Garden

Hamburg-Mitte (St. Pauli), the Japanese Gardens in the Planten
un Blomen on Stephansplatz
U1 Stephansplatz; S11, S21, S31 Dammtor; Bus 4, 5, 34, 36, 109,
112 Stephansplatz

Meaning 'plants and flowers' in Low German, Hamburg's Planten un
Blomen is a public garden occupying what was once an empty space
(glacis) outside the city walls of Neustadt, designed to deprive would-be
attackers of cover (see no. 20). It is named after a garden show staged
here in 1935 and has evolved gradually ever since, playing host to the
International Garden Exhibition (Internationale Gartenausstellung)
on no fewer than three occasions (1953, 1963 and 1973).

Incorporated into the design of the Planten un Blomen is the city's
former Old Botanical Garden (Alter Botanischer Garten), which was
established in 1821 between Stephansplatz and Marseiller Strasse
by the botanist Johann Georg Christian Lehmann (1792–1860). During the 1970s the traditional layout of the Old Botanical Garden was
swept away in favour of a grid of perennial flower beds broken up with
straight paths (only a handful of mulberries were left standing, together with a venerable plane (Platanus) planted by Lehmann at the
Dammtor entrance). When the taste for such rigid designs was itself
abandoned during the 1980s – cynical onlookers at the time re-named
the garden 'Platten und Beton' (paving stones and concrete) – this part
of the garden was reinvented with a more natural and landscaped feel.

Undoubtedly the most successful aspect of this overhaul has been
a pair of Japanese gardens, which continue to provide aesthetic and
spiritual sanctuary for those who value such precious places within an
urban context. The first, the Japanese Landscape Garden (Japanischer
Landschaftsgarten), was created in 1988 at the bottom of the access
ramp from the Dammtor station. Landscape gardener Professor Yoshi-
kuni Araki from Osaka utilised existing trees, as well as new plants and
rocks, to create a typical traditional Japanese garden. In keeping with
Shinto beliefs, each element in the garden is imbued with symbolism.
The group of boulders, for instance, over which life-giving water flows
from an eternal source marked by an inscribed stone, represents Mount
Fuji (in reality underground pumps keep the river flowing along its 150
meter-long course during the summer months). Similarly, the carefully
pruned, evergreen candelabra pines are a symbol of permanence, whilst

the cherry trees *(Prunus sargentii 'Accolade')*, which blossom fleetingly to stunning effect each April, are taken as a reminder of the transience of life.

The second Japanese garden lies beyond the first, alongside the pathway that connects the Hamburg Congress Centre (Congress Center Hamburg) with the Hamburg

Peace reigns at the Japanese Garden with Tea House (Japanischer Garten mit Teehaus) in the Planten un Blomen

Exhibition Centre (Hamburg Messe). The largest of its kind in Europe, the Japanese Garden with Tea House (Japanischer Garten mit Teehaus) was created in 1990. Once again the traditional combination of plants, rocks and water is used to create an idealised, miniature reflection of the Japanese natural world. The difference here is that a focal point is provided by a rustic tea house set at the edge of a small lake, a terrace leading out across the surface of the still water. Surrounded by flame-red maples and carved stone lanterns, the tea house is approached by means of a wooden gate, which creates a boundary between the garden and the ceremonial area beyond. Few locations in Hamburg offer a better place for personal contemplation. It is here on summer afternoons that visitors can take green tea, whilst learning more about the art of Japanese gardening (for details of traditional tea ceremonies and other events, including calligraphy and cooking, visit www.plantenunblomen.hamburg.de). The Japanese tea ceremony is also demonstrated each third weekend in the month at the Arts and Crafts Museum (Museum für Kunst und Gewerbe) on Steintorplatz (St. Georg).

Outside the Planten un Blomen, beneath the trees between Dammtordamm and Stephansplatz, there are a pair of monuments that could not be more different to each other. The Monument to the 76th Hamburg Regiment takes the form of a stone cube adorned with ranks of marching soldiers (it was erected in 1936 by the Nazi regime as a ripost to the cenotaph on the Kleine Alster, erected to a design by the anti-war sculptor Ernst Barlach (1870-1938) in 1931). An effective counterpoint to the monument is provided by the nearby Monument against War by the Austrian sculptor Alfred Hrdlička (1928-2009).

Other places of interest nearby:16, 62, 63, 64

16 The Old Alleyways of Neustadt

Hamburg-Mitte (Neustadt), the former *Gängeviertel* at
Bäckerbreitergang 49–58
U2 Gänsemarkt; Bus 3, 35 Johannes-Brahms-Platz

Although the Altstadt of Hamburg was surrounded by a protective wall
as early as the thirteenth century, it was not until the 1620s that the
burgeoning population of the port necessitated a major extension of
the wall westwards beyond the Herrengraben-Bleichenfleet moat (see
no. 20). The new area was called Neustadt and was soon densely inhabited by sailors, artisans, tradesmen, and soldiers. They lived in a warren
of narrow streets known as *Gängevierteln*, or alleyway neighbourhoods,
where inadequate sanitation did much to encourage the spread of disease, including the devastating cholera epidemic of 1892. Inevitably the
area became one of the most squalid in Hamburg.

Over time parts of the area were rebuilt to higher standards, with
much of the rest being obliterated during the Second World War. Despite this, one last example of a *Gängeviertel* street is still standing,
located in the north-western reaches of Neustadt. Surprisingly little-
visited, despite being just inside the busy Gorch-Fock-Wall ringroad,
Bäckerbreitergang 49–58 is a row of timber-framed tenements of the
type that would have been prevalent in Neustadt during the eighteenth and nineteenth centuries (numbers 49–50 were built in 1780;
numbers 51–58 date from the early nineteenth century). Still occupied
today, it is interesting to notice that the ground floor accommodation
had a separate entrance from the first floor accomodation. Unfortunately, only one side of the street is intact so it is difficult today to
imagine how narrow the street once was, suitable only for pedestrians
and hand carts (it is even more difficult to imagine that until the late
nineteenth century even the prestigious Mönckebergstrasse in Altstadt was a *Gängeviertel*).

Bäckerbreitergang runs south across Kaiser-Wilhelm-Strasse,
where it joins Breiter Gang, Rademachergang and Kornträgergang,
which together surround a pleasant leafy square. The uniform red-
brick houses here were erected in 1933–1937 as part of a programme
to replace the crumbling tenements of the *Gängevierteln*. Modern
sanitation and decorative features (including gable ends and maritime-

themed ornamentation) were a far cry from the old narrow streets that once stood here.

In the centre of the square is the Hummel-Denkmal, a fountain erected in 1938 depicting a traditional water carrier by the name of Johann Wilhelm Bentz (1787–1854). Children on the street taunted him with cries of "Hummel, Hummel" (meaning bumble bee), on account of the load he was carrying, to which he would respond "Mors, Mors", which in Low German means "Arses, arses!". A sculpture of one of the naughty children with his trousers down (!) can be seen on the corner of the nearby Memel-Haus, a hostel for retired seamen. Effigies of the water-carrier can still be found across Hamburg today (and his coarse response still heard), although the fountain also serves the more serious purpose of reminding the passer-by of the importance of fresh water in the fight against disease.

Streets such as Bäckerbreitergang in Neustadt were once home to soldiers and sailors

Other interesting buildings nearby include Kohlhöfen 29, where the philosopher Arthur Schopenauer (1788–1860) spent part of his youth, a pair of elaborate timber-framed buildings built in 1780 at Thielbek 12–14 and occupied simultaneously by multiple families, and a row of conventional late nineteenth century apartment houses on Brüderstrasse, of the type that would eventually replace so much of the *Gängevierteln*.

Other places of interest nearby: 13, 14, 17, 18, 20

17 The World's Oldest Terrace Houses

Hamburg-Mitte (Neustadt), the Kramer-Witwen-Wohnung
at Krayenkamp 10
S1, S3 Stadthausbrücke; U3 Rödingsmarkt, Baumwall;
Bus 37 Michaeliskirche

A terrace house is defined as a house that is one of a row of similar-looking buildings, situated side by side and sharing common side walls. Tucked away on Krayenkamp, in the lee of the Baroque Church of St. Michaelis (St. Michaelis Kirche), can be found the so-called Kramer-amtsstuben or Krameramtswohnungen ('Merchants' Almshouses'). This quaint ensemble of seventeenth century timber-framed buildings, which miraculously survived both the Great Fire of 1842 and the Second World War, represents the oldest extant row of terrace houses in the world.

The Krameramtsstuben comprise two rows of ten houses facing each other directly across a narrow enclosed courtyard (such courtyards were once commonplace in Neustadt until their wholesale destruction during the war). They are entirely hidden from the street by a large building erected in 1700 at Krayenkamp 10, through which a doorway provides access. The houses were commissioned in 1676 by Hamburg's prestigious Guild of Shopkeepers, in order to provide accommodation for twenty widows of deceased members. The guild, which was formed in 1375, was an association of well-to-do middle class retailers, all of whom maintained a permanent sales presence in the city, selling in particular spices, silk, and ironware. The guild's emblem, which can still be seen at the Krameramtsstuben today, depicts a pair of scales together with a measuring stick.

The oldest of the Krameramtsstuben can actually be traced back as early as 1620, to a trio of pre-existing houses (Houses A, M and N) that were re-used, although the rest are the result of an enlargement dating to 1676. It is interesting to notice how the floor space was maximised, due to the high cost of the building plots, by increasing the width of the upper floors by up to half a metre, resulting in a characteristic overhang running the length of the courtyard. With the introduction of the freedom of trade in 1863 the Guild of Shopkeepers was dissolved and the Krameramtsstuben were acquired by the City of Hamburg. The houses continued to be let to widows and pensioners until 1968, when they were renovated for commercial useage.

Although well hidden from the street the Krameramtsstuben today are a magnet for tourists visiting the nearby church, the crypt of which contains the grave of composer C.P.E. Bach (1714–1788), and the Old Commercial Room restaurant (see no. 18). Despite the presence of shops, a café and a restaurant to cater for them it is still possible to escape the bustle by visiting House C (Kramer-Witwen-Wohnung) (Almshouse for Merchant's Widow), which in 1974 was acquired by the Hamburg Museum (Museum für Hamburgische Geschichte). With only a handful of visitors permitted at any one time this particular house conveys a

Krayenkamp is said to be the oldest row of terrace houses in the world

good impression of the original internal layout of the Krameramtsstuben, enhanced by a collection of Late Biedermeier-era (1850–1860) furnishings both original and from the museum's own collection.

The ground floor of House C contains a small living room (now the ticket office) and kitchen, with an iron stove for cooking, as well as a water tap for washing (prior to the installation of water mains in the late nineteenth century the residents used two water pumps in the yard). From here a steep wooden staircase rises to a first floor parlour, furnished with a sewing table and an alcove bed with a chamber pot beneath it (a communal toilet shared by all residents was outside at the end of the yard). Further steps lead to a drying loft on the second floor, with a laundry rack attached to the outside of the window above the courtyard. The attic was also used to accept deliveries of wood and coal for the stove, which were brought up by means of a pulley. Whilst the facilities provided by House C might appear somewhat primitive by today's standards, at the time they were considered comfortable and progressive.

Other places of interest nearby: 10, 12, 13, 18, 19, 20

18 Food Fit for a Sailor

Hamburg-Mitte (Neustadt), the Old Commercial Room at
Englische Planke 10
U3 Rödingsmarkt, Baumwall; Bus 37 Michaeliskirche

As Germany's "Gateway to the World", Hamburg can boast a wide array of international cuisine. Yet despite so much foreign influence the city still offers its own unique local fare, which visitors should not miss.

It goes without saying that one of Hamburg's staple dishes is fish, from humble fish-filled bread rolls *(Fischbrötchen)* at pavement kiosks *(Kajüte)* on Bei den St.-Pauli-Landungsbrücken to a smart fish restaurant and oyster bar inside the International Maritime Museum Hamburg (Internationales Maritimes Museum Hamburg) (HafenCity). Late Spring is the time for *Maischolle* (spring plaice) and a summer favourite is herring *(Matjes)* served with green beans, bacon and fried potato slices *(Bratkartoffeln)*, both of which are served up in restaurants across the city. An upmarket speciality is *Finkenwerder Ewerscholle*, consisting of pan-fried plaice with bacon, boiled potatoes, salad and a sweet cream and lemon dressing. It can be found in dedicated fish restaurants such as Fischereihafen at Gross Elbstrasse 143 and Fischerhaus at St. Pauli Fischmarkt 14 in St. Pauli, and Deichgraf and Alt-Hamburger Aalspeicher at Deichstrasse 23 and 43 respectively, both in Altstadt.

There is much more to the North German kitchen, however, than simply fish, although many first-time visitors will be unfamiliar with it. This is perhaps because Hamburg's three signature traditional dishes – *Aalsuppe* (eel soup), *Birnen, Bohnen und Speck* (pears, green beans and bacon), and *Labskaus* (fish and meat stew) – do not sound at all appetising (the Hatari Pfälzer Stube at Schanzenstrasse 4 (St. Pauli) even offers cow stomach with Sauerkraut!). First impressions, however, can be misleading, since these three dishes can be delicious, drawing on local seasonal ingredients and reflecting both North German simplicity and the Danish taste for sweetness.

An unusual place to experience Hamburg cooking is the Old Commercial Room at Englische Planke 10 (Neustadt). The restaurant's name, along with that of the street it occupies, recalls the historic mercantile links between the ports of Hamburg and London. It is therefore not surprising that the Old Commercial Room was founded by an English ship owner in the style of an English pub and has lured hungry sailors to its tables since 1795. Today's visitors may be shown to one of

The healthiest fast food in Hamburg is undoubtedly the fish roll (Fischbrötchen)

the alcove tables *(Stammtisch)* reserved for established customers and celebrities: the walls are covered with signed photos of everyone from former chancellor Helmut Schmidt and The Beatles to singer Charles Aznavour and actor Clint Eastwood.

First dish on the menu is *Aalsuppe*. Whilst literally meaning 'eel soup' this dish started out as a frugal mélange of leftovers served up in a meat stock. The name is thought to derive from the Low German word *allns*, meaning 'all' rather than 'eel'. The base of *Aalsuppe* is ham broth flavoured with vinegar and sugar, to which *all* kinds of vegetables are added, including carrots, leeks, plums, and apples. Inch-thick slices of eel are today added at the end so as not to disappoint customers!

The second dish is the late summer speciality *Birnen, Bohnen und Speck*, a stew of green runner beans cooked with pears and bacon. A

To try Labskaus
reserve a table at the
Old Commercial Room
on Englische Planke

particular variety of pear that ripens in August is preferred, one which grows together with most of Hamburg's fruit in the so-called Altes Land south-west of the city (see no. 45).

The final dish, *Labskaus*, which dates back to the Middle Ages, is the most curious of all. In the days before refrigeration, fishermen could take only salted ('corned') beef with them on their long voyages, and they rendered it edible by boiling it into a thick broth with potatoes and onions. Mashed together with a herring, and served with beetroot and a pickled cucumber, the result was *Labskaus*. The dish is related to both Norwegian *Lapskaus* and Liverpudlian *Lobscouse*, all variants of the traditional one-pot meal consumed daily by the sailors of old.

Hamburg's local cuisine also includes several sweet delicacies, including the croissant-like *Franzbrötchen*, a pastry with a cinnamon, raisin, and sugar filling. *Rote Grütze*, a compote of red berries served with cream, resembles the Danish *rødgrød* and high-lights the strong connection between the cuisine of Hamburg and Denmark. Ordinary bread rolls in Hamburg are oval-shaped and called *Rundstück*, a relative of the Danish *Rundstykke*.

Other places of interest nearby: 17, 19, 20, 21, 22

19 A Street for Scandinavians

Hamburg-Mitte (Neustadt), the Swedish Gustav-Adolf Church
(Schwedische Gustav-Adolfskirche) at Ditmar-Koel-Strasse 36
U 3 Landungsbrücken; S1, S3 Landungsbrücken; Bus 112
Landungsbrücken; Harbour Ferry 62, 71, 73, 75 Landungsbrücken

Ditmar-Koel-Strasse, which runs diagonally from the shipping piers of Bei den St.-Pauli-Landungsbrücken into the former sailors' town of Neustadt, is named after a former sixteenth century mayor of Hamburg. Ditmar Koel (1500–1563), a statue of whom can be found on the nearby Kersten-Miles-Brücke, was also a successful sea captain and pirate hunter. The street reflects the maritime history of Hamburg in other ways, too. Although renowned today for its numerous Spanish and Portuguese restaurants, Ditmar-Koel-Strasse has for more than a century been the location of the city's Scandinavian seamen's missions.

The most visually impressive mission stands at number 36 and can be identified from afar by its tall steeple, looking out over the river like a lighthouse. The Swedish mission was constructed in polychrome brick in 1906–1907 to a plan by a Norwegian architect, which is not so surprising since for much of the nineteenth century Sweden and Norway shared the same ruler. As such the building is the oldest extant seamen's mission in Hamburg. Over the entrance hangs the Swedish flag, the design of which is repeated in a welcoming glass lantern hanging over the door.

Inside the Swedish mission on the ground floor there is a fine entrance hall, off which can be found a particularly cosy meeting room, with a library at one end and a crown-topped picture of the Swedish royal family at the other. The visitor quickly realises that

A glimpse into the Swedish Gustav-Adolf Church
(Schwedische Gustav-Adolfskirche) on Ditmar-Koel-
Strasse

such missions, provided originally for mariners and their families, are used today by the wider community. Indeed everybody whether Swedish, Scandinavian or otherwise will be made most welcome here, especially for tea and cakes on Saturday afternoon. The honorary Swedish consul is now based here, too.

Returning to the entrance hall, a staircase adorned with anchor motifs and illuminated by pastel-coloured glass windows rises to the first floor, where an arched doorway opens into the Swedish Gustav-Adolf Church (Schwedische Gustav-Adolfskirche; Swedish: Svenska Gustaf-Adolfskyrkan). The simple furnishings and blue-painted vaults of this tranquil space have the feel of a ship's interior, an impression reinforced by the model ship hanging from the ceiling, which is itself painted with the provincial coats of arms of Sweden.

The church is named after Gustavus Adolphus II (1594–1632), King of Sweden, whose bust can be seen on the staircase. Adolphus was a champion of the Protestant Lutheran cause in Germany against the Holy Roman Empire and its Catholic allies. Before his premature death in battle during the Thirty Years War he had made Sweden the third most powerful nation in Europe after Russia and Spain.

Hamburg's three other Scandinavian seamen's missions and their churches are all clustered together at the opposite end of Ditmar-Koel-Strasse. The Finnish Sailors' Church (Finnische Seemannskirche; Finnish: Suomalainen Merimieskirkko), for example, was erected in 1965–1966 at number 6. It is rendered in Finnish style in glazed brown bricks and, like other missions, stands alongside a meeting room and living areas. In Hamburg since 1901, the mission even has a sauna!

Immediately next door at number 4 is the Norwegian Sailors' Church (Norwegische Seemannskirche; Norwegian: Sjømannskirken) (1957). The original building was destroyed in the Second World War although the spire was reused in the new building in 1957 in the form of an unusual detached belfry. The Norwegian mission was established in Hamburg in 1907.

At the very end of the street is the Danish Sailors' Church (Dänische Seemannskirche; Danish: Danske Sømandskirke) (1951) at number 2. The church and mission were commissioned by the Bishop of Copenhagen in 1875 although the present structures date only from 1952. The open plan bell tower was inspired by the Adventskirche in Copenhagen.

A special time to visit the Scandinavian churches is during Christmas, when each hosts a traditional Christmas market.

Other places of interest nearby: 17, 18, 20, 21, 22

20 The Forgotten Walls of Hamburg

Hamburg-Mitte (Neustadt), the Hamburg Museum (Museum
für Hamburgische Geschichte) at Holstenwall 24
U3 St. Pauli; Bus 112 Museum für Hamburgische Geschichte

Hamburg's Altstadt was first surrounded by a wall during the thirteenth century, not long after it had been granted the status of an Imperial Free City by Holy Roman Emperor Frederick I (Barbarossa) (1155–1190). The Nikolaifleet, the original main arm of the Alster River, made up part of the moat, and in 1430 the wall was extended westwards to a line now occupied by the street Alter Wall. The new river port grew quickly and a larger wall was erected in the mid sixteenth century to protect it, recalled by the street name Neuer Wall; a new defensive moat was excavated beyond this wall, represented today by the Herrengrabenfleet and Bleichenfleet. This, too, was soon outmoded, not only by the burgeoning city but also by the growing threat from Denmark, which shared a border with Hamburg (in 1616 the Danish King Christian IV attacked the city in an attempt to gain control of the Elbe). This prompted the city to employ Dutch engineer Johan van Valckenburgh (1575–1625) to design an even larger and stronger wall, one which remained in place from the 1620s until the first half of the nineteenth century.

Today it is easy to forget that Hamburg ever had a city wall, so few are the remnants of it left in the landscape. One location that does preserve a reminder is the Hamburg Museum (Museum für Hamburgische Geschichte) at Holstenwall 24 (Neustadt), where the cobblestoned forecourt incorporates a mosaic depicting the former layout of the seventeenth century wall. Orientation is easy: standing in front of the mosaic, with the museum door directly ahead, one can see an inlet at the bottom left of the mosaic, representing the point where the Elbe joins the Alster; the third bastion moving clockwise from this point is the Casparus Bastion (on which the Bismarck Memorial was erected in 1906), whilst the fourth, beyond the old Millerntor gate (today Millerntordamm), is the Henricus Bastion on which the museum in front of you was constructed between 1914 and 1922.

On the first floor of the museum, which was designed by Fritz Schumacher (1869–1947), there is a splendid model showing how Hamburg

Hamburg's old city walls are depicted in a mosaic in front of the Hamburg Museum (Museum für Hamburgische Geschichte) on Holstenwall

would have appeared in 1644, two decades after the wall was completed. At the time the Dutch led in the development of new fortification techniques and the wall van Valckenburgh erected around Hamburg enabled the city to become one of the safest and most important commercial centres in seventeenth and eighteenth century Europe.

The model shows clearly an oval-shaped circuit wall pierced by several gateways. The line of the wall followed the ring road that today encircles the city centre, remembered in street names such as Holstenwall, Gorch-Fock-Wall, Glockengiesserwall, Steintorwall, and Klosterwall. Similarly, the gates are recalled in the street names Millerntordamm and Dammtordamm on the west, Steintordamm on the east, and Sandtorkai and Brooktorkai facing the Elbe (other gates such as Hafentor, Holstentor (on Sievekingsplatz), Klostertor and Deichtor were added later).

The wall was punctuated by twenty two individually-named, projecting bastions, distanced so as to be able to offer each other mutual support. The bastions were themselves protected by eleven independent bastions *(ravelins)*, erected on the far side of a 70 metre-wide, water-filled moat. Beyond the bastions lay the *glacis*, a broad belt of land kept

The walls of Hamburg are shown in a magnificent model inside the museum

free of buildings so as to deprive would-be attackers of any shelter (it is remembered in the street names Glacischaussee, Holstenglacis and Alsterglacis). An impression of the dimensions of the *glacis* can still be gained today, between Millerntor Damm and Dammtor Damm, where it is now occupied by three contiguous green zones (*Große Wallanlage, Kleine Wallanlage* and *Alter Botanischer Garten*), united as a public garden called Planten un Blomen (see no. 15). The lakes in the garden occupy parts of the former moat and still describe the zig-zag line of the bastions they once protected.

Construction of the wall lasted between 1616 and 1625, and when finished it encircled an area twice the size of the earlier walled Altstadt. Most significantly it encompassed Neustadt, to the west of Altstadt, which became densely populated with sailors, artisans, tradesmen, and soldiers. Many lived in the tightly-packed houses of the so-called *Gängeviertel*, where inadequate sanitation encouraged the spread of disease (see no. 16).

About a quarter of the city's revenues during the period were spent on the wall's construction, with entrenchment service made compulsory for all citizens. The wall was extended eastwards in 1697 to include the St. Georg district, which is remembered in the street names Wallstrasse, Berlinertordamm, Lübeckertordamm, and Sechslingspforte.

Military and administrative reorganisation occurred in line with the erection of the wall, notably the creation of a professional garrison in 1617, supported by a citizens' militia based on the city's five parishes. Different areas of the walled city were allocated to different trades and professions, some of which are still relevant today. Thus, important political and commercial institutions, such as the mint, town hall, stock exchange, and market place, were focussed around the Alster harbour (Binnenalster) into which timber and lime was delivered from upstream.

Where the Alster joined the Elbe was the Inner Harbour (Binnenhafen), defended not only by several bastions (including an additional fortification remembered in the street name Johannis Bollwerk) but also by timber posts embedded into the riverbed to prevent enemy ships from docking. The posts also served to narrow the harbour entrance, which could be closed off entirely by a timber boom, recalled in the street name Niederbaumbrücke. This harbour was used for docking by vessels too large to pass into the Alster, and a cargo handling centre was located here from the early fourteenth century onwards. As ships increased in draft they were moored at the timber posts, from where goods were ferried ashore by barge, giving rise to the street name Vorsetzen.

Until the Great Fire of 1842 most goods were transferred from the Inner Harbour to warehouses on the Nikolaifleet (see no. 10). Building materials, grain and flammable goods were taken eastwards along the Dovenfleet and Mührenfleet to the Upper Harbour (Oberhafen), where another timber boom (remembered in Oberbaumbrücke) protected Hamburg's upstream entrance to the Elbe.

The island of Grasbrook, south of the walled city, was used to graze cattle, dry textiles, and for public executions, the most famous being that of renowned pirate Klaus Störtebeker. By the early nineteenth century the wall had been deemed unecessary and was demolished piecemeal thereafter, the island of Grasbrook eventually becoming the location for Hamburg's famous warehouse district (Speicherstadt), which was inaugurated in 1888 (see no. 7).

Other places of interest nearby: 16, 17, 18, 19, 21

An Important Institute for Tropical Medicine

Hamburg-Mitte (St. Pauli), the Bernhard Nocht Institute for Tropical Medicine (Bernhard-Nocht-Institut für Tropenmedizin) at Bernhard-Nocht-Strasse 7 (note: the institute is not open to visitors)
S1, S3 Landungsbrücken; U3 Landungsbrücken; Bus 112 Landungsbrücken; Harbour Ferry 62, 72, 73, 75 Landungsbrücken

For those interested in the likelihood of ingesting worms whilst eating Sushi in Japan, or the dangers of eating uncooked Maniok in Central Africa, or which vaccinations are recommended for a pilgrimmage to Mecca, there's only one place to go: Hamburg's Bernhard Nocht Institute for Tropical Medicine (Bernhard-Nocht-Institut für Tropenmedizin) at Bernhard-Nocht-Strasse 7. Whilst the institute itself, which is dedicated to the treatment of tropical and infectious diseases around the world, is *not* open to casual visitors, the results of over a century of research *are* available to everyone through the institute's fascinating Travel Medicine Centre, which offers a mass of practical advice online (visit www.gesundes-reisen.de). Everything for the modern traveller is included, from how dangerous it is to stand on a Blue-ringed Octopus and the risk of alcohol poisoning in Russia, to the likelihood of contracting Yellow Fever whilst on safari in Kenya.

Bernhard-Nocht-Strasse is named after the first director of Hamburg's Institute for Tropical Medicine (Bernhard-Nocht-Institut für Tropenmedizin)

The Institute for Maritime and Tropical Diseases (Institut für Schiffs- und Tropenkrankheiten) was opened on 1st October 1900 in a former naval hospital administration building. Bernhard Nocht (1857–1945), a naval physician and medical officer for the Port of Hamburg, was appointed its first director, an honour reflected in the fact that the institute was re-named in honour of his 85th birthday in 1942. Nocht believed that Hamburg was the ideal location for such an institute because of the city's vast network of maritime overseas contacts. Between 1910 and 1914 a new red-brick building was erected on the site to a design by the renowned architect Fritz Schumacher (1869–1947), a tireless promoter of Brick Expressionism in Northern Germany (see no. 3).

The list of achievements made in the field of tropical medicine at the Bernhard Nocht Institute is impressive and includes the improvement of malaria therapy by the use of quinine derivatives (1911–1926), and the identification of the causative agents of epidemic typhus (1916), trench fever (1918), and bird malaria (1943). Despite being damaged by air raids in the Second World War, during which time the clinical department served as a military hospital, Germany's most important research facility for tropical medicine has continued to make historic contributions to the understanding and control of communicable diseases and emerging infections. Subsequent milestones have included immunisation research into bilharzia (1950), identification of the Marburg virus (1968), and the demonstration that patients infected with HIV experience massive viral replication in the lymph nodes (1985). In 2003 virologists at the institute identified the Severe Adult Respiratory Syndrome (SARS) virus as a so-called coronavirus. On the same day as their discovery they posted details on the Internet crucial to diagnosis, a selfless decision that garnered them the Order of Merit of the Federal Republic of Germany.

The near pandemic of the SARS virus served well to remind the institute's detractors, who questioned the ongoing need for such facilities in the West, that globalisation and climate change is bringing tropical disease closer to home (for example the Asian tiger mosquito was identified in the Upper Rhine valley in 2008). Domestic considerations aside, the industrialised West has a moral responsibilty to conduct biomedical research on behalf of the world's poorer nations, moreso since many of these nations were once colonised and exploited by Europe. Stamping out poverty-related disease will help reduce poverty itself, currently one of the main threats to global peace.

Many important discoveries have been made at the Institute for Tropical Medicine

The library at the Bernhard Nocht Institute for Tropical Medicine is as old as the institute itself, making it the oldest and largest library relating to tropical medicine in Germany. With collections pertaining not only to tropical medicine but also parasitology, immunology, virology and molecular biology the library contains approximately 43 000 books, 48 000 printed articles, and 160 current journals (including 38 e-journals). Visits can be arranged through the institute's website at www.bni-hamburg.de.

Other places of interest nearby: 19, 22, 23, 29

22 Hamburg's Favourite Hidden Place

Hamburg-Mitte (St. Pauli), the Old Elbe Tunnel (Alter Elbtunnel) at Bei den St.-Pauli-Landungsbrücken (note: the tunnel is open to cars Mon–Fri, but only to pedestrians Sat & Sun)
S1, S3 Landungsbrücken; U3 Landungsbrücken; Bus 112 Landungsbrücken; Harbour Ferry 62, 72, 73, 75 Landungsbrücken

Since the early nineteenth century, large passenger ships arriving in Hamburg have docked at Bei den St.-Pauli-Landungsbrücken. In 1907 the original riverboat quay of 1839 was replaced by a 688 metre-long landing stage, made up from a series of floating pontoons. Despite being seriously damaged during the Allied air raids of the Second World War, the landing stage was rebuilt in the 1950s, although the luxury liners of yesteryear have now been replaced by much smaller ferry boats and pleasure cruisers (liners now dock at the Cruise Center in HafenCity).

Passengers disembarking in the old days would have made their way along the pontoons and out to waiting taxis, buses and trains through the stretched-out former terminal building. Built between 1907 and 1909 from rough hewn volcanic tufa the building is still standing, its distinctive profile comprising two cupolas, and a tower at the eastern end. Called the Pegelturm, the tower indicates the level of the Elbe, which is tidal in Hamburg despite being a hundred kilometres from the North Sea. At the western end of the building there is a detached structure with a weathered copper dome. Constructed of finely cut masonry the building forms a suitably imposing entrance to the Old Elbe Tunnel (Alter Elbtunnel), Hamburg's favourite hidden place.

The first bridges to cross the Elbe in Hamburg were built in the late nineteenth century but in the busy harbour area of St. Pauli a bridge was not feasible due to the volume of high-masted sailing vessels. By the turn of the century some 40 000 dock workers were employed in the burgeoning shipyards on the south shore of the Elbe, and they were transported back and forth from their homes on the opposite shore by a fleet of ferries (see no. 29). This inevitably created traffic problems, and in 1901 it was decided to construct a tunnel like the one beneath the River Clyde in Glasgow.

Two tunnels were excavated, set side-by-side, stretching 426.5 metres from Bei den St.-Pauli-Landungsbrücken to the shipyards of

Steinwerder on the southern shore (see no. 29). The excavation work was carried out by 4400 workers, the majority of whom were professional miners from Silesia and the Ruhr area. At either end of the tunnels was built a terminus, where four large lifts were used to transfer vehicles to pavement level twenty four metres above.

The tunnel opened in 1911 and was immediately hailed as a technical masterpiece. Since then little has changed and it is still used today, especially by tourists. To get a good look at the lifts in action descend to the tunnels by means of the staircase that spirals down the inside of the vertical shafts. The way down, as well as the white-tiled tunnels themselves, are adorned with numerous ceramic ornaments, mostly on a marine theme, such as fish, lobsters, and sailing boats; there is

The lift shaft of the Old Elbe Tunnel (Alter Elbtunnel) is both functional and graceful

even one depicting a sailor's old boot, surrounded by rats! It is worth remembering that vehicles are not allowed to use the tunnel at weekends, which makes it easier to scrutinise at leisure the sign in the middle of the tunnel announcing that the average high tide level of the Elbe lies exactly twenty one metres above one's head.

Re-emerging in Steinwerder one notices that the entrance building on that side has a flat roof rather than a cupola. This is because both buildings were damaged during the Second World War but so far only the cupola on the St. Pauli side has been restored, using approximately seven tons of copper sheeting. To save money the Steinwerder entrance was given a simple (and cheaper) flat roof. However, the Steinwerder entrance building is able to boast the tunnel's service areas including

The Old Elbe Tunnel (Alter Elbtunnel) connects St. Pauli with the shipyards of Steinwerder

a control room, machine hall, and power plant, the latter containing a small museum illustrating the history of the tunnel.

The construction between 1968 and 1975 of a new 3.1 kilometre-long Elbe Tunnel, carrying the A7 Autobahn between the districts of Othmarschen and Walthershof, has meant that the St. Pauli-Steinwerder tunnel is now referred to as the Old Elbe Tunnel (Alter Elbtunnel) or St. Pauli-Elbtunnel. Lacking the charm and history of its predecessor the new tunnel is nonetheless an engineering marvel, as witnessed by the colossal cutting wheel used to excavate it, which is now on permanent display outside the Museum of Work (Museum der Arbeit) at Wiesendamm 3 (Barmbek-Nord) (see no. 78).

Other places of interest nearby: 19, 21, 23, 29

23 Along the Sinful Mile

Hamburg-Mitte (St. Pauli), a tour of the red-light district
between Reeperbahn and Bernhard-Nocht-Strasse
S1, S3 Reeperbahn; Bus 36, 37 Davidstrasse, 112 St. Pauli
Hafenstrasse

"In Hamburg sind die Nächte lang" (In Hamburg the nights are long)
go the words of a song popular in the 1950s, and nowhere are they
longer than in St. Pauli, home to the city's famous red-light district.
The suburb of St. Pauli, originally called Hamburger Berg, originated
during the first half of the seventeenth century beyond the city walls,
initially as a means of guaranteeing a clear line of fire between Hamburg and Altona (the latter administered from 1640 until 1864 by Denmark). Gradually workhouses, hospitals, and undesirable industries
were moved here, amongst them the city's ropemakers, attracted by the
availability of open ground on which to twist their ships' ropes. Up to
300 metres in length the ropes were known locally as *Reep*, giving rise
to the name of St. Pauli's best known street – the Reeperbahn.

The first public entertainment in St. Pauli consisted of a modest
row of booths on Spielbudenplatz but these were destroyed by Napoleon when he occupied Hamburg in 1806. In 1833 St. Pauli was incorporated into Hamburg and the booths were gradually replaced by theatres,
dance clubs, beer halls, and officially-sanctioned brothels, which even-

The Reeperbahn has
long been popular with
visitors

Modesty screens are in place at either end of Herbertstrasse

tually spread along the Reeperbahn between Davidstrasse and Große Freiheit. Known as Hamburg's "Sinful Mile" this part of St. Pauli was long popular with sailors on shore leave but is now a tourist attraction in its own right.

Understandably many of St. Pauli's more overt attractions are not for the prudish, and are of necessity hidden places. This short tour of three more salubrious locations visible to all begins on the landward side of the Reeperbahn on Große Freiheit, a street famous for being the place where The Beatles first made their mark in the early 1960s (see no. 25). Since 1718 the lovely Baroque Catholic Church of St. Joseph (St. Josephs Kirche) has stood here, surrounded by bars and sex clubs. This setting is perhaps not so incongruous when one recalls that Große Freiheit (meaning 'great liberty') once stood in Altona, and was so-named by the Danish to reflect the freedom of religion and trade not offered in neighbouring Hamburg (see no. 58). Today, the presence of the church here reflects a new type of openness.

Our second location is the Davidwache, a police station at the corner of Spielbudenplatz and Davidstrasse. After St. Pauli was incorporated into Hamburg the police responsible for safeguarding the area were housed in a wooden hut. As the district grew more popular further police were needed to keep the peace, and in 1868 a police station was built here. It was replaced in 1914 with the current brick building designed by renowned architect Fritz Schumacher (1869–1947).

This tour finishes a couple of streets south of the police station on Herbertstrasse. During the 1930s the Nazis arrested prostitutes and threatened to demolish St. Pauli's red-light district. Eventually they compromised by permitting striptease shows to take place, but *only* on Herbertstrasse, and only if the short street was screened at either end to protect the public. The screens are still in place today (beyond which scantily-clad girls parade their wares in glass-fronted booths) and remain an interesting relic from the Nazi period. It is said that uninvited women, under-18s, and troublemakers attempting to enter will be greeted with a bucket of cold water!

Other places of interest nearby: 21, 22, 25

24 Harry's Hamburger Hafenbasar

Hamburg-Mitte (Altstadt), Harry's Hamburger Hafenbasar
in the GREIF floating crane at Sandtorhafen
U1 Meßberg; Bus 3, 4, 6 Auf dem Sande (Speicherstadt);
Harbour Ferry 72 Elbphilharmonie

Harry's Hamburger Hafenbasar was founded in 1954 by Harry Rosenberg (1924-2000), a well-travelled sailor forced into early retirement by a lung disease. Initially he opened a shop on Bernhard Nocht Strasse selling old coins and stamps, the premises of which he adorned with colourful souvenirs from his travels. It soon became apparent, however, that his customers were far more interested in the spears on the wall and the stuffed crocodiles than in the coins and stamps!

Inspired by the popularity of a similarly-adorned tavern in St. Pauli, operated between the 1930s and 1950s by the legendary 'Käptn Haase', Rosenberg decided to transform his shop into Harry's Hamburger Hafenbasar, a singular combination of ethnological museum, warehouse, and shop. Such was the success of the business that it soon transferred to larger premises on the same street, then to Große Freiheit, and in 2001, after Rosenberg's death, to Erichstrasse in St. Pauli.

From 1996 onwards the business was ably managed by Rosenberg's daughter, Karin. Whereas her father replenished his stock by purchasing artefacts from fellow sailors returning periodically to port, Ms. Rosenberg used foreign intermediaries acting on her behalf. The relatively short time that ships stay in port these days, combined with the introduction of container shipping, means that long gone are the days when a mariner would amble into the Hafenbasar looking to sell his souvenirs.

The death of Karin Rosenberg in 2011 might well have meant the end of the Hafenbasar. Instead long-time fan, Dr. Gereon Boos, stepped in to save the day. Strong in the belief that the collection should be closer to the sea, whence much of the collection heralded, he took the bold decision to move it once again – and to premises that could not be more suitable. Harry's Hafenbasar is today housed inside a floating crane!

The GREIF floating crane dates from 1947 and is moored at Sandtorhafen. Its cavernous interior provides 200 square metres of space divided up into thirty three separate compartments. This means that

Harry's Hamburger Hafenbasar is a world apart!

the Hafenbasar can for the first time be displayed thematically, with a different compartment dedicated to a different type or provenance of object. By contrast, in the days of Harry Rosenberg the collection was displayed fairly chaotically, although admittedly this was part of its charm. When anyone asked Harry Rosenberg how many items were in his collection he would always answer the same: 81,283! Of course, he didn't know the exact number but his tongue-in-cheek response was indicative of just how big the collection had become.

Entering the Hafenbasar today is still an overwhelming experience. The sight of so many exotic objects transports the visitor immediately to strange and far-off lands. The compartments are crammed with ethnic crafts and souvenirs, stuffed animals and other natural curiosities, old tools and musical instruments, and ceremonial and religious objects. The smoky aroma is the result of some carvings having been singed by medicine men, and the lack of natural daylight only adds to the mystique.

Compartment after compartment takes the visitor on a journey worthy of Jules Verne. One is filled with wooden masks, statues and other carvings from West Africa, another stashed with colourful Asian masks, rows of seated Thai Buddhas, and paper-thin Indonesian shadow puppets. There is even rumour of a South American shrunken head! A particularly intriguing compartment contains maritime oddities such as sharks' jaws, dried Asian fish with painted eyes, ships' portholes, mast lanterns, and an example of the legendary Seychelles' *Coco de Mer*.

Like the Rosenbergs before him, Gereon Boos encourages visitors to touch the artefacts on display – something that sets the Hafenbasar apart from other museums – since this keeps the dust from gathering. After all, who would want to dust 81,283 exhibits?

Other places of interest nearby: 7, 8, 9, 10, 11

25 In John Lennon's Doorway

Hamburg Mitte (St. Pauli), John Lennon's doorway at
Wohlwillstrasse 22, Jägerpassage 1
S1, S3 Reeperbahn; U3 St. Pauli; Bus 36, 37 Davidstrasse

On 17th August 1960 a previously unknown 5-piece band from Liverpool – comprising John Lennon, Paul McCartney, George Harrison, Stuart Sutcliffe, and Pete Best – took to the stage of Hamburg's Indra Club at Große Freiheit 64 (St. Pauli), a side street off the Reeperbahn made famous by the actor Hans Albers in the wartime film *Große Freiheit Nr. 7*. It would be the start not only of a 48-night residency at the club (during which time the band would adopt the name The Beatles) but also of a ten year career during which they would become the most successful pop group in history.

Fans of The Beatles have been coming to Hamburg ever since those early days to follow in the footsteps of their idols. The Indra Club still exists as a music venue, as does the Kaiserkeller at Große Freiheit 36, where The Beatles played for a further 58 nights, after the Indra Club was closed temporarily. It was here that they met their new drummer Ringo Starr. Between August and September they lived in gloomy unheated rooms above the Bambi Kino, a cinema around the corner at Paul-Roosen-Strasse 33. Containing only a single wash basin John Lennon described the windowless premises, which are still standing, as a "pigsty".

The group returned to Hamburg in 1961 to play at the Top Ten Club at Reeperbahn 136 (also still extant), and three more times in 1962 to work the now legendary Star Club at Große Freiheit 39. The Beatles' last concert in Hamburg was played here on 31st December 1962. Unfortunately, after a fire in 1987 the derelict Star Club was pulled down and there is now only a stone memorial to mark the spot, inscribed with the name of The Beatles, as well as those of other famous performers such as Bill Haley, Jerry Lee Lewis, Ray Charles, and Jimmy Hendrix.

Today's Beatles pilgrim would do well to take the excellent 'Beatles in Hamburg' tour of St. Pauli (visit www.beatles-tour.com), during which all the sites detailed above are visited. Also namechecked is the record-shaped sculpture on Beatles-Platz.

There is one secret location on the tour, however, which is not listed in the mainstream guidebooks. This is the doorway depicted

In the early 1960s John
Lennon posed for an
iconic photograph in
this doorway

on the front cover of John Lennon's sixth post-Beatles solo recording
Rock'n'Roll. Despite being released in 1975 the album's black-and-white
image of a young leather-jacketted Lennon leaning in a doorway was
taken in 1961, after the band had returned to Hamburg and were exploring the seedy but exciting back streets of St. Pauli. As Lennon himself
later admitted: "I was born in Liverpool, but I grew up in Hamburg".

The doorway is to be found on Wohlwillstrasse, an atmospheric
street of alternative cafés and craft studios, which one imagines Lennon would approve of were he still alive today. At number 22 a pair of
wooden gates open onto Jägerpassage, a narrow thoroughfare lined
with brick-built tenements. The doorway depicted on *Rock'n'Roll* is at
Jägerpassage 1, although there is nothing to identify it as such, thereby

preserving the mystique of the location. Long may this continue.

The photograph itself was taken by the Hamburg photographer Jurgen Vollmer (b. 1941), whose name is credited on the album sleeve. Vollmer had befriended The Beatles when they first arrived in Hamburg in 1960, and remained in touch with them after he relocated to Paris' influential Left Bank. Lennon

The little-known Jägerpassage is still a site of pilgrimage for many John Lennon fans

and McCartney visited him there in 1961, emulating not only Vollmer's fashionable suits but also his 'mop top' hair cut. The Beatles early iconic style was born.

Vollmer went on to become one of the most acclaimed fashion, celebrity and film stills photographers of the 1960s, settling eventually in New York in 1971. It was here in September 1974 that he encountered John Lennon's personal assistant, May Pang, at the first Beatlefest convention. She explained that the singer was struggling to select suitable artwork for the cover of his forthcoming *Rock'n'Roll* album. Vollmer, who was at the convention selling his pictures, reached into his portfolio and pulled out the photo he had taken of Lennon in the doorway on Wohlwillstrasse over a decade earlier. When Lennon eventually saw it for himself he knew immediately that he need look no further.

Other places of interest nearby: 20, 21, 23

26

Across the Sea to Neuwerk

Hamburg-Mitte (Neuwerk), the island of Neuwerk northwest
of Cuxhaven (note: if crossing by foot it is imperative to check
the tide times)
Metronom train from Hamburg Hauptbahnhof to Cuxhaven,
then Bus 1006 either to Alte Liebe for boat crossing at high
tide, or Sahlenburger Strand for horse-drawn carriage at
low tide

In the shallow coastal waters northwest of Cuxhaven lies the tiny North
Sea island of Neuwerk. Despite being 105 kilometres away from Hamburg it belongs administratively to the city – specifically the borough of
Hamburg-Mitte – and a trip to visit it can be a real adventure. The car-
free island is best reached across the mud flats at low tide by means of
a specially adapted horsedrawn carriage *(Wattwagen)*. Carriages depart
once a day from Wattwagenplatz at Sahlenburger Strand (depending
on the tide times), with the round journey taking about four hours (including one hour on the island). It is advisable to book a seat in advance
(visit www.wattwagen-cux.de) and to bring warm weatherproof clothing, as the weather can be very changeable in the channel.

Neuwerk originated as a sandy island as recently as the first century BC, during what geologists term the Holocene period. The oldest
documentary evidence for Neuwerk dates from 1286, detailing summer
grazing rights on the island, which is referred to only as 'O', that being
Old Frisian for island. At the time the island belonged to the Dukes
of Saxe-Lauenburg, who in 1299 granted Hamburg the right to build a
tower on the island. The mouth of the Elbe river was vital to the commercial livelihood of Hamburg and the tower would act as a defence
against pirates and would-be invaders. The occupants of the nearby
East Frisian Islands thereafter referred to the island as *Dat Werk* or *Nige*
(new) *Werk*, leading eventually to the name Neuwerk. Incidentally, the
sturdy 35-metre-high, brick-built tower seen on the island today, surrounded by a protective embankment, was built between 1367 and 1369,
after a fire destroyed the earlier one; it is officially Hamburg's oldest
building, as well as its last extant fortification. The original doorway
was situated eight metres above ground and could only be reached by
means of a rope ladder.

Since its formation the shape of Neuwerk has changed completely. After the building of the first tower the island continually lost
ground to violent winter storms necessitating the construction of a

Horsedrawn carriages bound for the island of Neuwerk

protective ring dyke around the tower in the mid sixteenth century. Within the security of the dyke several farmsteads were established, together with all-year-round arable land. The dyked-in area, the so-called *Binnengroden*, was kept dry by the construction of a series of smaller channels known as *Grüppen*. Outside the dyke, however, which can still be made out today, the land was only fit for seasonal grazing. The dyke was still sometimes breached at high tide and from the late eighteenth century until the 1930s the island's shoreline was comprehensively stabilised.

In the middle of the seventeenth century a coal-fired navigational light was added to the tower for the first time, and by the end of the eighteenth century the tenant farmers on the island were allowed to purchase their farms. Eventually, in 1814 the defence tower was converted into a lighthouse proper, and the lamp, which has been remote-controlled from Cuxhaven since 1971, became visible for miles around due to a system of parabolic mirrors.

With the development of seaside tourism in the early twentieth century Neuwerk became a visitor attraction, periodically swelling the tiny indigenous population. Farming started to wane after the first hotel opened in 1905, and in 1924 the lighthouse, with its fine all-round

The water gets deep in the centre of the channel

views, was listed as a historic monument. Alongside it there is a poignant seamens' cemetery dubbed the Cemetery of the Nameless.

Neuwerk didn't always belong to Hamburg though. In 1937 under the terms of the Greater Hamburg Law, Prussia traded Altona, Harburg and Wandsbek with Hamburg in return for Cuxhaven and Neuwerk. After the Second World War these Prussian rights passed to the new state of Lower Saxony, which in 1969 transferred Neuwerk back to Hamburg, in readiness for the construction of a deepwater harbour. It was never constructed and instead Neuwerk, together with the lonely seabird sanctuaries of Scharhörn and Nigehörn, became part of the Hamburg Wadden Sea National Park (National Park Hamburgisches Wattenmeer), one of three national parks along the German North Sea coast that share and protect the Wadden Sea ecoregion.

27

A Cemetery for Submarines

Hamburg-Mitte (Finkenwerder), the remains of U-boat dock
Fink II in the Rüschkanal, visible from Rüschweg
Bus 150, 611 Nordmeerstrasse, then walk to the Rüschkanal;
Harbour Ferry 64 Rüschpark

Anyone interested in submarines will certainly want to make a visit to the U-Bootmuseum Hamburg at Versmannstrasse 24 (HafenCity), where the B-515, a Russian Tango Class submarine launched in Gorky (now Nizhny Novgorod) in 1976, lies moored in the Baakenhafen. Powered by diesel and battery-powered engines and measuring just over 90 metres in length the submarine was the largest non-atomic powered submarine in the world, patrolling the Arctic Ocean on surveillance missions with the Russian North Sea fleet. With a crew of eighty four it was able to descend as deep as 400 metres and had a special rubberised outer coating rendering it almost invisible to radar detection. After being decomissioned in 2002 the B-515 was brought to Hamburg where it was re-numbered U-434.

Not surprisingly for a port, Hamburg's connection with submarines goes back much further than the U-434. After the First World War the Kiel-based company Howaldtswerke, which had constructed the world's first modern submarine in 1850, avoided bankruptcy by expanding to Hamburg. In 1940 they took over the Vulcan Works on Roßhafen (Steinwerder), one of Germany's leading shipyards. Shifting production exclusively to submarines, in 1941 the company completed a 140 metre-long wet dock on Am Vulkanhafen under the codename Elbe II. Consisting of two docks side-by-side, protected by a three metre-thick roof of reinforced concrete, the company's two hundred mostly-German workers built thirty three submarines here before the end of the Second World War.

When British Royal Engineers eventually demolished the Elbe II dock in November 1945 there were three state-of-the-art Type XXI U-boats still inside (U-2505, U-3004 and U-3506), which became permanently entombed. Daring salvage workers subsequently made the dangerous descent through layers of shattered concrete to visit the trapped submarines, which still rose and fell with the daily tide, until the entire Vulkanhafen basin was filled with sand in the 1990s and converted into a lorry park. Few people today are aware that the submarines still lie somewhere beneath the ground.

The shattered remains of Hitler's U-boat dock Fink II in the Rüschkanal

To get an impression of an extant U-boat dock one must travel west to Finkenwerder, where the Deutsche Werft AG shipyard was founded in 1918. Despite being a major employer it did not prosper greatly until the Second World War, when large orders were received from the German Navy, mainly for the construction of submarines. As at Elbe II, the workforce was protected from possible air raids by the construction of a huge fortified wet dock, this time under the codename Fink II. It was constructed from 130 000 cubic metres of concrete, and, despite being of a similar length to Elbe II, consisted of five parallel docks with a holding capacity of fifteen boats. The biggest U-boat dock in Germany it also differed from Elbe II in that most of its labourers were prisoners of war, housed in an on-site satellite camp of the Neuengamme Concentration Camp (Konzentrationslager Neuengamme).

The 3.6 metre-thick roof of the Fink II dock was damaged in April 1945 by powerful British 'Grand Slam' bombs. The remains were then further dismantled in October of the same year, and in 1956 they were covered over and forgotten about. However, during the construction of the runway for the Airbus factory on Finkenwerder the ruins of the old U-boat dock were revealed, and they have subsequently been preserved as a reminder of the violence of war. The remains can be viewed from Rüschweg, which runs along one side of the Rüschkanal, where the dock was located.

A collection of wartime submarine memorabilia is on display in the U-boat gallery of the International Maritime Museum Hamburg (Internationales Maritmes Museum Hamburg) at Koreastrasse 1 (HafenCity). A piece of anti-submarine netting once used to protect the Port of Hamburg from attack by Allied submarines coming up the Elbe is displayed outside the German Customs Museum (Deutsches Zollmuseum) at Alter Wandrahm 16 (Altstadt).

Other places of interest nearby: 28

28   Strolling on the Island of
        Finches

Hamburg-Mitte (Finkenwerder), a walk around the island
of Finkenwerder starting on Auedeich
Bus 146, 150, 251 Auedeich; Harbour Ferry 62 Finkenwerder

Finkenwerder, meaning 'island of finches', is the westernmost of
Hamburg's Elbe river islands. It was wrought from the old island of
Goriesswerder during a violent storm flood (the Allerkindleinsflut) in
December 1248. Whereas islands such as Steinwerder, Kleiner Grasbrook, Wilhemsburg, Veddel, and Rothenburgsort are dominated by
docks, canals, and railways, Finkenwerder retains a more rural feel. It
is also home to a significant permanent population numbering more
than 11 000, unlike neighbouring Altenwerder, for example, which
despite being similarly sized supports a population of just two (see
no. 43)! Finkenwerder is also unusual in that its western part is given
over entirely to the private Hamburg Finkenwerder Airport, and the
Airbus works it services (see no. 44). The construction of a land bridge
southwards across the water to Neuenfelde, across which the Airbus
runway has been constructed, means that Finkenwerder is techically
no longer an island.
    Of far greater interest to the explorer, however, is old Finken-
werder, which occupies the central and eastern parts of the island,
where it makes for an pleasant few hours to stroll along the old streets
and rural thoroughfares. We begin where the bus stops on Auedeich, a
narrow street set on top of an ancient embankment that winds northwards through this part of the island. The buildings lining the street
are a charming mixture of ornately-plastered late nineteenth century
structures (such as the former butcher and baker at numbers 30 and 22
respectively), and timber-framed red-brick houses dating back to the
early nineteenth century. A good example of the latter, which is typical
for the area, stands at number 24. Dating to 1817 it has a broad ground
floor storey, over which rises a magnificent, gently-sloping thatched
roof, containing two upper storeys. Other houses on the street have lost
their thatched rooves but still retain their timber-framed construction,
whilst several twentieth century buildings mimic the traditional style
using modern materials.
    Continuing northwards Auedeich runs into Sandhöhe and Ka-
nalstack to join Köhlfleet Hauptdeich, where a charming little harbour

This old thatched house stands at one end of Auedeich on Finkenwerder

can be found in which are moored several old fashioned, single-masted North Sea fishing boats *(Hochseekutter)*. Fishing was once the main occupation in this part of the island and Finkenwerder plaice *(Scholle)* is still renowned (see no. 18). From here follow Köhlfleet Hauptdeich northwards onto Benittstrasse, passing on the right a maritime firefighting school with an old water jet in the front garden. On the left is a former sports hall designed by the architect Fritz Schumacher (1869–1947) and named in honour of Finkenwerder's most famous author, Gorch Fock (real name Johann Wilhelm Kinau) (1880–1916), who died at the Battle of Jutland. Beyond is a former sailors' school, now a police station, erected originally in 1913 for use by the Deutsche Werft AG shipyard.

In front of the police station is the landing stage for the harbour ferries (although it is recommended to approach Finkenwerder by bus from Neugraben, so as to better appreciate the settlement's geographical setting). Looking out across the Köhlfleet from here it is easy to make out the red-brick pilot's house *(Lotsen-Haus)* from where pilots would escort shipping into the Port of Hamburg farther upstream.

Returning to the bus route it is only a couple of stops to Rüschweg, from the end of which it is possible to see the ruins of a former Second

World War U-boat dock (see no. 27). It is worth remembering that Finkenwerder was once a satellite labour camp of the Neuengamme Concentration Camp (Konzentrationslager Neuengamme), in which six hundred prisoners of war toiled under harsh conditions (see no. 51).

From Rüschweg Bus 251 continues onwards to its terminus on Norderkirchenweg, in the rural heart of Finkenwerder, where the island's churches and burial grounds are located. Running east to west is Finkenwerder Landscheideweg, which until 1937 divided the island in two: the northern part having belonged to Hamburg since 1445, the southern part being in the possession of Braunschweig-Lüneburg until 1814, the Kingdom of Hanover until 1866, and thereafter to Prussia. During the cholera epidemic of 1892 those in

Traditional fishing boats are moored in the tiny harbour of Finkenwerder

the north of the island risked not only disease but also the death penalty by entering the south in order to attend Protestant services at the St. Nikolaikirche, which still stands just inside the former southern territory. From here it is a brisk walk eastwards along Finkenwerder Landscheideweg to finish at our starting point on Auedeich.

Other places of interest nearby: 27

29   The Greatest of Shipbuilders

Hamburg-Mitte (Steinwerder), the Blohm & Voss shipyard at
Hermann-Blohm-Strasse 5
S1, S3 Landungsbrücken or U3 Landungsbrücken, then walk
along the Old Elbe Tunnel (Alter Elbtunnel); Harbour Ferry 75
Steinwerder

The name Blohm & Voss has long been synonymous with shipbuilding in Hamburg, and the company's sprawling shipyards on Steinwerder still dominate the Elbe when viewed from the old passenger liner terminal at Bei den St.-Pauli-Landungsbrücken.

Hermann Blohm and Ernst Voss first became acquainted in England, whilst studying the techniques of iron shipbuilding. On 5th April 1877 they founded the Blohm & Voss Shipyard & Machine Factory (Blohm & Voss Schiffswerft & Maschinenfabrik) at Kuhwerder, an area used previously for grazing cattle, on the western side of the Elbe island of Steinwerder. Their first workshop was little more than a wooden shed. Despite the big Hamburg shipping lines of the day ordering their steamers from Britain, Blohm & Voss slowly carved out a name for themselves. The construction of a dry dock in which they could carry out ship repairs was a significant turning point, and during the late nineteenth century the company came to the notice of the German Navy. Business began booming and by 1905 the Blohm & Voss shipyard was one of the largest in the world, covering an area of 560 000 square metres and with a three kilometre-long waterfront.

The fact that so many workers were employed by Blohm & Voss, as well as other shipyards on Steinwerder, prompted the decision in 1901 to excavate Hamburg's famous Old Elbe Tunnel (Alter Elbtunnel), creating a direct connection between the shipyards and the workers' homes in Neustadt (see no. 22). Until the tunnel's opening in 1911 the 40 000 or more workers were ferried daily across the Elbe, which not only took longer but was also an inconvenience to shipping. The tunnel still delivers pedestrians and vehicles to the Blohm & Voss shipyard at Hermann-Blohm-Strasse 5, where today a large rusting anchor marks the main entrance. Although not open to the public it is a suitable place to pause and reflect on some of the great ships constructed here, most of which have subsequently been either scrapped or else consigned to the ocean floor.

In the early decades of the twentieth century Blohm & Voss con-

A huge anchor lies outside the main entrance to the Blohm & Voss shipyard

structed both steam ships as well as sailing ships, the latter represented by the four-masted barque *Pamir*. Launched in 1905 the *Pamir* was commissioned by the company of Ferdinand Laeisz, whose eighteen-strong fleet of sailing ships (the so-called Flying P-Liners) operated in the lucrative nitrate and guano trade with Chile. All the names of the ships began with the letter 'P' in honour of Carl Laeisz's curly-haired wife, whose nickname was Poodle (see no. 2)! Converted into a training vessel in 1952 the *Pamir* eventually capsized with the loss of most of its crew during an Atlantic storm in 1957.

In 1913 Blohm & Voss launched the *Vaterland*, the second of a trio of transatlantic passenger liners commissioned by Albert Ballin of the Hamburg-America Line (HAPAG). Arriving in New York just as the First World War broke out the ship was impounded, and then requisitioned as the *SS Leviathan* by the United States after they entered the war in 1917.

Blohm & Voss concentrated on the production of submarines during the First World War after which they lost all their navy contracts. Despite this the company avoided bankruptcy and in 1927 launched the *Cap Arcona* for the Hamburg-Süd shipping company. A luxury liner it also served as an emigrant ship, sailing regularly between Europe and

Elbe 17 is one of the largest dry docks in Europe

South America. During the Second World War the ship served as a troop transporter for the German army, and in April 1945 most remaining prisoners from the Neuengamme Concentration Camp (Konzentrationslager Neuengamme) were placed aboard the ship in Lübeck Bay. It seems the intention was to sink the ship in an attempt to conceal the crimes of the SS. Tragically, on 3rd May the unmarked ship was spotted by Allied bombers, and destroyed with the loss of over 4000 lives.

Blohm & Voss was an important builder of both warships and passenger liners during the years of the Third Reich. The *Wilhelm Gustloff*, for example, was launched in 1937 and named after the German leader of the Swiss Nazi Party, who had been assassinated in 1936 by a Jewish student. With space for 1400 passengers it was part of the "Strength through Joy" (Kraft durch Freude – KdF) fleet, designed to take German workers on pleasure cruises whilst under the ever-watchful eye of the Nazi state. On 30th January 1945, whilst the ship was being used to evacuate German refugees from East Prussia, it was sunk by a Soviet submarine resulting in the death of over 9000 passengers.

Blohm & Voss spent most of the Second World War building submarines for the German Navy but not before they had built the *Bismarck*, the most powerful battleship in the world. Launched on 14th February 1939 in the presence of Adolf Hitler the 250 metre-long ship was rendered impervious to torpedoes by a hull made of reinforced Krupp steel. The *Bismarck* set sail on 18th May 1941 and encountered the British fleet in the

The battleship *Bismarck* in the docks at Hamburg in 1940

North Atlantic. After quickly sinking the *HMS Hood* the *Bismarck* was hit by an airborne torpedo and her rudder jammed. Unable to manouvre it is assumed that her admiral gave the order to open the seacocks and the great battleship was sent to the bottom, together with 2000 of her crew. A solitary 16-tonne armour plate surplus to requirement is the only reminder of the *Bismarck* at Blohm & Voss today, displayed alongside the dock (Werfthafen) where she was built.

It is sometimes wrongly assumed that the *Bismarck* was constructed in the massive dry dock Elbe 17, clearly visible from Bei den St.-Pauli-Landungsbrücken. With a length of 351 metres and a width of 59 metres it was commissioned in 1938 to repair ships such as the *Bismarck* and to construct the even larger H-Class battleships. None of this ever happened and instead the sturdy structure served as an air raid shelter for up to 6000 workers. One of the largest dry docks in Europe it has subsequently been used by some of the world's longest liners, including the *MS Freedom of the Seas* (339 metres), the *Queen Mary 2* (345 metres), and the *Sovereign Maersk* (347 metres).

Blohm & Voss today is a part of ThyssenKrupp Marine Systems and specialises in the construction of luxury yachts.

Other places of interest nearby: 22

30   Hitler's Concrete Castles

Hamburg-Mitte (Wilhelmsburg), a former Second World War
anti-aircraft tower *(Flakturm)* on Neuhöfer Strasse
S1, S31 Wilhelmsburg, then Bus 252 Neuhöfer Strasse

In September 1940, Adolf Hitler issued a *Führerbefehl* (Führer Order)
stipulating that Berlin, Hamburg and Vienna be protected from possible air raids by a series of colossal anti-aircraft towers *(Flaktürme,*
where *Flak* is an acronym of *Fliegerabwehrkanonen,* meaning 'aircraft
defence guns'). Hamburg was an obvious target for the Allies because
of the presence of shipyards such as Blohm & Voss, H.C. Stülcken,
Howaldtswerke, and Deutsche Werft AG, in which most of Germany's
submarines were produced (see no. 27).

The towers were commissioned by Hitler's architect Albert Speer
(1905–1981), who tasked the motorway architect Friedrich Tamms
(1904–1980) and the Organisation Todt (the Third Reich's military
engineering division) to design and build them in just six months using forced labour. Each *Flak* installation consisted of a heavily-armed
attack tower *(Gefechtsturm)* approximately 40 metres high, and with
walls of reinforced concrete up to 3.5 metres thick, together with a
smaller control tower *(Leitturm)* equipped with retractable radar for
direction finding and ranging purposes. The installations were posi-
tioned so as to form a mutually-supportive defensive ring designed to
prevent enemy bombers getting close to factories and civilian areas.
Once operational the towers were manned by Hitler Youth *Luftwaffen-
helfer* under the command of experienced Luftwaffe officers and NCOs
of the *Turmflak-Abteilung.*

Three *Flak* installations were planned for Hamburg, of which only
two were completed: *Flakturm IV* in 1942 on Feldstrasse (Heiligengeistfeld) in St. Pauli, and *Flakturm VI* in 1943 on Neuhöfer Strasse in the
suburb of Wilhelmsburg; a third installation covering the eastern side
of the city was never built. (Roman numerals were allocated chrono-
logically to the installations as they were completed regardless of the
city in which they were built).

The Wilhelmsburg *Flak* installation is now a forlorn place to visit,
and speaks powerfully of the futility of Hitler's war. Having been
deemed instruments of war after Germany's surrender British engineers attempted to demolish the towers in 1947. They only succeeded in
removing the control tower in Wilhelmsburg, leaving the attack tower

Vegetation is slowly smothering this abandoned anti-aircraft tower (Flakturm) in Wilhelmsburg

virtually intact; today it is abandoned except for a handful of telephone masts and is gradually being engulfed by vegetation. The visitor can only imagine the same scene during the Second World War when the tower was fully operational. Measuring 57 metres square and rising nine storeys it has four cylindrical gun emplacements on the roof, each provided with twin-barrelled, 128mm anti-aircraft guns; between them they could fire 2900 shells an hour with a range of 21 kilometres and to a height of 15 000 metres. The guns were fed continuously by shell hoists that reached down inside the tower. On the projecting balconies below were further 20mm and 37mm guns, designed to bring down low-flying aircraft. Being impervious to explosives and gas, and having their own wells and power stations, the huge towers could also double as civilian shelters during air raids; the Wilhelmsburg attack tower alone could shelter up to 30 000 people if necessary.

The Heiligengeistfeld *Flak* installation suffered a different post-war fate. Considered too dangerous to demolish with explosives the attack tower, which measured a colossal 70.5 metres square, was converted into accomodation in 1946, with a series of windows cut into the concrete façade. In 1992, after serving as a potential civilian shelter once more during the Cold War, the tower was converted into a media centre

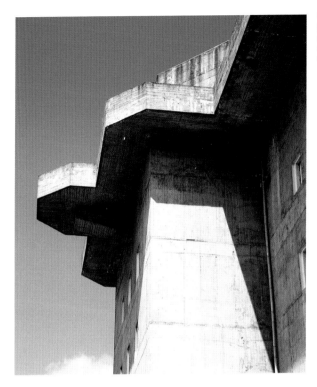

The former Heiligengeistfeld anti-aircraft tower now serves as a media and events centre

and events venue. The control tower, which was eventually demolished in the early 1970s, was used in 1950 to transmit the first television signal for Northwest German Television (Nordwestdeutscher Rundfunk), after which a regular programme was broadcast from the tower.

In military terms the *Flak* installations were quickly rendered obsolete by the introduction of mass Allied bombing raids, as well as the dropping of aluminium foil (called Window) to confuse German radar. Their presence, however, undoubtedly had a certain propaganda value in convincing the civilian population of Germany's invincibility. It is worth noting that had Germany won the war there were plans to clad the redundant *Flak* towers with marble, on which would have been inscribed the names of every member of the Luftwaffe who had died in action.

Other places of interest nearby: 31

A Handful of Historic Windmills

Hamburg-Mitte (Wilhelmsburg), a tour of old windmills
beginning with the Windmill 'Johanna' (Windmühle Johanna)
at Schönenfelder Strasse 99a
S3, S31 Wilhelmsburg, then Bus 154 Wilhelmsburger Mühle

Anyone strolling through Hamburg's green belt will notice the increasing presence of wind turbines. Flat geography and reliable prevailing winds mean that the city is well-placed to take advantage of this renewable form of energy. It is little wonder that Hamburg was the setting for the WindEnergy International Trade Fair in 2004 (at which the world's longest windmill blade (61.5 metres) was unveiled), and that in 2009 Siemens Wind Power opened their new European headquarters in the city's district of St. Georg.

The history of Hamburg's windmills, however, stretches back much farther. From the twelfth century onwards several hundred mills were constructed in Hamburg, powered not only by the wind, but also by water and by horses. Watermills especially had a considerable impact on the landscape, since they often necessited the diversion of rivers and the construction of dams. The former existence of these mills is recalled in street names such as Mühlendamm, Mühlenkamp and Neumühlen.

Although the majority of Hamburg's mills are long vanished the city is still blessed with a handful of historic windmills. This short tour begins on the island of Wilhelmsburg, which, together with the neighbouring islands of Kleiner Grasbrook, Steinwerder and Veddel, is located between the northern and southern branches of the Elbe. Despite being marred today by extensive road, rail and dock facilities, Wilhelmsburg has a long and interesting history, which is detailed at the Museum Elbinsel Wilhelmsburg at Kirchdorfer Strasse 163. The island also contains one of the most charming vistas in all Hamburg, namely the view across the millpond on Bei der Windmühle towards the Windmill 'Johanna' (Windmühle Johanna) at Schönenfelder Strasse 99a.

Windmill 'Johanna', like all Hamburg's extant windmills, is a Dutch-style smock mill, consisting of a tapering, thatched or weatherboarded tower, topped with a cap that rotates to bring the sails into the wind (the sails can be opened or closed by the miller from the gallery running around the base of the tower, hence the German name *Galerieholländer*). The mill was built in 1875 on a site occupied previously by four earlier mills, each lost over the years to age or fire. The first was constructed in 1585 and survived until 1705, when it was replaced: this new mill lasted only until 1718. A third mill lasted almost a century, from 1719 until 1813. The fourth mill was in operation between 1814 and 1874, when the mill seen today was finally erected. Restored in the late 1990s it is still used to produce flour and today contains a café on the ground floor. Alongside the windmill there is the timber-framed former home of the mill owner Christoph Cordes, whose son Johann Wilhelm designed Ohlsdorf Cemetery (Friedhof Ohlsdorf) in the 1870s (see no. 83).

Three of Hamburg's five remaining windmills are to be found in the borough of Bergedorf, south-east of Wilhelmsburg. The Windmill 'Glück Zu' (Windmühle 'Glück Zu'), for example, was built in 1831 at Chrysanderstrasse 52a, in the district of Bergedorf itself. Used to grind corn until 1968 it features a single-cylinder steam engine installed in 1926.

Inside the Riepenburger Windmill (Windmühle Riepenburger Mühle) in Kirchwerder

To the southwest lies the region known as the Vier- und Marschlande, where a pair of windmills can be found. The Reitbrook Windmill (Windmühle Reitbrook) at Vorderdeich 11 (Reitbrook) is a three-storey mill constructed in 1870 to replace an earlier mill of 1773 destroyed by fire. It is not open to the public, so to understand the inner workings of such a mill visit the Riepenburger Windmill (Windmühle Riepenburger Mühle), a little farther south at Kirchwerder Mühlendamm 75a (Kirchwerder). Built in 1828 this is Hamburg's oldest and largest working corn mill; it also occupies the oldest site of any windmill in the city, dating back to 1318. The mill's grinding machinery can be observed at close quarters.

This tour concludes in the borough of Altona with the Osdorf Windmill (Windmühle Osdorf) at Osdorfer Landstrasse 162 (Osdorf), built in 1890 and now used as a restaurant.

Most of Hamburg's historic windmills can be visited during Deustche Mühlentag, an annual open day hosted on Whit Monday by the German Society for Millers and Mill Preservation (Deutsche Gesellschaft für Mühlenkunde und Mühlenerhaltung (DGM) e.V.). For further details visit www.muehlen-dgm-ev.de.

Other places of interest nearby: 30

32 A Lonely Little Lighthouse

Hamburg-Mitte (Wilhelmsburg), the Bunthaus Lighthouse
(Leuchtfeuer Bunthaus) on Moorwerder Hauptdeich at
Bunthäuser Spitze
S3, S31 Wilhelmsburg, then Bus 351 to Freilichtschule
Moorwerder and follow the path marked 'Wanderweg'

The mighty Elbe river stretches for almost 1100 kilometres, from its source in the Krkonoše mountains on the northwest borders of the Czech Republic, down to the North Sea at the German fishing town of Cuxhaven. First recorded by the Roman geographer Ptolemy in the second century AD as the *Albis* (Germanic for 'river'), the Elbe has long been an important delineator of European geography, forming the eastern limit of the Frankish empire of Charlemagne (Charles the Great), King of the Franks (742–814), and proving vital in the Late Middle Ages to the commercial success of the Hanseatic League.

The Elbe's tidal estuary stretches from the North Sea upstream to the Port of Hamburg and is marked by more than seventy lighthouses *(Leuchttürme)* along the way – the largest number of lighthouses on any inland waterway in the world. They are often built in pairs, the front light being designated the *Unterfeuer*, and the rear light the *Oberfeuer*. Fifty of these lighthouses are located above the town of Brunsbüttel, where the Elbe waterway narrows from the broader waters of the *Elbemündung* (the mouth of the Elbe), and where one of the entrances to the Kiel Canal is located. Downstream from Hamburg those on the south bank of the Elbe are in Lower Saxony (Niedersachsen) and those on the north bank are in Schleswig-Holstein.

Fortunately, despite navigators relying less and less on lighthouses these days, the lighthouses of the Elbe are administered and protected by a federal agency, the Wasser- und Schifffahrtsamtverwaltung des Bundes (WSV). As a result, most of them are maintained and in good condition. The fact that lighthouses on the Elbe come in all shapes and sizes has generated strong interest in these structures, from the pair of traditional-looking, iron-framed towers (1900) on the north bank of the Elbe at Wittenberge (Altona) and the ultra-modern, red-and-white striped tower (1984) on the beach at Blankenese (Altona) to several historic lightships moored along the river (see nos. 11 & 50).

Of especial interest, and considerable charm, is the Bunthaus Lighthouse (Leuchtfeuer Bunthaus) on the island of Wilhelmsburg,

The charming
Bunthaus Lighthouse
(Leuchtfeuer Bunthaus)
stands at the southern
tip of Bunthäuser
Spitze

Europe's largest river island. The lighthouse is Hamburg's smallest and stands on the southern tip of the Bunthäuser Spitze, a narrow spur of land in the southeastern corner of the island, dividing the Norderelbe and Süderelbe. It can be found at the end of a tree-lined embankment erected in the 1870s surrounded by dense reed beds, which are today a part of the Heuckenlock Nature Reserve (Naturschutzgebiet Heukenlock).

The lighthouse was constructed in 1914, and takes the form of a seven metre high, hexagonal wooden tower, topped by a galleried lantern that is reached by an external staircase. Built originally to guide boats heading downstream it has been inactive since 1977 and now contains equipment used to monitor the flow rate of the river. A victim of vandalism this historic little lighthouse was restored in 1989, as part of the 800th anniversary of the harbour of Hamburg, and today sports colourful red, green and white paintwork.

33 The Rebuilding of BallinStadt

Hamburg-Mitte (Veddel), BallinStadt Emigration City at
Veddeler Bogen 2
S3, S31 Veddel (BallinStadt); Bus 13, 154, 254, 354
S-Bahn Veddel

The neo-Classical façade of the Hapag-Lloyd shipping office at
Ballindamm 25 (Altstadt) dominates the eastern bank of the Binnenalster. The grandeur of the building (called Ballin-Haus) and the name
of the street bear witness to the entrepreneurial genius of Albert Ballin (1857–1918), a German Jew who transformed the face of Hamburg's
shipping industry during the early years of the twentieth century. So
successful was he that his luxurious villa at Feldbrunnenstrasse 38
(Rotherbaum) was nicknamed "Little Potsdam", and boasted a drive-
way wide enough to accommodate the entourage of his friend Emperor
William II (1888–1918).

Although not open to the public it is possible to catch a glimpse of
the imposing foyer of Ballin-Haus from the street, which helps explain
the background to Ballin's success. Inscribed across a marble lintel is
the phrase "Mein Feld ist die Welt" (My field is the world), the motto
of the Hamburg-American Line (Hamburg-Amerikanische Paketfahrt-
Aktiengesellschaft – HAPAG), which was founded in 1847 (the merger
with Norddeutsche Lloyd only came in 1970). The company benefitted
greatly from the fact that Hamburg was fast becoming one of the most
important emigrant centres in Europe, predominantly for Russians
and East European Jews fleeing poverty and persecution in the hope of
a better life in America. One of the agencies selling passages belonged
to Albert Ballin's father, which young Albert inherited in 1874, and developed into an independent shipping line. His success brought him to
the attention of HAPAG, where he was employed in 1886. By 1899 he
had risen to managing director – and HAPAG had become the largest
transatlantic shipping line in the world.

Albert Ballin's phenomenal success was two-fold. Firstly, under
his management HAPAG offered luxury cruises around the globe in
specially-commissioned passenger liners, such as the *SS Imperator* and
SS Vaterland, which featured novelties such as onboard newspapers,
cinemas, and swimming pools. Secondly, and more importantly, Ballin introduced steerage class on his ships, which made transatlantic
crossings not only affordable for emigrants but also highly profitable

35 A Hindu Temple in the Suburbs

Hamburg-Mitte (Rothenburgsort), the Afghan Hindu Temple
(Hindu Tempel) at Billstrasse 77
S21 Rothenburgsort; Bus 130 Haus des KFZ-Gewerbes,
154 Billstrasse

At first glance the island of Rothenburgsort, located between the north
arm of the Elbe (Norderelbe) and the River Bille, appears to be one of
Hamburg's less attractive neighbourhoods. The flat landscape, dominated by bridges, canals, railways and chimneys (notably that of the
nearby Tiefstack power station), marks the transition between the agricultural land of the Billwerder marshlands to the east, and the industrial hinterland of the Port of Hamburg to the west. It comes as a pleasant surprise, therefore, to discover that Rothenburgsort is home to one
of the city's most surprising places of religious worship.

The temple of Hamburg's Afghan-Hindu community is tucked
away amongst industrial enterprises at Billstrasse 77, along the northern shore of the island, well away from the main area of habitation.
Seen from the outside the building appears like any other on the street
and gives little suggestion of the temple inside, with its Hindu deities
and sacred atmosphere.

Until 1980 Hindus had been living in Afghanistan for many centuries, where they formed a prosperous urban minority working mainly
as traders in Kabul. Forced to flee because of civil war many headed to
Germany, a country with which Afghanistan had maintained a special
bond since King Amanullah (1892–1960) visited Berlin in 1927. However, of the approximately 100 000 Afghans living in Germany today,
only a minority of around 5000 are Hindus.

Germany's Association of Afghan Hindus (Afghanische Hindu
Gemeinde e.V.) was established in 1991, and in 1994 the first Hindu
temple was opened in Hamburg in a rented building on Lindenstrasse
(St. Georg). With the need for larger premises the two-storeyed building on Billstrasse was purchased in 1996, and fitted out with new sacred statues of Hindu deities *(Murtis)* financed by London-based Pujya
Shree Rambaba, the so-called 'Saint of the Thames'. The association
today comprises around eight hundred families for whom the temple is
their main place of worship and a point of social contact.

Open daily to people of all religious persuasions a special time to

An idol in the prayer room of Hamburg's Afghan Hindu Temple in Rothenburgsort

visit the temple is on Sunday, when up to four hundred Afghans from across the city congregate for a special celebration. The proceedings begin with live music and prayers from 2pm to 3.30pm in the prayer hall, which is located on the first floor. Along the far wall stand the deities, who are revered as living gods: Hanuman, who led an army of monkeys to fight the demon king Ravana; Lakschmana, a hero of the epic *Ramayana*; the supreme goddess Radah Krishna; the elephant-headed Ganesha; and Lakshmi, goddess of wealth and wisdom. In the middle sits the mother goddess Durga clutching a tiger. To the left is a small pool containing two *Lingam*, symbols for the worship of the Hindu deity Shiva. Afterwards, between 3.30pm and 5pm, hot sweet tea and *Langar* (free vegetarian food) is served in the ground floor dining room to all people irrespective of their caste, creed, colour or status. It is taken whilst sitting on the floor.

The temple also functions as a means of reaching out to other religious communities, and spreading knowledge of the fascinating Afghan culture. Other Afghan Hindu temples in Germany can be found in Frankfurt, Cologne and Essen.

Other places of interest nearby: 36

36 An Englishman and his Sewers

Hamburg-Mitte (Rothenburgsort), Kaltehofe on Kaltehofe
Hauptdeich
S21 Rothenburgsort, then walk along Billhorner Deich and
Ausschläger Elbdeich

Beneath Hamburg's elevated railway line *(Hochbahn)* on Vorsetzen, close to the station at Baumwall, there stands the statue of a Victorian gentlemen with frock coat and whiskers, clutching a plan. It commemorates the English engineer Sir William Lindley (1808–1900), who designed waterworks and sewerage systems in cities across Europe, including that of Hamburg.

As a trained engineer William Lindley first arrived in Hamburg in 1834, when he was commisioned by a group of wealthy merchants to build the Hamburg-Bergedorf Eisenbahn, the first railway ever constructed in Northern Germany. Although the official opening of the line was abandoned, after parts of Hamburg were destroyed in the Great Fire of 1842, Lindley was asked to stay on to help re-build the city, and to install a new water and sewerage system. Taking London as inspiration it would be the first in continental Europe.

Within three years Lindley had constructed an 11 kilometre-long network of brick-built sewers beneath central Hamburg, using gravity to carry wastewater and excess rainwater southwards to the Elbe. Alongside Lindley's statue today there is a sturdy little kiosk, which gives access to his main sewer – the so-called *Geest-Stammsiel* – which transferred wastewater down to St. Pauli-Hafenstrasse, from where it was deposited untreated into the middle of the river (in later years the wastewater would be pumped to the Köhlbrandhöft gas plant on the opposite side of the Elbe). In 1877 the German Crown Prince, later Emperor William II (1888–1918), navigated the sewer by boat, and commented on the purity of the air. Although rarely open to the public it is said that the sewer still contains the berthing dock built especially for his visit.

During the 1840s Lindley had also been tasked with draining the Hammerbrook marshes east of the city centre, primarily for industrial use. He completed the task using a grid of canals connected by locks to the Elbe, creating Hamburg's first modern suburb in the process.

Immediately to the south of Hammerbrook is the island of Rothen-

This statue at Baumwall commemorates the English engineer Sir William Lindley

burgsort, which Lindley chose as the best location for his waterworks, since the island lies upstream from the city, where the river runs purest. Water taken from the river was first stored in a series of basins, in which sediments were removed, and then pumped into a water tower erected in 1848, from where it was distributed around the city using gravity. The tower and the waterworks are still there today, next to Trauns Park on Ausschläger Elbdeich, and there are plans to open a waterworks and sewerage museum here in the future (Lindley himself has a nearby street named in his honour).

Despite Lindley departing Hamburg in 1860, his water and sewer system continued to be developed, for example the construction of a subterranean water reservoir in Sternschanzenpark (1863), and the installation of a junction beneath the eastern pier of the Lombardsbrücke, bringing together sewers coming down from the suburbs east and west of the Außenalster (1870) (see no. 76). Despite such improvements, however, for the next thirty years Hamburg suffered numerous outbreaks of water-born cholera, especially in the built-up areas known as the *Gängeviertel* (see no. 16). The quality of the city's drinking water needed to be improved and it was decided to build a large filtration plant on Kaltehofe, a small island south of Rothenburgsort.

A visit to Kaltehofe today can be a poignant experience. One can't help but recall the more than 8500 victims of Hamburg's worst outbreak of cholera in 1892, who perished just a year before the opening of the plant that might have saved them. And then there is the plant itself, which after filtering out bacteria and impurities from the waters of the Elbe for almost a century was finally decommissioned in 1990. The twenty two former filtration beds are now gradually silting up, the tiled

The Kaltehofe
filtration plant on
Rothenburgsort is now
a nature reserve

roofs of their little red-brick valve houses slowly falling into disrepair. Despite such dereliction, however, the island is fast becoming a haven for plants and wildlife, and a walk around its perimeter on a summer's day can prove surprisingly pleasurable.

Hamburg's water and sewerage system as envisaged by William Lindley was largely complete by 1910, at which point it was several hundred kilometres long, punctuated by a series of pumping stations. They still form the backbone of the system today, although the addition of a new main sewer in 1967 has increased the total length of tunnels to an impressive 950 kilometres.

In the courtyard of Hamburg's Town Hall (Rathaus) there stands a fountain depicting Hygeia (Hygeia-Brunnen), the Greek goddess of health. She was selected for the fountain over the god Mercury as a reaction to the 1892 cholera epidemic, and the subsequent installation of a safe and secure water supply for Hamburg.

Other places of interest nearby: 35

37 For Painters and Varnishers Only

Bergedorf (Billwerder), the German Painters' and Varnishers'
Museum (Deutsches Maler- und Lackierer Museum) in the
Glockenhaus at Billwerder Billdeich 72
U2, U4 Billstedt, then Bus 330 Maler- und Lackierer Museum

One of the most unusual museums in Hamburg – and also one of
the most remote – is the German Painters' and Varnishers' Museum
(Deutsches Maler- und Lackierer Museum) in Billwerder. Document-
ing the long and venerable history of the commercial painter and var-
nisher's craft, the museum is housed in the so-called Glockenhaus at
Billwerder Billdeich 72, on the banks of the gently flowing River Bille.
Whilst making the journey out to visit the museum it is worth recalling
that until the 1930s it was possible in winter to skate along the frozen
Bille, all the way back into Hamburg.

The building housing the museum, which is so named on account
of its rooftop belfry, is interesting in itself. It was transformed into a
country house in 1780 from what had originally been a sixteenth century farmhouse. As such, it is an important example of an early country
house in the Hamburg region, hence its careful restoration in 1972. To
one side of the house there is an intricate Baroque-style *parterre*, with a
well-stocked herb garden beyond.

The museum is set across two floors, although the ground floor,
which contains various regalia, flags and certificates pertaining to the
800 year-long history of Germany's painters' and varnishers' guilds, will
probably only appeal to the specialist. For the general visitor the exhibits on the first floor will prove to be of far greater interest, since it is here
that the traditional tools and techniques of these trades are displayed.

Starting in the hall at the top of the stairs there are pattern books
for wall decorators, boxes of professional wax crayons, jars of powdered
paint pigments, sample books, and paint brushes of all shapes and
sizes. One cabinet contains the delicate equipment used by a gilder,
while another contains the many brushes of a theatre set decorator.

Off the hall are located several rooms devoted to specific tasks. One
is for signwriters (marked *Schildersaal*) and contains some fine examples of nameplates painted with gold letters on black glass as well
as numerous typeface catalogues and writing equipment; in one corner of the same room there is an old hand-powered wallpaper print-

ing machine. Another room (the *Malersaal*) contains examples of artificial wall coverings, such as timber effects and marbling, each achieved using paint and varnish. Also displayed here are stencils, and lacquer boxes in the *Chinoiserie* style. A final room (the *Kontorsaal*) contains the administrative equipment required in a painter and decorator's office, including sample books, typewriters, and other office equipment.

Of especial interest is the ceiling of the first floor rooms, which not surprisingly is painted (!), and dates back to around 1650. It consists of brown-painted river scenes surrounded by blue-painted scrolls and garlands. Such riverine themes remind the viewer that Billwerder is one of

The unusual German Painters' and Varnishers' Museum (Deutsches Maler- und Lackierer Museum) in Billwerder

the seven parishes that make up the so-called Marschlande region (the others are Allermöhe, Moorfleet, Ochsenwerder, Reitbrook, Spadenland, and Tatenberg), and was drained during the twelfth century for the growing of hops and grain for brewing. Billwerder was acquired by Hamburg in 1395 in order to help secure the lucrative Elbe river trade and the land was eventually turned over to vegetables, notably after the privations of the Thirty Years War (1618–1648).

Returning downstairs cross the road now to where the museum continues in a thatched barn and outbuilding, which contain several painters' wagons and a magnificent, red-painted three-wheeled painter's van from the 1950s. Alongside it is an old carriage with a finely lacquered leather cab and wheel spokes. Around the barn there are several reconstructed artists' studios, a stained glass workshop, a wallpaper printing shop, and a paint shop, the latter including a collection of paint mills *(Farbmühle)* dating back to 1850. There is also a display of hand-stencilled wallpaper borders, of which sample number 7, depicting birds and roses and requiring twelve individually stencilled colours, is a reminder of the considerable effort involved in creating the interior decorations of yesteryear.

38 Sand Dunes in the City

Bergedorf (Lohbrügge), the Boberger Flatlands Nature
Reserve (Naturschutzgebiet Boberger Niederung) on
Boberger Furt
U2 Mümmelmannsberg, then Bus 232 Am Langberg and by
foot to Boberger Furt

Barely more than ten kilometres east of Hamburg's bustling city centre lies the Boberger Flatlands Nature Reserve (Naturschutzgebiet
Boberger Niederung), which despite being surrounded on all sides by
urban sprawl is considered one of Germany's richest areas of biological
diversity. Established in 1991 it supports 110 endangered plant species.
The reserve is best reached from the north by U-bahn and bus, from
where Schulredder leads past Weidemoor onto Boberger Furt. Here at
number 50 can be found the Naturschutz-Informationshaus Boberg,
which tells the story of this fascinating and beautiful urban Eden.

Although the Boberger Flatlands Nature Reserve covers an area
of only 350 hectares it contains elements of four distinct geographical and ecological zones. Leading away from the information centre
are four different walking routes, of between three and five kilometres
in length, enabling the visitor to explore the four zones. Each route is
marked with a different and pertinent symbol.

To the north and northeast there rises a 30 metre-high slope known
as Geest. During the penultimate glacial period in northern Europe
(the Saale Ice Age) glaciers deposited loamy moraines forming such
slopes, which can be seen across Northern Germany, the northern
Netherlands, and Denmark. The extraction of clay from the slope for
brickmaking in the mid nineteenth century has subsequently revealed
the underlying stepped limestone, creating the distinctive terraced
contours seen today. The remaining pockets of warm clay are favoured
by orchids, such as the Marsh Helleborine *(Epipactis palustris)* and the
Broad-leaved Marsh Orchid *(Dactylorhiza majalis)*, which is why the
route is marked by a flower symbol.

In the centre of the reserve, at the end of Walter-Hammer-Weg,
there are sand dunes bordered by dry heathland. It comes as something of a surprise to see sand dunes within the boundaries of a city.
The dunes were left by the retreating glaciers, although they have been
greatly reduced in size by sand extraction for building purposes. The
dry grassy heathland covering parts of the dunes supports plants such

as German Pink *(Dianthuis carthusianorum)* and Sheep Scabious *(Jasione montana)*, and is the habitat of warmth-loving bees, beetles, ants, and butterflies such as the Common Blue *(Polyommatus icarus)*. The symbol of a butterfly marks this particular route.

On the periphery of the dunes there is a mixed wood of oak and birch trees, populated with Woodlark *(Lullula arborea)* and Skylark *(Alauda arvensis)*. There is also a small rectangular lake called the Haarteich, which is the only lake in the Boberg valley that lies within the dune area. As a result its water is relatively poor in nutrient, which has provided the ideal habitat for the endangered Natterjack Toad *(Epidalea calamita,* formerly *Bufo calamita)*, whose noisy mating call can be heard during the summer months.

Sand dunes are the most surpising aspect of the Boberger Flatlands Nature Reserve (Naturschutzgebiet Boberger Niederung)

To the west of the dunes lies a boggy moorland created when the former glacial valley was flooded by rising sea levels, depositing marine clay and peat, the latter up to a depth of six metres. There are several lakes here on which can be found the Grey Heron *(Ardea cinerea)*, the carnivorous floating Greater Bladderwort *(Utricularia)* plant, as well as the Moor Frog *(Rana arvalis)*, which in the mating season turns almost as blue as the local Kingfishers! The lakes are surrounded by stands of alder trees inhabited by grass snakes *(Natrix natrix)* and birds such as Siskin *(Carduelis)*, Golden Oriole *(Oriolus oriolus)*, Penduline Tit *(Remiz)*, and Hamburg's greatest concentration of Nightingales *(Luscinia megarhynchos)*. Not surprisingly the symbol of a bird marks this route.

The fertile peat of the moorland has in the past been extracted for

The River Bille, a tributary of the Elbe, skirts the edge of the nature reserve

agricultural purposes, which explains the fertility of the lush meadows of Billwerder, watered by the winding River Bille, a tributary of the Elbe. Home to the Common Snipe *(Gallinago gallinago)* and the rare Whinchat *(Saxicola rubetra)* the winding lanes and dense hedgerows are also popular with small mammals, which is why this final route is marked by the symbol of a rabbit.

39 The Castle on the Water

Bergedorf (Bergedorf), the Bergedorf and Vierlande Museum
(Museum für Bergedorf und die Vierlande) in Schloss Berge-
dorf at Bergedorfer Schlossstrasse 4
S2, S21 Bergedorf; Bus 135 Schillerufer

The small town of Bergedorf, situated just inside Hamburg's border with Schleswig-Holstein, has been a part of Hamburg since 1868. Despite this the town retains an atmosphere all its own and its history before this date recalls a time when Hamburg played second fiddle to Lübeck, some 60 kilometres to the north-east. Arriving in Bergedorf by S-Bahn today, however, gives little hint of the historical treasures awaiting the visitor.

Not until one reaches Alte Holstenstrasse does old Bergedorf begin to reveal itself. Here can be found several delightful timber-framed buildings, including a former corn mill in use until 1939 (now a Starbucks café), the turreted Hasse-Haus in which the composer Johann Adolf Hasse (1699–1783) was born, and the higgledy-piggledy Church of Sts. Peter and Paul (St. Petri und Paul), with its painted wooden balconies, built originally in 1500. The nineteenth century is represented around the corner on Bergedorfer Schlossstrasse by a former tobacco factory now used as apartments, as well on Chrysanderstrasse where the Windmill 'Glück Zu' (Windmühle 'Glück Zu') was used to grind corn until 1968 (see no. 31). Both of these structures overlook Schloss Bergedorf, the only extant castle in Hamburg (except for the pitiful remains of the former Harburger Schloss at Bauhofstrasse 8 (Harburg)). The castle today contains the Bergedorf and Vierlande Museum

Neo-Classical statuary at the doorway of Schloss Bergedorf

Schloss Bergedorf is today home to the Bergedorf and Vierlande Museum (Museum für Bergedorf und die Vierlande)

(Museum für Bergedorf und die Vierlande), detailing the full history of the town and its surroundings.

The origin of Bergedorf typifies the way in which several Hamburg boroughs have come into being, namely through a gradual acquisition by Hamburg of outlying territories, once under the sway of various dukes and kings. In the case of Bergedorf the story begins in the twelfth century, when the land stretching southwards as far as the Elbe – the so-called Vier- und Marschlande – was drained by the Dukes of Saxe-Lauenburg to create arable land. In 1202 the area fell to the Danish king, whose governor, Earl Albert II of Orlamünde (1182–1245), granted permission to the inhabitants of Bergedorf to dam the River Bille and construct a water mill.

In time Bergedorf became a regional court of government, to which the local peasantry rendered taxes and labour, and in 1275 the settlement was granted town status. The first documentary reference to the castle is in around 1350, in the annals of the Schloss Bergedorf's then owners, the Dukes of Saxe-Lauenburg (once again). The dukes' lack of finance, however, saw the castle occupied by troops from Lübeck between 1370 and 1401. Lübeck in the late Middle Ages was one of Europe's richest cities, and far more important than Hamburg at the time. Its wealth came from its position as head of the Hanseatic League – the trading alliance of Dutch and North German cities made in 1266 – which controlled the highly lucrative Baltic Sea trade routes; from 1398 Lübeck also had access to the Elbe by means of the first manmade canal in Northern Europe.

Despite Duke Eric IV of Saxe-Lauenburg (1368–1412) re-capturing the castle he was forced out by a military alliance between Hamburg and Lübeck, as a result of which the control of Bergedorf was shared between the victors. The damaged castle was strengthened and enlarged, and in 1512 the large corner turret seen today was added. This emphasised the strategic importance of Bergedorf, not only in controlling traffic between Hamburg and Lübeck but also in protecting both the River Bille (which was important for the rafting of Hamburg's building timber from the forests of Saxony) and the Vierlande region (from where Hamburg sourced hops and grain for brewing), as well as in guarding the trade and military route running south to the Elbe river crossing at Zollenspieker (see no. 41).

During the seventeenth and eighteenth centuries Schloss Bergedorf was ruled feudally by a bailiff, elected alternatively by the councils of Hamburg and Lübeck. It was never used militarily, however, and gradually became more decorative, with the addition of two pretty stepped gables. The earth ramparts became rose-filled gardens and except for the period 1806–1813, when it served as barracks for occupying French troops, the castle continued to serve as a bailiff's residence. This ended in 1868 when Hamburg purchased Lübeck's share of Bergedorf, and the castle became the office of the local mayor. By this time Lübeck's star had long since waned in the wake of the European colonisation of North America, when the Hanseatic League lost out to new trade routes in the North Sea and Atlantic, enabling Hamburg and Bremen to finally come into their own.

The mayor's mahogany-lined meeting room with tiled oven is today a part of the museum inside Schloss Bergedorf, which illustrates the history of this important borough from prehistoric times until the present day. Before leaving don't forget to visit the delightful wood-panelled café dating back to the mid nineteenth century.

40

From Hamburg to the Stars

Bergedorf (Bergedorf), Hamburg Observatory (Hamburger
Sternwarte) at Gojenbergsweg 112 (note: for tours, which are
by appointment only, visit www.hs.uni-hamburg.de)
S2, S21 Bergedorf, then Bus 335 Sternwarte Eingang

Straddling the eastern boundary of Hamburg on August-Bebel-Strasse
(Bergedorf) lies the New Bergedorf Cemetery (Neuer Friedhof Bergedorf). The western perimeter fence of the cemetery doubles as the eastern perimeter fence of Hamburg University's astronomical observatory,
which is located alongside it. One of the graves in this part of the cemetery is of particular importance to astronomers, so much so that its
headstone faces *away* from the cemetery, through the fence *towards* the
observatory. It is the grave of the Estonian optician Bernhard Schmidt
(1879–1935), who worked tirelessly at the observatory from 1916 until
his early death in 1935. Schmidt's greatest contribution to astronomy
was the invention in 1930 of the Schmidt Telescope (Schmidtspiegel),
a wide-angled astronomical camera used to record broader swathes of
the universe – and with far greater accuracy – than had previously been
possible. The invention revolutionised astronomical research.

When Bernhard Schmidt first came to the Hamburg Observatory
(Hamburger Sternwarte) it was located in open countryside. Due to
increasing light pollution and traffic vibration in the city centre the
observatory had relocated here in 1906 from Holstenwall (Neustadt),
where the Hamburg Museum (Museum für Hamburgische Geschichte)
now stands. (Hamburg's first observatory had been built at nearby
Millerntor in 1802 but was destroyed by Napoleon in 1811; the Holstenwall facility opened in 1825).

Touring the astronomical park in Bergedorf today is a fascinating
experience, not only for a glimpse of Bernhard Schmidt's grave but
also for the many historic telescopes still located here. The oldest is
the Equatorial (Äquatoreal), a 26 centimetre refractor telescope constructed in 1867 for the Holstenwall site and later moved to Bergedorf.
It can be seen at the far end of the path after entering the grounds from
the main entrance at Gojenbergsweg 112. Along the way are two other
venerable telescopes on the right-hand side. The first is the imposing
60 centimetre diameter Great Refractor (Grosser Refraktor), housed
inside a whitewashed building with a neo Classical portico. The telescope was assembled in 1914 by the firm of Johann Georg Repsold

(1770–1830), the observatory's founder. Beyond it is the curious hump-backed Meridian Circle (Meridiankreis), built in 1907 again by Repsold, and used for observing the time of stars passing the meridian.

In the centre of the park is the 1m-Spiegelteleskop, a one metre reflector telescope constructed in 1911 by the firm Carl Zeiss. Until 1920 it was the largest telescope in Germany, and the fourth largest in the world. Close-by is the so-called Schmidt-Gebäude, a modest-looking whitewashed building in which Bernard Schmidt once worked. Since 1979, a decade after the observatory became part of Hamburg University, a small museum to Schmidt has been installed in the building, where pride of place goes to the first Schmidt Telescope ever constructed. Ranged around the rest of the park are numerous other telescopes both old and new, including the triple-refractor Lippert-Astrograph (1911), the Salvador Reflector (Salvadorspiegel) (1960), the Oskar-Lühning-Teleskop (1975), and the Hamburg Robotic Telescope (2005).

The so-called Great Refractor (Grosser Refraktor) at the Hamburg Observatory (Hamburger Sternwarte) in Bergedorf

Few visitors are aware that one of the buildings at Hamburg Observatory is currently used to store a statue of Hermann von Wissmann (1853–1905), Imperial Commissioner of German East Africa. The statue had originally been erected in Dar es Salam in Tanzania but after its capture by the British it was transferred via London to Hamburg. In 1922 the statue was placed in front of the University of Hamburg, which had been founded in 1919 through the merging of a scientific foundation and the city's former Colonial Institute. In the light of critical discussion about Germany's colonial legacy the statue was toppled by students in 1968 and has remained in storage ever since.

41

A Short Walk Through One of the Four Lands

Bergedorf (Kirchwerder), a walk in the Vierlande region
beginning in Kirchwerder
S2, S21 Bergedorf, then Bus 124 Kirchwerder Kirche

Stretching southwards from the district of Bergedorf, down as far as the northern shore of the Elbe, lies the region known as the Vierlande, or Four Lands. This relatively remote area of Hamburg, which has been so-named since the mid sixteenth century, comprises the four ancient parishes of Curslack, Neuengamme, Altengamme, and Kirchwerder. Mentioned usually in the same breath as the neighbouring Marschlande region (Vier- und Marschlande), the area was drained as early as the twelfth century by the Dukes of Saxe-Lauenburg to create land for habitation and agriculture (see no. 39). Originally used to cultivate hops and grain for brewing, the Vierlande is now renowned for its fruit, vegetables, and flowers.

The bus journey south through the Vierlande, from the S-Bahn station in Bergedorf, reveals a landscape shaped entirely by the presence of water: dykes, embankments and ponds create a patchwork of fields, market gardens, and orchards, punctuated by traditional thatched and timber-framed farm buildings. A half day's walk through this land from the bus stop in Kirchwerder on the banks of the Gose Elbe takes in not only some lovely countryside but also several unusual landscape features.

The walk begins at the Church of St. Severin (St. Severini zu Kirchwerder) at Kirchenheerweg 12. This distinctive late eighteenth century church is noteworthy for its detached and weatherboarded belfry, an unusual feature found elsewhere in the area (for example the Church of St. Johannis zu Curslack and the Church of St. Nicolai zu Altengamme). From the churchyard gate the narrow Alte Twiete leads onto Kirchwerder Hausdeich, and the countryside, where a wooden post on the roadside supports a nest used by white storks.

At the junction where Kirchwerder Hausdeich joins Kirchwerder Mühlendamm the walker has a choice. A left turn leads out to Hof Eggers, a farm first recorded in 1548, and in the hands of the same family since 1620. The current building dates from 1834 but the outbuildings are older, one particular barn dating back to 1631 and a gra-

nary to 1535. Hof Eggers is not a museum but rather a working farm using eco-friendly practices. (To experience a traditional Vierlande farm visit the Rieck Haus Open Air Museum (Freilichtmuseum Rieckhaus) at Curslacker Deich 284 (Curslack); built in 1533 it is one of Germany's oldest examples of a timber-framed *Haubarg*, a Dutch-style elongated farmhouse shared by man and beast, in which hay was also stored.)

A right turn at the junction, on the other hand, leads past the Riepenburger Windmill (Riepenburger Mühle), Hamburg's oldest corn mill (see no. 31). Farther on is a crossroads with Kirchwerder Marschbahndamm, a name that recalls a railway that once ran this way. Be-

Ferries have been calling at Zollenspieker since the thirteenth century

yond the crossroads is a peaceful stretch of woods, which is a protected nature reserve and bird sanctuary.

At the far end of Kirchwerder Mühlendamm there is a T-junction facing the river. On the left there can be made out a hill surrounded by ditches. This is all that remains of the Riepenburg, a medieval fortress constructed in the thirteenth century to guard a river crossing that once existed here. Turn right onto Zollenspieker Hauptdeich and cross to the other side of the flood embankment. The dense reed beds fringing the Elbe here are an important and protected tidal plant zone.

This walk ends at the Zollenspieker Fährhaus, a much storied former ferry and customs terminal first recorded in 1251. The building was reconstructed in 1621 after being ransacked by troops from Lüneburg, sent to destroy the dykes constructed in the area by Hamburg, in an attempt to gain a monopoly on river trade along the Elbe. After the customs station closed in 1806 the building was converted to an inn, a function it continues to serve to this day. Its leafy terrace is the perfect place to sit and watch the car ferry toing and froing from one side of the river to the either, whilst keeping an eye open for the bus back up to Bergedorf.

42

Evidence for Hamburg's Earliest Inhabitants

Harburg (Neugraben-Fischbek), the Archaeological Footpath Fischbeker Heide (Archäologischen Wanderpfad Fischbeker Heide) at Fischbeker Heideweg 43
S3, S31 Neugraben, then Bus 250 Fischbeker Heideweg

Although the history of Hamburg officially begins in 808AD, when Charlemagne (Charles the Great), King of the Franks (742–814) commissioned the enigmatic fortress known as the Hammaburg, to prevent unwanted Slavic and Viking incursions into the region after his expulsion of the Saxons, man had already long been active in the area (see no. 1). In the first centuries AD, for example, the Hamburg region had been populated by the Suebi (or Suevi), a group of Germanic tribes who came from Scandinavia and eventually moved southwards into Southern Germany, Italy and Spain. They left behind them large cemeteries in Fuhlsbüttel to the north (where the names Stellingen and Schnelsen date from this time), and in Marmstorf, Eissendorf and Langenbek in the southern district of Harburg.

The very first settlers arrived during the Late Stone Age (Upper Paleolithic), which occurred towards the end of the most recent glacial period (the Weichsel Glaciation). They were semi-nomadic reindeer hunters who would have encountered a landscape resembling the Arctic tundra. Their distinctive stone arrowheads and bone-working chisels, dating to between 13500 and 11000BC, have been unearthed by archaeologists all across northwestern Europe, from northern France and southern Scandinavia, eastwards as far as Poland. Such sites in Northern Germany feature layers of habitation debris including much horn and bone suggesting the repeated occupation of small seasonal hunting camps during this period. Circles of large pebbles have been interpreted as weights to hold down the coverings for tents. The excavation of one such site during the 1930s in Meiendorf in the Hamburg district of Rahlstedt (Wandsbek) led to the entire culture being termed the Hamburg Culture.

There are two locations in Hamburg where it is possible to confront these early peoples. The first is the Archaeological Footpath Fischbeker Heide (Archäologischer Wanderpfad Fischbeker Heide) in the district of Neugraben-Fischbek, which can be reached by walking south from the terminus of Bus 250 along Fischbeker Heideweg. Be sure to pick up

This wooden sarcophagus is a highlight of the Archaeological Footpath Fischbeker Heide (Archäologische Wanderpfad Fischbeker Heide)

a map at the thatched information centre (Naturschutz-Informations-haus 'Schafstall') and then proceed deep into the dense Beech forests. Just beyond a signpost marked 'Fischbektal' will be found the largest and oldest group of archaeological monuments in Hamburg. Since 1974 the dozen or so prehistoric monuments dating from the Stone Age onwards have been connected by a 2.5 kilometre-long woodland path. Information boards alert the passer-by not only to the presence of the monuments, predominantly Bronze and Iron Age burial mounds, but also to the importance of each in the prehistory of the Hamburg region. Of particular interest is a reconstruction of a sarcophagus crafted from a hollowed-out tree trunk.

The Fischbeker Heide itself is a surprisingly rugged natural conser-vation area of forests and heathland, lying fully within the city bound-ary of Hamburg. It forms a part of The Black Hills (Die Schwarzen Berge), which themselves represent the northern extremity of the Harburg Hills (Harburger Berge). The area contains the Hasselbrack, which at 116 metres above sea level is the highest point in Hamburg.

The second location is the Archaeological Museum Hamburg (Archäologisches Museum Hamburg) at Harburger Rathausplatz 5 (Harburg), the city's official museum of archaeology since 1898. The earliest history of man in Northern Germany is illustrated here very ef-fectively by means of a selection of exhibits drawn from the museum's collection of 1.5 million catalogued artefacts. Aimed squarely at school parties but of equal interest to adults, too, the museum is spread over two floors. The ground floor represents the past, with archaeological

The Helms-Museum in Harburg makes archaeology accessible to all ages

artefacts divided into themes such as innovation, mobility, war, and death. Each theme is mirrored on the floor directly above, only this time by artefacts from the present. Thus, a domestic dump of nineteenth century waste, including broken pots and clay pipe bowls, is reflected in the present by a pile of empty plastic water bottles; similarly, a pagan burial site is mirrored by a pile of wooden Christian grave markers; and so on. For visitors keen to see a more traditional museum approach, both floors include a series of slimline glass display cases containing some fascinating objects, including the oldest implement in Northern Germany (a Neanderthal flint hand axe dated to 3800 BC), a skull fragment from the oldest Hamburger yet discovered (6500 BC), and even Northern Germany's oldest piece of bread (unearthed in Stade and carbon dated to 500 BC). In a separate room called the Archaeologicum, decorated to resemble the painted caves of Altamira, visitors are encouraged to try their hand at flint knapping, fire making, potting, weaving, and cereal grinding.

43 The Lost Village of Altenwerder

Harburg (Altenwerder), the Church of St. Gertrude
(St. Gertrud Kirche) on Altenwerder Kirchweg (note: the
church is only open once a month)
S3 Neugraben, then Bus 250 BAB Ausfahrt Waltershof, then
follow signs to the church

The most isolated church in Hamburg is undoubtedly that of St. Gertrude (St. Gertrud Kirche) in Altenwerder. Visiting the church can be a disconcerting experience, since it is located on a narrow strip of woodland, accessible by crossing some of the busiest roads in Hamburg. Standing in the churchyard, with rarely another person in sight, it is difficult to imagine that until as recently as the 1970s the surrounding area was home to some 2000 people. Their homes were swept away to make room for the construction of the nearby Altenwerder Container Terminal, and by 2006 the official population of Altenwerder had dropped to just two persons!

The story of Altenwerder begins on 28th December 1248, when the Elbe island of Gorieswerder was broken up by a powerful storm tide (the event was christened the *Allerkindleinsflut* after the Biblical Massacre of the Innocents, which is marked by Christians on the same day). The new island of Altenwerder lay in the southern arm of the Elbe (Süderelbe), with the Kohlfleet to the north and the Old South Elbe to the south, both of which have long since disappeared.

Undated records suggest that Altenwerder was first settled around 1250, the newcomers making a living from fishing, agriculture, boatbuilding, and sail making. The island continued to be a victim of flooding, however, and so in 1418 it was dyked by order of the landlords, the Duke of Brunswick-Lüneburg and the Archbishop of Bremen. Fields for growing fruit and vegetables were established inside the protective dyke, with less vulnerable meadows and pasture land placed outside the dyke. Houses were also built along the dykes and in the 1430s the island's first church was constructed (it was rebuilt in 1769 then damaged by a serious flood in 1825 and rebuilt again in its present form in 1831, with a spire added in 1895).

By 1803 there were 133 residential buildings registered in Altenwerder with a population of one thousand. There were also four hundred cows, whose milk was taken to market in Hamburg by sailing barge *(Fracht-Ewer)*. By 1925 the human population had risen to 2010, consisting of 493 households occupying 243 houses.

Plans to extend Hamburg's port facilities to Altenwerder were first mooted before the First World War but as the land was still part of Prussia only the district of Waltershof was developed. Altenwerder was incorporated into the City of Hamburg in 1937 but again port expansion plans were thwarted, this time by the Second World War. The island fell victim to Allied air raids because of its proximity to the Elbe II submarine dock, and on 8th April 1945 the Church of St. Gertrude was badly damaged in what was one of the last air raids of the war (see no. 27). Several gravestones in the churchyard still carry the scars from this period. The building was restored in 1948 becoming one of the first churches in Hamburg to reopen after the war.

The Church of St. Gertrude (St. Gertrud Kirche) is all that remains of the village of Altenwerder

The first law regarding the port extension to Altenwerder was passed in 1961. Although private development on the island was henceforth restricted, few inhabitants believed the plans would ever be carried out. That feeling changed in 1973 when the City of Hamburg announced plans for the formal expropriation of all property in the village (which at the time covered fourteen square kilometres) in return for compensation and resettlement elsewhere. By the end of the 1970s many residents had departed, their former homes razed immediately to prevent reoccupation. A second port extension law passed in 1982 sounded the death knell for the old village. Despite opposition from the remaining inhabitants together with 8000 supporters the demolition

A wind turbine stands where once there were houses

and clearance continued, and the last residents of Altenwerder departed in 1998. In 2003 the long-planned container terminal was finally inaugurated.

A visit to Altenwerder today is tinged with sadness for what is gone. Only the church has been left standing (now a part of the parish of Hausbruch), dwarfed by a pair of colossal wind turbines. It is approached along Altenwerder Kirchweg, which, together with its southern extension, Kirchdorfweg, was once lined with brick-built houses with tiled hipped roofs and neat front gardens. Only the overgrown pavements and leaning telephone posts hint at the lost community. Running eastwards from the church a country road (Querweg) once led through fields to Altenwerder harbour, although most traffic reached the harbour along Altwerder Elbdeich, which ran from the top of Altenwerder Kirchweg. A map from 1975 shows clearly that this was the route taken by the number 451 bus, as it serviced the old harbour and ferry dock. Together with a post office and public telephone this too has been obliterated by today's container terminal.

At the time of writing there are an estimated seventeen million reusable shipping containers in the world, and a large proportion of the world's long distance freight is transported inside them. Hamburg is one of the largest container ports in Europe, with around 300 shipping lines docking regularly to transport goods to and from a thousand ports all over the world. Lorries and trains then transfer the goods overland into Poland, the Ukraine, the Baltic States, and beyond.

A Baroque Musical Masterpiece

Harburg (Neuenfelde), the Church of St. Pankratius (Pankratiuskirche) on Organistenweg, off Arp-Schnitger-Stieg
S1, S3, S11 Neugraben, then Bus 257 Arp-Schnitger-Stieg or
S1, S3, S21 Altona then Bus 150 Neuenfelde Kirche

The rural community of Neuenfelde lies on the banks of the Mühlenberger Loch, an inlet of the Elbe between the districts of Finkenwerder and Cranz. Created in 1929, Neuenfelde comprises the historic settlements of Hasselwerder and Nincop, the former settled by the Saxons in the eleventh century, the latter settled in the twelfth century by Dutch settlers brought in to drain the land for farming and fruit growing. Neuenfelde is geographically a part of the extensive cultural landscape known as the *Altes Land*, a mosaic of orchards, drainage dykes, embankments, and traditional farm buildings (see no. 45).

What sets Neuenfelde apart, however, is the Church of St. Pankratius (Pankratiuskirche) on Organistenweg. Work on the distinctive red-brick church began in 1682, during a period of prosperity in the wake of the Thirty Years' War (1618–1648). An earlier church on the same site was demolished except for its tower, which was incorporated into the new building. The tower remained in place until it was hit by lightning in 1786, after which the tower seen today was constructed.

The interior of the church is an excellent example of North German rural Baroque, with a barrel-vaulted wooden ceiling covered with painted angels and cherubs. Of particular note is the richly carved altar pulpit created in 1688 by the Hamburg sculptor Christian Precht. Amongst the various biblical scenes on

The lovely Church of St. Pankratius (Pankratiuskirche) in Neuenfelde

The interior of the Church of St. Pankratius (Pankratiuskirche) is a fine example of North German rural Baroque

the pulpit can be found the coat of arms of Count Otto Wilhelm von Königsmarck (1639–1688), Governor General for Swedish Pomerania (on what is now the Baltic coast of Germany and Poland), who helped pay for the church. Note also the ornate font cover, and the full figure painting of Provost Johann Hinrich von Finckh, who instigated the rebuilding of the church.

The greatest treasure in the Church of St. Pankratius is undoubtedly a magnificent organ built by master craftsman Arp Schnitger (1648–1719), whose name and achievement is celebrated in the local street names. Located in a specially-constructed wooden loft at the west end of the building the organ was constructed between 1683 and 1688. Unfortunately, during the eighteenth and nineteenth centuries the organ was reconditioned in line with prevailing tastes, as a result of which the sound of the original Baroque organ was lost. A costly restoration in 1978 restored the sound and today it is one of the few Baroque organs still operated by means of a bellows. Visitors can hear the organ by attending one of the free recitals given on the first Sunday of the month at 4.30pm (another Schnitger organ can be heard every Thursday at noon in the Church of St. James (Jacobikirche) at Jakobikirchhof 22 (Altstadt)).

Considering the historical fabric of Neuenfelde it is difficult to believe that the area has been threatened with destruction by plans to extend the runway for the nearby Airbus factory on Finkenwerder. The latter was once an island until being connected to the mainland at Neuenfelde by an artificial landbridge (creating the Mühlenberger Loch on one side and the Alte Süderelbe on the other), over which part of the runway is now located. Fortunately, the runway is still several fields away from the Church of St. Pankratius, so that the roar of aircraft engines only intermittently breaks the peace of this hidden corner of Hamburg.

Other places of interest nearby: 45

45   A Taste of the Altes Land

Harburg (Cranz), a walk through the *Altes Land* from Cranz
to Neuenfelde
S1, S3, S31 Altona, then Bus 150 Cranz; Elbe Ferry
Blankenese-Cranz

Downstream from Hamburg, on the southwestern bank of the River Elbe, there is a vast area of reclaimed marsh known as the *Altes Land*. The name is derived from the word *'olland'*, meaning Dutch, and reminds the visitor that the area was drained by Dutch settlers brought into the area almost nine hundred years ago. Although much of the region is centred around the town of Jork in Lower Saxony, a significant part lies within the boundaries of Hamburg, where it includes the districts of Cranz, Finkenwerder, Francop, and Neuenfelde. A walk from Cranz to Neuenfelde provides an enjoyable taste of this intriguing historical landscape.

Although the starting point in Cranz can be reached by ferry from Blankenese, an altogether more interesting means is by bus from distant Altona; the journey reveals numerous examples of the abrupt transition from urban to industrial to rural landscapes so typical of Hamburg. Once at the bus terminus in Cranz walk back along Estebogen and Estedeich by means of the sturdy earth embankments erected to contain the flood waters of the River Este on which Cranz is situated. Notice along the way the numerous timber-framed farm buildings dating back to the seventeenth century, some of which are still thatched.

The Este is crossed by means of a bridge at Am Alten Estesperrwerk, leading onto Neuenfelder Fährdeich. The view from this point is dominated entirely by apple orchards, stretching away as far as the eye can see. Best witnessed in either late spring, when the trees are in blossom, or during the harvest season, when the boughs are heavy with red fruits, it is a powerful reminder that the *Altes Land* is the largest contiguous fruit orchard in Central Europe. Covering more than 14 000 hectares (35 000 acres) the orchards comprise 77% apples, 13% cherries, with the rest made up by plums and other fruits.

By turning right for a short distance along Neuenfelder Fährdeich an ornately carved wooden gateway can be seen. Such gates, often

The orchards of the Altes Land are famous for their apples

A traditional Altes Land farmhouse on Nincoperstrasse

leading to similarly ornate farm-houses, are a proud reminder of how successfully the fruit farmers of the *Altes Land* have exploited the rich al-luvial soil of the region, their produce now dispatched far beyond the markets of Hamburg.

Turning back and proceeding left along the Neuenfelder Fährdeich embankment reveals some astonishingly diverse scenery: on the right-hand side are seemingly endless, neatly planted orchards whilst on the lefthand side, between the road and the Elbe, are a series of busy factories and shipyards. Where the embankments are broken to enable traffic to pass, vertical slots can be seen in which flood barriers are inserted when necessary. Tucked safely inside the landward side of the embankments are further traditional farm buildings, strung out along the street, with their orchards and fields behind them. Such linear village settlement patterns are known in the region as *Marschhufendörfer*.

Continuing along Neuenfelder Fährdeich, enjoying the often breezy open countryside, an unexpected sight is the modest Moschee Klein Istanbul, opposite Neuenfelder Damm, used by the Islamic community of Neuenfelde. Another place of worship is the Church of St. Pankratius (Pankratiuskirche) in Neuenfelde, the spire of which is just visible in the distance (see no. 44). Rather than entering Neuenfelde, turn right onto Marschkamper Deich and then left onto Nincoper Strasse, along which are many more imposing timber-framed farmhouses, the more recent of which have neo-Classical elements, such as columns and pediments, bizarrely worked into into their otherwise rustic façades.

Bus number 257 south to Neugraben can be caught anywhere along the road, from where the S-Bahn runs back into central Hamburg.

On the first weekend in May a Blossom Festival is staged in Jork, the 'capital' of the *Altes Land*, including a parade and the crowning of the Fruit Blossom Queen. In winter several of the frozen orchard paths are used for the sport of curling, the participants keeping warm with mugs of mulled fruit wine.

Other places of interest nearby: 44

Ups and Downs in the Staircase District

Altona (Blankenese), the Staircase District (Treppenviertel) in Blankenese
S1 Blankenese or Bus 36 Blankenese, then Bus 48 Strandweg; Elbe Ferry Cranz-Blankenese

The quickest way to get to Blankenese (pron. Blanken-ay-zer) using public transport is by S-Bahn. Bus 36 takes ten minutes longer but follows a more scenic route, hugging the north bank of the Elbe for much its journey from Altona Altstadt. The river and parkland views provided by the bus, as well as those of the many grand houses in this part of the city, are well worth seeing. Both S-Bahn and bus arrive in Eric-Blumenfeld-Platz, from where Bus 48 shuttles visitors down to Strandweg on the riverbank, where this short tour begins.

The name Blankenese is derived from two North German words, namely 'blanc' meaning white or shiny and 'Neß' meaning promontory. Between them they refer to the 75-metre high Süllberg, which dominates Blankenese when viewed from Strandweg. It was the presence of this little hill – a rare feature in the predominantly flat geography of Hamburg – that prompted Archbishop Adalbert von Bremen (c. 1000–1072) to first build a fortified priory on the hill in 1060, to safeguard an important ferry link across the Elbe. The ferry still calls here although it is dwarfed by the huge container ships that ply the Elbe today, accounting for the presence of the tall lighthouse at the water's edge (the numerous wrecks on the shoreline a little further downstream are a reminder of the Elbe's destructive power).

At Strandweg 79 directly opposite the lighthouse is Kajüte SB12, a friendly little café renowned for its fried potato dishes *(Bratkartoffel-gerichte)*; in the summer months its tables spill onto the golden sands as if it were the seaside. Rather more grand is the Strand Hotel at Strandweg 13, a former *Jugendstil* villa built in 1902. When the wealthy merchants of Hamburg first discovered Blankenese in the late seventeenth century it was little more than a simple fishing village spread across the slopes of the Süllberg. An independent town within Schleswig-Holstein until 1927, and theafter a part of Altona until 1938 (when Altona was absorbed into Hamburg), wealthy outsiders have been embellishing Blankenese with their holiday homes ever since.

Tourism came to Blankenese during the nineteenth century and

the first restaurant was opened on the Süllberg in 1887. Visitors were drawn by the picturesque thatched fishermen's cottages on the steep slopes, reached by means of stone steps and narrow alleyways accessible only to pedestrians. So many steps are there – 4864 at the last count – that the area has been dubbed the *Treppenviertel*, or Staircase Quarter. It can be reached by walking east along Strandweg and then climbing the 217 steps of Rutsch.

At the top of Rutsch turn right onto Elbterrasse; half way along turn left up Schnudts Treppe, and then left again along Süllbergterrasse, which winds its way to the Hotel Süllberg at the top. Built like a castle this 5-star hotel occupies the spot where the archbishop built his priory, and the Dukes of Holstein later built their own castle, although

A traditional Blankenese fisherman's cottage

the views have changed considerably since then: what was once open countryside is now covered by shipyards and the Airbus works.

Passing over the top of the Süllberg, with the hotel on the right, drop down the other side along Bornholdts Treppe, taking in the vista of the many houses clinging to the hillside. At the bottom join Hans-Lange-Strasse, which to the right joins up once again with Elbterrasse, where at number 4–6 can be seen the last example of a traditional Blankenese fishermen's cottage. Built in 1880 this charming thatched property was originally occupied by three families and today contains a museum.

This tour finishes at Der Treppenkraemer at Hans-Lange-Strasse 23, a nautical-themed café offering hot drinks, herring sandwiches, and homemade cakes to those in need of sustenance. At the bottom of the hill is Blankenese Hauptstrasse, from where a bus can be caught back up to the S-Bahn and bus stations.

Downstream from the Süllberg, between Falkentaler Weg and Falkensteiner Weg, lies the Römischer Garten, a secret Italianate garden established by the founder of the Holsten brewery in the nineteenth century. It was reworked in 1913–1925 by Germany's first female head gardener, Else Hoffa, for the Hamburg banker Max Warburg (1867–1946), whose family bequeathed it to the city in 1951 (see no. 72). Not far away at Grotius Weg 79 is a striking whitewashed Bauhaus-style villa erected in 1923, which contains a gallery and a puppet museum (Puppenmuseum Falkenstein).

47 Subterranean Hamburg

Altona (Nienstedten), a tour of cellars beginning at the Hotel
Louis C. Jacob at Elbchaussee 401–403
Bus 36 Sieberlingstrasse

Of the many aspects of subterranean Hamburg, including tunnels, bunkers and the pneumatic post, perhaps the least well known are the city's ice cellars *(Eiskeller)* (see nos. 5, 12, 22 & 36). In the days before refrigeration the preservation of perishable foods in their original state was a luxury made possible only by using ice. The successful fermentation of beer also required the use of ice, in order to maintain temperatures of between 8 and 14° C. The sourcing and storage of ice was a costly process, requiring considerable manpower and the construction of a dry subterranean chamber close to a source of freshwater winter ice. Ice cellars could thus only be afforded by wealthy country house estates, hotels, and breweries.

A fine example of an ice cellar used for catering purposes can be found at the Hotel Louis C. Jacob at Elbchaussee 401–403 in Nienstedten. Situated on the banks of the Elbe this historic hotel was established in 1765 by Margaretha Catherina Burmester. In 1791 she married the nurseryman Daniel Louis Jacob, after whom the hotel is named. It was Jacob who added the lime tree terrace, which provides welcome shade to those fortunate enough to stay at this charming hotel during the summer months. Visitors may not be aware that the limes also keep the ground beneath them cool, which was important because it is here that the hotel's ice cellar was constructed around 1850.

Lost for many years the remains of the ice cellar were only uncovered in 1994, when the hotel was extended. The ice cellar has subsequently been restored and is now used for special functions but can be visited upon request. It takes the form usual for European ice cellars, which were introduced in the seventeenth century, namely a sturdy, conical brick-built chamber the majority of which is subterranean. At ground level, towards the top of the chamber where the domed roof begins, there is a doorway through which ice collected from the Elbe would be delivered. Once inside the chamber the ice would be packed with straw or sawdust for insulation, so as to reduce the rate of melting. A drain at the bottom of the cellar would allow any meltwater to drain away rapidly into a sump below. This was an important feature since water transfers heat more quickly than ice: it was thus necessary to keep the ice as dry as possible. A well-packed ice cellar might stay frozen for many months and even years. Another ice cellar, dating back to 1870, can be found at Lessers Passage 4 (Altona Altstadt), and it can be visited on occasional tours conducted by the Hamburg Underworlds Association (Hamburger Unterwelten e.V.).

Ice cellars used in breweries were of necessity far larger structures, in order to accommodate the brewing equipment. A good example exists in Bergedorf, where until the First World War there were nine breweries taking both water and ice from the local River Bille (see no. 59). There are few remains today although on Chrysanderstrasse there can still be found the extensive former ice cellars of the Actien Brewery (Actien-Bier-Brauerei) constructed in 1864. Unfortunately not open to the public the cellars with their metre-thick brick vaults can

be visited on occasional tours made by the Under Hamburg Association (unter-hamburg e.V.). The old brewery buildings themselves burned down in 1965 and modern apartments have subsequently been built over the cellars, parts of which are used today as garages and storerooms. In the past they were used for growing mushrooms and as a civilian air raid shelter during the Second World War. (The former Hastedt's Brewery ice cellar at Buxtehuder Strasse 35 (Harburg) suffered a similar fate by having a neo-Baroque villa built on top of it in the late nineteenth century.)

The oldest beer cellar *(Bierkeller)* in Hamburg is the Gröninger Brauereikeller at Willy-Brandt-Strasse 47 (Altstadt). A series of low, red-brick vaulted cellars run beneath one of the last Ba-

An ice cellar beneath the Hotel Louis C. Jacob on Elbchaussee

roque buildings in the city. Furthermore, behind the Baroque façade, which was added in the 1760s, are structural elements first mentioned in 1260 making this the oldest inn in Hamburg. Until the construction of Willy-Brandt-Strasse in the 1950s the building faced onto the Gröningerstrassenfleet, which was subsequently infilled. A brewery has existed here almost continuously since 1793, and a microbrewery has been in place since the early 1980s producing approximately 200 000 litres of Gröninger Pils a year (the copper brewing vessels can be seen to the rear of the building at Zippelhaus 4). The beer and the rustic ambience are the perfect accompaniment to traditional German beer drinking fare, such as Schweinshaxe (roast pork knuckle), Kasseler (dried and salted pork), and Fleischkäse (baked sausage meatloaf).

This tour of Hamburg cellars finishes farther along Willy-Brandt-Strasse at number 60, where an atmospheric wine cellar *(Weinkeller)* exists beneath the ruined Church of St. Nikolai (Nikolaikirche) (see no. 70). The cellar dates from the reconstruction of the church following the Great Fire of 1842 and from the start was deliberately intended to be let out to help finance the building costs. Hamburg's oldest wine distributor used the cellar from 1928 until 2005, and it can be visited on occasional tours conducted by the Hamburg Underworlds Association (Hamburger Unterwelten e.V.).

Other places of interest nearby: 48

48 An Eden on the Elbe

Altona (Gross Flottbek), the New Botanical Garden
(Neuer Botanischer Garten) at Hesten 10
S1, S11 Klein Flottbek; Bus 15, 21 Klein Flottbeck

Almost half of Hamburg is taken up with either water, forest, or farm-land giving credence to the claim that the city is Europe's greenest. Not surprisingly Hamburg can boast more than 1400 parks and gardens, many of which are little-known. There is something to satisfy all tastes, from the neatly clipped lawns and tidy flower beds of the Botanischer Sondergarten Wandsbek at Walddörferstrasse 273 (Wandsbek), to the wild and rugged heathland of the Duvenstedter Brook Nature Reserve, far to the north on Duvenstedter Triftweg (Wohldorf-Ohlstedt).

If there is a Garden of Eden anywhere in Hamburg, however, it prob-ably lies on the north bank of the Elbe in Altona, where there are three highly individual gardens within easy reach of each other. Two of them, the Hirschpark at Elbchaussee 409 (Nienstedten) and the Jenischpark at Elbchaussee 50 (Othmarschen), have aristocratic origins dating back to the late eighteenth century. The Hirschpark is known for its herd of deer, the Villa Godeffroy, a two hundred year old Sycamore tree, and the Witthüs Teehaus, a charming thatched tearoom at Elbchaussee 499a. The Jenischpark is an English-style landscape garden contain-ing Hamburg's oldest oak tree (thought by some to have been planted during the fifteenth century) and the Jenisch-Haus, a former country residence built in the 1830s and now used as a museum of aristocratic art and furnishings.

The third garden in the trilogy is this author's personal favourite. The New Botanical Gardens (Neuer Botanischer Garten), which cover an area of approximately 57 acres (23 hectares) in the district of Gross Flottbek, contain over 20 000 plant species exhibited in more than a dozen self-contained gardens. Not only do these gardens provide a unique recreational area in which the visitor can get happily lost for hours, but also as part of Hamburg University's Institute of General Botany they serve an important educational and research function.

Hamburg's Old Botanical Garden (Alter Botanischer Garten), which was founded in 1821 at Stephansplatz (St. Pauli), was swept away during the 1970s to make way for the more user-friendly Planten un Blomen (see no. 15). The New Botanical Garden, which opened to the public in 1979, set out to be something very different.

The garden is divided into three main areas. The first to be encountered after passing through the main entrance at Hesten 10 is perhaps the most unusual. Marked MEN (for Mensch = people) on the garden plan this area focusses on the longstanding relationship between man and plants. To illustrate the many ways in which people live, use, and work with plants the area features a farmer's garden, a Biblical garden, and a pharmacist's garden, in which fragrance, taste and textures are paramount. A highlight are the dense groves of the ever-useful bamboo plant, which young and old will certainly want to explore.

The theme of plants useful to man is developed further by the Museum für Nutzpflanzen housed inside the Loki Schmidt Haus, a near windowless cube clad in bright blue tiles that sits surprisingly well in the garden. Alongside is a greenhouse containing tropical and desert plants, including carnivorous plants and epiphytes suspended from the ceiling. Man's selective breeding of plant species is demonstrated by attendant rose, rhododendron and conifer gardens.

It's fun to explore the bamboo groves of the New Botanical Gardens (Neuer Botanischer Garten)

The centre of the garden, beyond the lake containing some very friendly carp, is marked SYS on the plan, meaning sytematic relationships. This area of the garden reveals the biological relationship between seemingly disparate species of plants, regardless of geographical distribution. Species or groupings are connected to each other, quite literally, by curving stone paths, making accessible to all a subject usually perceived as academic.

The unusual Loki Schmidt Haus fits surprisingly well into the New Botanical Gardens (Neuer Botanischer Garten)

The third and final area, towards the rear of the garden, is the largest and most traditional. Marked GEO on the plan it is divided into four zones representing the four geographical areas on Earth most like Hamburg in terms of plant diversity. They are Europe (including forest, heath, moorland, and coast), Asia (including China, Japan, and the Steppe), and North and South America. Walking through this part of the garden is like taking a short trip around the world!

At Kupferredder 45, on the edge of the Duvenstedter Brook Nature Reserve (Wohldorf-Ohlstedt), stands the Neuer Kupferhof. During the Second World War it was home to Abwehrstelle X, a German military intelligence centre in which twenty five transmitters maintained contact with German agents around the world. The building today serves as a training centre for the City of Hamburg.

Other places of interest nearby: 47

49 A Gigantic Reminder of the Ice Age

Altona (Othmarschen), Der Alte Schwede on Hans-Leip-Ufer,
at the end of Övelgönner Hohlweg
Bus 36 Liebermannstrasse; Harbour Ferry 62 Neumühlen

Around 20 000 years ago, during an era called the Pleistocene by geologists, the great glaciers of the last ice age began slowly retreating from north-west Germany. Stone Age (Palaeolithic) man was already living nomadically in the area, and the disappearance of the ice allowed him to settle more permanently. The resulting landscape would have resembled the arctic tundra, and archaeologists have found evidence of where reindeer hunters built summer camps at this time (see no. 42).

It is difficult to imagine that Northern Europe during the Pleistocene era resembled how Greenland appears today. The land was covered by huge glaciers, often several hundred metres thick, which spilled southwards from Scandinavia reaching as far as Central Europe. They brought with them great masses of rocky debris, which together with the sheer weight of the ice, ground the land below until it was flat.

As the temperature rose so the glaciers withdrew, leaving in their wake not only fertile loamy soil, which man has subsequently used to his great advantage, but also occasional huge boulders that even the glaciers were unable to crush. Such a boulder is known as a glacial erratic, or *Findling* in German (meaning an abandoned child).

On the sandy northern

Der Alte Schwede is a huge glacial boulder sitting on the bank of the Elbe in Othmarschen

bank of the Elbe, on Hans-Leip-Ufer (named after the author of the love song *Lili Marleen*), just beyond Schröders Elbpark, there can be found a spectacular example of a glacial erratic. Discovered during dredging work in the Elbe in 1999 it weighs an impressive 217 tons, and is nearly five metres in height. Geologists from the

A display in the Geology and Palaeontology Museum (Geologisch-Paläontologisches Museum) in Rotherbaum

Mineralogical Institute of the University of Hamburg have studied the boulder and agree that it is grey Småland granite, brought here by glaciers all the way from Sweden.

Having been designated the oldest glacial erratic ever found in Germany, the Hamburg boulder has been dubbed *Der Alte Schwede*, or the Old Swede. By way of celebration it was baptised with water from the Elbe in the summer of 2000, in the presence of the mayoress of Hamburg at the time, Krista Sager, whose Danish ancestry meant she shared a common Scandinavian ancestry with the rock. Also in attendance was the Swedish Consul Leif H. Sjöström, and the minister of the Swedish Gustaf-Adolf Church, Ernst-Arne Detert. Despite having survived being crushed by glaciers the Old Swede has not escaped the unwanted attention of graffiti artists and has subsequently been given a protective coating. Only in Hamburg!

The full story of Germany's geology is told in a pair of museums at the University of Hamburg. The little-visited Geology and Palaeontology Museum (Geologisch-Paläontologisches Museum) at Bundesstrasse 55 (Rotherbaum) contains fascinating examples of insects preserved in amber, dinosaur eggs, as well as fossils from the famous quarries at Solnhofen. The Mineralogical Museum (Mineralogisches Museum) at nearby Grindelallee 48 (Rotherbaum) includes an intriguing collection of meteorites. Not too far away, on the banks of the Außenalster, can be found another meteorite, near the junction of Milchstrasse and Harvestehuder Weg. This one, however, which has been located in the Alsterpark since 2000, is artificial. Painted silver it is one of a series by the artist Thomas Stricker (b. 1962), renowned for his "Kunst im öffentlichen Raum" (Art in public spaces).

Other places of interest nearby: 50, 51

50 The Treasure of Käppn Lührs

Altona (Othmarschen), Käppn Lührs Museum & Oevelgönner
Seekiste at Övelgönne 61 (note: open by appointment only)
Bus 36 Liebermannstrasse; Harbour Ferry 62 Neumühlen

Historians are undecided about the origin of the name Övelgönne, which today is a small riverside community strung out along the north bank of the Elbe, west of Ottensen. Indeed, even the spelling is a moot point, with some people preferring Oevelgönne. The name appears to be derived from the German word *Übelgunst*, meaning "evil grace". Perhaps it refers to the attitude of the first settlers here and the poor quality of the land they encountered, or else the bad feeling roused in the people of neighbouring Ottensen over salvage rights to goods washed up on the shoreline? As good a place as any to find the answers is the curious Käppn Lührs Museum & Oevelgönner Seekiste at Övelgönne 61.

Housed in a former single-storied river pilot's house the museum is a tribute to the self-styled Käppn Lührs, whose family were originally wreckers on Heligoland. After moving to Övelgönne the family outgrew the little house and so replaced it with a larger, two-storied house. The old house was dismantled, brick by brick, and rebuilt in the back garden, where it still stands today.

Käppn Lührs was in fact a boat-builder by trade, having been prevented from becoming a real captain through having impaired vision. Instead, he lived out his dreams by collecting anything and everything to do with the sea, and showing the collection to anyone who was interested. On his death bed in 1989 the captain instructed his son

The idiosyncratic Käppn Lührs Museum in Othmarschen holds many surprises

Hannes not to dispose of the collection for at least a decade, during which time a new caretaker could be sought. Almost exactly ten years later Hannes met his future wife Uschi Lewen, and the two of them have managed the museum ever since.

Amongst the captain's many treasures on show are antique navigational instruments, boat-building tools, ships' log books, an old diving suit weighing 130 kilos (complete with diver's telephone), and a frightening set of sharks' jaws. One room contains a cosy captain's quarters dating back to 1860. There are also several maritime curiosities in the museum, including a container used by sailors to preserve locks of hair of their favourite girls, the preserved eye of a whale (the unfortunate creature's dried penis is suspended from the ceiling!), a nail reputed to come from Noah's Ark, and a human leg bone said to be that of the notorious pirate Klaus Störtebeker (see no. 20). The museum also makes an unusual venue for birthday parties, weddings, and other events.

This deep sea diving suit is a feature of the Käppn Lührs Museum

After visiting the museum either walk back along Övelgönne, taking note of the other charming cottages and houses that line the street, or else walk down to the beach to marvel at a huge Ice Age boulder (see no. 49). The beach was once the site of a timber-built dockyard and leads onwards to the Museumshafen Övelgönne. This small, privately-owned collection of ships moored at the Neumühlen quay comprises vessels that once worked on the Elbe but which otherwise would have been scrapped. The collection includes several traditional, single-masted fishing boats *(Fischkutter)*, the steam-powered icebreaker *Stettin* (which makes occasional cruises through the Kiel Canal into the Baltic), the Elbe 3 lightship *(Feuerschiff)* (the oldest lightship in the world), and the *Bergedorf*, a 1950s Hadag passenger ferry that once shuttled between Bei den St.-Pauli-Landungsbrücken and Finkenwerder; it is now used as a floating café and restaurant.

Whilst standing on the Neumühlen quayside, which boasts an old-fashioned wooden waiting room, don't be too surprised to see a man standing on a marker buoy floating in the middle of the Elbe; it is a life-sized work of art by famous German sculptor Stephan Balkenhol (b. 1957).

Other places of interest nearby: 49, 51

51 How Hamburg Might Have Looked

Altona (Ottensen), the Augustinum at Neumühlen 37
S1, S3, S31 Altona, then Bus 112 Neumühlen/Övelgönne;
Harbour Ferry 62 Neumühlen

Between 1933 and 1945 the Port of Hamburg, together with Berlin, Munich, Nuremberg and Linz, was designated a Führerstadt (or City of the Führer of the Reich). Such cities were to be completely redesigned architecturally, in Hamburg's case as the Third Reich's new "Gateway to the World". Of the many plans for this transformation none ever left the drawing board. Had they done so Hamburg would look very different today.

In June 1936 Adolf Hitler took a cruise down the River Elbe. Approaching the old fishing village of Övelgönne he waved his hand from one side of the river to the other, and announced that here would be built the world's longest suspension bridge. The north bank of the river down to this point would be lined with skyscrapers, he said, emulating the great metropolis of New York, including a gigantic regional Nazi headquarters. "Hamburg feels so American", the dictator proclaimed enthusiastically, and anything that stood in the way of his plans would simply be swept away.

To facilitate Hitler's grandiose scheme tenders were invited and a competition announced to secure a suitable architect. The winner was Konstanty Gutschow (1902–1978) on whom in 1939 Hitler bestowed the grandiose title 'Architect of the Banks of the Elbe'. Despite Gutschow's efforts soon being diverted to coordinate the removal of rubble resulting from Allied air raids, he and his staff continued to develop their plans throughout the war, although they must have seemed increasingly futile.

At the heart of Gutschow's plan was the North-South axis, a spectacular boulevard in Ottensen, connecting a new railway station in the north with a 250 metre-high skyscraper on the riverbank housing the Nazi headquarters *(Gauhochhaus)*. Gutschow had been greatly impressed by the Empire State Building during a visit to America in the autumn of 1937, and sought to replicate such structures on the banks of the Elbe.

Around the *Gauhochhaus* he planned an open air ceremonial fo rum *(Gauforum)*, and behind that a "Strength through Joy" (Kraft durch Freude – KdF) hall capable of holding 50 000 spectators. The "Strength through Joy" organisation, founded in 1933 by Robert Ley, head of the German Work Front (Deutsche Arbeitsfront), was an attempt to bring Germany's leisure activities under the control of the state. A fleet of KdF cruise ships was launched to take holidaymakers to Italy, Greece and Norway, and Gutschow included a terminal for them in his plan (see no. 29).

Between the *Gauhochhaus* and the old liner terminal at Bei den St.-Pauli-Landungsbrücken Gutschow planned a series of imposing high-rise buildings, designed to impress visitors arriving in Hamburg by ship. Downstream from the *Gauhochhaus* would stand the suspension

The Augustinum at Neumühlen was once a cold store for Argentinian beef

bridge, straddling the Elbe between Övelgönne and the harbours of Waltershof. With one level for cars and another for trains the bridge would be supported on pylons soaring 180 metres into the air. A single 12 metre-deep watertight *caisson* was actually constructed on the beach at Övelgönne to support one of the pylons but was demolished in the 1950s.

To gain an impression of the planned height of the suspension bridge visit the Elbewarte rooftop restaurant on top of the ten-storey high Augustinum at Neumühlen 37 (Ottensen). This unusual retirement home was constructed originally in 1924 as the Cold Store 'Union' and used mainly by a British trading company to store meat from Argentina. In 1939 Konstantin Gutschow and his team erected a greatly

Under the Hitler regime the beach at Neumühlen would have been the site of the world's longest suspension bridge

reduced scale model of one of the bridge's pylons in the harbour alongside the building, to test its visual effect. The test pylon (which was dismantled in the 1950s) was a similar height to the cold store: the finished pylons would have been more than three times this height.

To ensure a constant supply of cheap building materials for the construction of the "Führer City Hamburg" a disused brickworks was reactivated by prisoners at the Neuengamme Concentration Camp (Konzentrationslager Neuengamme) on the banks of the Dove Elbe at Jean-Dolidier-Weg 75 (Neuengamme). The camp was established by the SS in 1938, as a satellite camp of the Sachsenhausen Concentration Camp. Together with more than eighty five sub-camps, Neuengamme would become the largest concentration camp in north-western Germany, where more than 40 000 people would die through the Nazi's policy of "extermination through work". The clay pits also provided material for a modelling workshop in which prisoners cast busts and reliefs of Hitler, as well as candlesticks given by SS officers as Christmas gifts. The former brick factory is today preserved as a memorial (KZ-Gedenkstätte Neuengamme).

Other places of interest nearby: 49, 50, 52

History Between the River and the Sea

Altona (Altona-Ottensen), the Altona and North German State
Museum (Altonaer Museum – Norddeutsches Landesmuseum)
at Museumstrasse 23
S1, S3, S31 Altona

Sometimes overshadowed by the Hamburg Museum (Museum für
Hamburgische Geschichte) in the city centre, the Altona and North
German State Museum (Altonaer Museum – Norddeutsches Landes-
museum) at Museumstrasse 23 (Altona-Ottensen) is one of the finest
regional museums in Germany. When it first opened in 1863, however,
Altona lay in the Duchy of Holstein, which had been under the admin-
istration of the Danish monarchy since 1640 (see no. 58). This situa-
tion changed in 1867 when war forced Denmark to cede Schleswig and
Holstein to the Kingdom of Prussia, although it was not until 1938 that
Altona was eventually merged into Hamburg.

Such vicissitudes are reflected in the history of the museum itself,
which began as a purely local and natural history collection. In 1901
it moved into a fine neo-Renaissance building, which was seriously
damaged during the Second World War. In the 1970s it was decided to
separate the existing collections – the prehistoric holdings, for example, went to the Archaeological Museum Hamburg (Archäologisches
Museum Hamburg) (Harburg) – leaving the museum to concentrate
on the history and culture of Northern Germany, hence the museum's
current subsidiary name – Norddeutsches Landesmuseum.

Bounded by the River Elbe, the North Sea and the Baltic the area
of Northern Germany includes the city state of Hamburg, Lower Saxony, and Schleswig-Holstein (the most northerly of Germany's sixteen
federal states). Not surprisingly, therefore, maritime history features
highly in the museum's collections, Altona having been founded in
1535 as a fishing village, and becoming later one of the Danish monarchy's most important harbour towns (it was connected by railway
to the Baltic port of Kiel). Included are nautical instruments, fishing
equipment, and ships's figureheads, as well as curiosities such as a bone
taken from the inner ear of a whale, a model ship made entirely from
cloves, and the effigy of a Native American smoking a pipe, once used
to advertise a tobacconist's shop.

Something unique on the second floor of the museum is a series

This old fashioned shop is reconstructed in the Altona and North German State Museum (Altonaer Museum – Norddeutsches Landesmuseum)

of charming furnished living rooms from North German farmhouses *(Bauernstuben)*. They include an eighteenth century example from the island of Sylt in Nordfriesland (a district of Schleswig-Holstein) adorned with ornate wall tiles and painted wood ceilings. From closer to home comes a room from the Kirchwerder district in the Vierlande region of south-east Hamburg, constructed around 1800 and identified by its pretty blue-and-white tiled oven and inlaid wooden doors. Also here is a more modern room containing early twentieth century cleaning and cooking utensils, including wickerwork carpet beaters, fruit preserving jars, lamp wicks, and flour sieves. Alongside it is an old general store selling everything from jars of bonbons and sausages hanging from the ceiling to powdered pudding mixes and tins of biscuits.

On the first floor of the museum are a series of grander eighteenth century rooms, with wainscotted walls, leaded windows, and fine carved furniture. Most unusual of all is an entire traditional timber-framed farmhouse, again removed from the Kirchwerder district, and reconstructed in the museum where it is used as the restaurant Vierländer Kate. Originally constructed in 1745 it consists of one large single hall divided up into areas for animals, storeage, and living quarters, with a central fireplace.

The museum also cares for the Heine Haus at nearby Elbchaussee 31, a quaint summerhouse of the 1830s that once belonged to the banker Salomon Heine, an uncle of the poet Heinrich Heine (1797–1856).

Other places of interest nearby: 51, 53

53 The Jewish Stones Speak

Altona (Altona-Altstadt), the Altona Jewish Cemetery
(Jüdischer Friedhof Altona) at Königstrasse 10a
S1, S3 Königstrasse, Reeperbahn; Bus 36, 283 Blücherstrasse

Anyone interested in the four hundred year-long history of the Jews in Hamburg should begin their quest on the second floor of the Hamburg Museum (Museum für Hamburgische Geschichte) at Holstenwall 24 (Neustadt), where a permanent exhibition tells the full story. A fascinating fold-out map available free in the museum foyer identifies many historic locations associated with the city's Jews, including synagogues, schools, memorials, and cemeteries. Undoubtedly one of the most unusual is the Altona Jewish Cemetery (Jüdischer Friedhof Altona) at Königstrasse 10a (Altona-Altstadt).

The Altona Jewish Cemetery is Hamburg's oldest Jewish cemetery. It was established in 1611 by Sephardic Jews driven out of Spain and Portugal by the Inquisition, where many of them had been forcibly converted to Catholicism. They began arriving in Hamburg around 1580, where they were permitted to settle because they no longer 'looked' Jewish and had useful trading connections. However, distrust and severe restrictions on the numbers of Jews permitted to live in Hamburg meant they were expelled in 1603. Having reverted to Judaism they settled in neighbouring Altona, a town renowned for its tolerance towards minorities, where they were granted generous privileges, initially by the Counts of Holstein-Schauenburg and from 1640 onwards by the Danish crown (see no. 58).

Ashkenazi Jews, with roots in Eastern Europe and Russia, were also arriving in Hamburg, and in 1616 they were permitted to bury their dead in the cemetery on Königstrasse. However, except for the fact that the graves of both communities faced eastwards in the direction of Jerusalem, the communities shared little else in common. They attended different synagogues and schools, disagreed over prayer books and services, and had segregated burial plots.

The Altona Jewish Cemetery was eventually closed in 1869 after which Jews were allowed burial in Ohlsdorf Cemetery (Friedhof Ohlsdorf), although they were refused the guarantee of an eternal resting place. It is precisely this Jewish concept of a burial ground in which no gravestone is ever removed that enables the Altona Jewish Cemetery to preserve forever the memory of such a longstanding and major centre

Ashkenazi graves in the Altona Jewish Cemetery (Jüdischer Friedhof Altona)

of Jewish life and scholarship, destroyed so recently at the hands of the Nazi regime.

Upon entering the cemetery visitors will find the Sephardic graves on the left-hand side. They consist of horizontal marble slabs and chest-like tombs, inscribed in Spanish and richly decorated with biblical imagery and family crests. They include Rodrigo Castro, personal physician to the King of Denmark. By contrast the Ashkenazi graves on the right-hand side are mostly standing stones with Hebrew inscriptions, adorned more frugally with icons reflecting the name and profession of the deceased. A water jug, for example, refers to the priesthood, whilst a goose refers to the family name of Gans. Throughout both parts of the cemetery are renowned rabbis and Talmudic scholars, teachers and preachers, as well as distinguished and successful families.

In 1865 Hamburg's Jewish community consisted of 14 000 members (including Orthodox and Reform groups) and had been given full civil rights. Small Jewish neighbourhoods had existed in Wandsbek and Harburg since the seventeenth century, and now a new, well-to-do Jewish quarter known as the Grindel was established between Rotherbaum and Harvestehude. This area was ransacked during Reichskristallnacht, the Nazi's anti-Jewish pogrom in 1938, and then

The water jug carved on this headstone signifies a priest

further damaged during Allied air raids. By May 1945 only 647 Jews
were left in Hamburg.

After the war the ruins of the Grindel were swept away and the area
used for the construction of a series of high rise apartment blocks (see
no. 67). Despite this Hamburg's Jewish community rebuilt itself and in
1960 a new synagogue was consecrated at Hohe Weide 34. The former
Thalmud-Torah-Schule at Grindelhof 30 reopened as a school, and the
Café Leonar at Grindelhof 59 now offers coffee and enlightenment to
those interested. Of the many memorials to the Grindel the so-called
Stolpersteine (stumbling stones) are the most affecting. Inserted into
the pavement of streets such as Grindelallee, Grindelweg, and Hallerstrasse they mark the former homes of Jews who were deported and
murdered. As Gunter Demnig, the initiator of the *Stolpersteine* project
points out "The horror didn't start in Auschwitz, Treblinka or in other
camps ... it started in our neighborhood, in our house, outside our
door".

Other places of interest nearby: 23, 25, 52

54 Adaptive Reuse in Altona

Altona (Ottensen), Medienzentrum Zeise Hallen at
Friedensallee 7–9
S1, S3, S21 Altona; Bus 37, 150 Friedensallee

In 1867, as a result of wars between Denmark and Prussia over control of Schleswig-Holstein, the independent city of Altona was ceded to Prussia. This triggered a growth in population, accompanied by rapid industrialisation, so that by the time Altona was incorporated into Hamburg in 1937 it had changed dramatically in appearance. Several of the borough's old industrial-era structures can still be seen, and it is interesting to see how they have been adapted for modern reuse.

The most famous example of a reused building in Altona is undoubtedly its former Fish Auction Hall (Fischauktionshalle) at Grosse Elbstrasse 9 (Altona-Altstadt). Fish had been successfully traded in Altona since the sixteenth century and the erection of the hall in 1894 continued this trend, despite the erection of a similar hall in Hamburg. Both were damaged during the Second World War, and after the storm tide of 1967 the Hamburg hall was demolished. Altona's restored auction hall is now a popular venue for Sunday breakfast, when the fish market (Fischmarkt) outside is in full swing. (Amidst the bustle few visitors will be aware that the market was once connected to the Altona railway station by a special railway line, part of which ran through the so-called Schellfischtunnel, occasional tours of which are conducted by the Hamburg Underworlds Association (Hamburger Unterwelten e.V.).

A less well known example of adaptive reuse in Altona is the Gaswerk Hotel Hamburg at Beim Alten Gaswerk 3 (Bahrenfeld). It is difficult to imagine that this modern, stylish and comfortable 141-room hotel occupies the former coal depot of a gasworks. Only the red-brick outer walls (and of course the name!) offer any clue as to the building's original use. (Of similar construction are the halls of Hamburg's old slaughterhouse (Alte Rinderschlachthalle), strung out between Neuer Kamp and Lagerstrasse (St. Pauli), whose former function is recalled in the formidable statue of a bull at one end of Sternstrasse.)

The Altona district of Ottensen is rich in industrial history and contains two fine examples of adaptive reuse, in which original fabric and fittings have been preserved to great effect. The first is the Medienzentrum Zeise Hallen at Friedensallee 7–9, a cinema, gallery and retail venue installed inside the former Theodor Zeise marine propellor

Fabrik on Barnerstrasse in Ottensen is a concert venue inside a former machine hall

factory, which went bankrupt in 1979. The main hall, with its battered brick walls, huge arched windows and chimney stump, makes an especially atmospheric setting for a selection of artists' studios, shops and cafés. On the floor can still be seen the iron tracks along which powerful cranes once transported the heavy propellors.

The second site in Ottensen is Fabrik at Barnerstrasse 36, a concert venue built in 1971 inside a 150-year old former machine hall. The conversion of the building (a joint project between the artist Horst Dietrich and the architect Friedhelm Zeuner) was considered groundbreaking at the time, with the timber-framed interior being opened out like the nave of a church. Since then many famous entertainers have performed

The Medienzentrum Zeise Hallen on Friedensallee occupies a former marine propellor factory

here from Miles Davis and B.B. King to AC/DC and Meat Loaf. Flea-markets are held here on Saturdays in the winter, and as a reminder of the building's history there is a large crane perched on the roof.

Before leaving Ottensen and ending this tour visit the children's playground at the corner of Nöltingstrasse and Am Born, which is the former site of the Menck & Hambrock mechanical excavator factory. Once Ottensen's largest industrial concern the factory has now been demolished but a solitary excavating machine reminds the passer-by of what once went on here.

The fish market in Altona is probably Hamburg's best known market but there are several others also worth experiencing. They include the Isemarkt on Isestrasse (Eppendorf) (Tuesday and Friday mornings), a farmers' market which is stretched out beneath a viaduct connecting two U-Bahn stations; there are claims that it is the longest and narrowest market in the world. Other farmers's markets are held on Lange Reihe (St. Georg) (Friday) and Goldbekplatz (Winterhude) (Tuesday, Thursday & Saturday). For antiques and collectibles visit the Flohcampus at Hamburg University's Von-Melle-Park (Rotherbaum) (Saturday).

Other places of interest nearby: 52, 55

55 Bonbons, Cigars, and Sailors' Hats

Altona (Ottensen), a tour of unusual shops beginning with
Bonscheladen at Friedensallee 12
S1, S3, S21 Altona; Bus 37, 150 Friedensallee

Although the high streets of Europe look increasingly similar these days, being dominated by the same powerful brands, Hamburg has managed to retain a healthy number of independent specialist retailers. These idiosyncratic bastions of local colour are manned by knowledgeable staff, each with a passion for their products.

This tour of just a few of them begins at Friedensallee 12 in the district of Ottensen, where the confectioner Bonscheladen has been operating since 2005. The word *Bonsche* is regional slang both for 'bonbons' and for 'treat', and it is certainly a rare treat to visit a sweet shop as traditional as this one. The hard candy bonbons and soft fudge sold here are crafted lovingly by hand in the old fashioned way, using only the best quality ingredients (such as organic cane sugar) and without artificial additives. Best of all it is possible to see the bonbon-making process first hand, during the daily demonstration (4.15pm weekdays and 2.30pm Saturdays). It is intriguing to watch how a blackcurrant-flavoured 'anchor' motif is made to run through a long red and white bonbon, which is then chopped up into many small ones.

Moving eastwards into Altona-Altstadt we find Otto Hatje at Alte Königstrasse 5, Hamburg's last cigar maker, established in 1922. The premises are lined with wooden shelves containing not only cigars but also all the paraphernalia that goes with them. There is also a smokers' lounge where cigars and suitable alcoholic beverages can be enjoyed by customers.

Beyond, in Sternschanze, at Schulterblatt 57 is another specialist, Stüdemann's Tea Shop. There is a timeless quality about this old-fashioned shop, and the staff have endless patience and knowledge. It is proof that the city's expertise in shipping coffee extends to tea as well, since behind the old-fashioned counter are containers filled with both. On wooden racks can also be found local specialities such as *Schanzensekt* (Schanze sparkling wine) and *Hamburger Rote Grütze* (Hamburg red cherry compote). Also to be found in St. Pauli is Freiheit & Roosen at Paul-Roosen-Strasse 41, a haven for film and music nostalgia buffs.

See sweets made the traditional way at Bonscheladen in Ottensen

Moving eastwards again we halt briefly in Neustadt to visit Benjamin Klemann Schumacherei at Poolstrasse 9, where shoes are handcrafted to fit exactly the foot of the customer. One wall of the workshop is filled entirely with different-sized wooden forms. Book lovers will want to call at Joachim Lührs Kunstantiquariat at Michaelisbrücke 3, an extravagant nineteenth century building every bit as interesting as the books it contains.

We finish in Altstadt, where there are three traditional outfitters. One of them, Ladage & Oelke at Neuer Wall 11, lays claim to being Hamburg's oldest established outfitters, having been founded in 1845 (not far away at Neuer Wall 57 is the shop FahnenFleck, which since

Tropen Brendler in Altstadt has been supplying naval uniforms for more than a century

1882 has kept Hamburg and its ships well-stocked with flags). The other two outfitters reflect Hamburg's role as an international port. Walther Eisenburg at Steinstrasse 21 has been supplying beautifully hand-crafted sailor's caps *(Mützen)* to mariners since 1892, but for the rest of the outfit a visit to Tropen Brendler at Grosse Johannisstrasse 15 is a must. Since 1879 this has been the place to buy a naval officer's uniform or to get kitted out for a trip to the tropics. On the ground floor can be found safari suits made to Brendler's own specifications, as well as sandproof desert boots, and even pith helmets. Seamen, on the other hand, will go to the first floor, where there are neat racks of naval jackets and sturdy traditional all-wool sailor's coats *(Stutzer)*, as well as glass-fronted cabinets containing captains' hats and gold embroidered cap badges.

The tour concludes just around the corner at Kleine Johannisstrasse 6, where gents hairdresser Knut Harms operates from tiny premises that are as much a museum as a salon.

Other places of interest nearby: 52, 54

56 From Crystals to Quarks

Altona (Bahrenfeld), the German Electron Synchrotron
(Deutsches Elektronen-Synchrotron) at Notkestrasse 85
(note: tours are not suitable for visitors under 16 years of age;
for tours in English, which are available only by special request,
visit www.desy.de)
S1, S3, S31 Altona, then Bus 1 Zum Hünengrab/DESY

A highly unusual Hamburg visitor attraction, one which is well away from the normal tourist routes, can be found in the Altona district of Bahrenfeld. The German Electron Synchrotron (Deutsches Elektronen-Synchrotron), or DESY for short, is one of the world's leading centres for research into the structure of matter using particle accelerators. Guided tours of the extensive DESY facility, which occur at 10am on the first Saturday of each month, offer a fascinating glimpse of a scientific world rarely seen by the general public.

After announcing their arrival at the main gate at Notkestrasse 85, visitors make their way to Building 01. Here they are greeted by one of DESY's 1500 or more employees, and given an easygoing 45-minute lecture on the history of particle physics, from man's first classification of the elements over two thousand years ago, and the discoveries of Galileo, Newton and Einstein (including gravity and electromagnetism), right up to the identification of quarks, which are a fundamental constituent of matter and an important object of investigation by particle physicists in facilities such as DESY.

The main functions of the DESY facility are then outlined by the lecturer, namely the development, construction and operation of large particle accelerators. The special intense light generated by the accelerators using certain crystals is used to conduct research into both elementary particle physics as well as photon science, a combination unique in Europe. The resulting spectrum of research at DESY is diverse, drawing more than 3000 guest scientists annually from around the world.

The two-hour tour proper now begins, with a first stop in the foyer of Building 01, where there are numerous displays, models and experiments relating to work at the DESY facility, which was founded in 1959. Of particular interest are the aerial photographs of the site on which have been superimposed the subterranean location of the two main accelerator rings. The smaller of the two (PETRA) can be seen to encircle

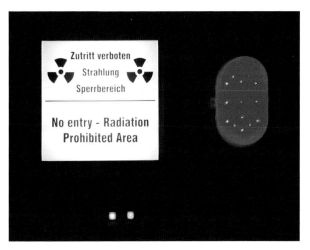

the campus, whereas the larger (and older) ring (HERA) stretches far beyond the campus, encompassing the Altonaer Volkspark, Hauptfriedhof Altona and HSH Nordbank Arena.

Once outside, the next stop on the tour is a small garden in which several disused laboratory components are on display, including a test section of an accelerator ring. Moving onwards past DESY's power plants (designed not to drain the power supply of surrounding residential neighbourhoods) the tour arrives at the facility's main control room, where a row of consoles and television monitors give the impression of a scene from a science fiction film.

Two storeys beneath the control room is an experimental hall containing a display of cut-away accelerator rings. Here the technical specifications of DESY's two main accelerator rings are described in detail. The HERA ring, for example, measures 6336 metres in length, making it the third longest accelator ring in the world. Built during the 1980s it occupies a 5.3 metre-wide tunnel built 30 metres below the ground. Although it cannot be visited it helps to know that its dimensions resemble those of an average underground railway tunnel. Although HERA has not been active since 2007 it will be dwarfed in 2015 by the opening of the 3.4 kilometre-long XFEL tunnel, reaching across the border from Hamburg into Schleswig-Holstein.

Another experimental hall nearby is home to DORIS III, a storage ring used to hold charged particles generated during synchrotron radiation, prior to them being sent onwards to other experimental research facilities outside the DESY campus. The tour concludes not far away

A disused piece of an accelarator ring in the grounds at DESY

with a colossal, gently-curving experimental hall built directly over the PETRA ring; the building is said to have the largest single-piece concrete foundation in the world.

A stroll past numerous other buildings returns visitors back safely to Building 01, where before departing they might be shown DESY's video conference room, linked permanently to the control rooms of similar facilities around the world, including Chicago and Switzerland.

Other places of interest nearby: 57

A Day at the Races

Altona (Bahrenfeld), the Trabrennbahn am Volkspark at Luruper Chaussee 30
S1, S3, S31 Altona, then Bus 2 Trabrennbahn Bahrenfeld

The history of spectator sport in Hamburg is a long and varied one, which
has left some interesting and unusual marks on the urban landscape.
The Hamburger Turnerschaft, for example, which was founded in 1816
is Germany's oldest athletic club. Perhaps it is therefore not surprising
to find a Nordic Walking Park in the city, offering ten different routes of
varying severity along the beautiful Alstertal (Wellingsbüttel). Similarly,
Germany's first rowing club was founded in Hamburg in 1836 and a year
later participated in the country's first rowing race against the English
Rowing Club, formed by members of Hamburg's English community.
The many boathouses along the city's rivers today bear witness to the
continuing popularity of watersports in the city. Hamburg's number one
spectator sport, however, remains football, the first match being played
in the city in 1881. Local team Hamburg SV (Hamburger Sport-Verein),
which was formed in 1919, is one of the top teams in the *Fußball-Bundes-
liga* and all fans will want to pay homage to it at the HSV-Museum inside
the HSH Nordbank Arena at Sylvesterallee 7 (Bahrenfeld).

One sport with a particularly colourful history in Hamburg is horse
racing. The Hamburger Rennclub (Hamburg Race Club) was founded
in 1852, and in 1869 the first North German Derby was run at the
newly-built Horner Rennbahn (Horn). Since 1889 the German Derby
(Deutsches Derby), as it is called today, has been staged on the first Sunday of July, and is the culmination of a week of competitive horse-racing.

Another annual equestrian event staged in Hamburg is the German
Jumping and Dressage Derby (Deutsches Spring- und Dressurderby)
in May. Billed as one of the world's longest and most difficult jumping
courses the event has occured at Derby Park on Baron-Voght-Strasse
(Klein Flottbek) since 1920. Horses and jockeys come from around the
world and the audience is often in excess of 25 000, with a further ten
million watching on television.

Less glamorous but no less exciting is Hamburg's third equestrian venue. The Trabrennbahn am Volkspark at 30 Luruper Chaussee (Bahrenfeld) is a no-frills track used to stage races in which light,
two-wheeled gigs are pulled at considerable speeds by a single horse.
This is the place where horse-racing experts, bookmakers, gamblers,

A unique atmosphere awaits visitors to the Trabrennbahn am Volkspark in Bahrenfeld

and the general public alike gather twice-weekly to place bets and enjoy the atmosphere (race days are Thursday 6.15–11.30pm and Sunday 1.30–6.30pm; for further details visit www.trabhamburg.de). Placing a modest bet on one of the horses can be an exhilirating pleasure quite unknown to many Hamburg visitors.

The ancient Greeks are credited with having first created a *Hippodrome* 2500 years ago, around which lightweight carriages were pulled at breakneck speeds by a harnessed horse, much to the delight of the spectators. Not until the late eighteenth century, however, did Russian Count Alexey Grigoryevich Orlov (1737–1808) breed the perfect carriage horse, the so-called Orlov Trotter, whose hereditary speed and stamina was much appreciated by Tsar Alexander I (1777–1825).

The farmers and industrialists of Hamburg began to take note of such equine developments on 31st May 1874, when the newly-founded Hamburger Traber-Club (Hamburg Trotting Club) staged their first meeting in Groß-Jüthorn (Wandsbek). The horses raced on that day were a cross between American Standardbred stallions and Orlov mares known as Russian Trotters. On 20th June 1880 the club opened their own track in Bahrenfeld, where the Trabrennbahn am Volkspark has been located ever since.

Despite initially high admission prices the Bahrenfeld track proved immensely popular, and soon the services of a full-time coach called Anthony Mills were secured. Mills lived in a house next to the main gate of the track, and it was here that his son, the legendary trainer Charlie Mills (1888–1972), was born in 1888; although the house is long gone a small stone memorial in the bushes still marks the spot, unveiled when the track was reopened after the war in July 1953. Charlie Mills won his first trophy as a jockey aged just twenty and went on to win many more in both the German and Austrian Derbys. He eventually became a pioneering coach and breeder relocating to France in 1947 after losing most of his horses in the war. Despite this he always received a warm welcome on his frequent visits back to the track where he was born, and it's a welcome that continues to be offered to race-goers today, as well as to those who come to attend the outdoor concerts also now staged here.

Other places of interest nearby: 56

58 Altona, Land of the Free

Altona (Bahrenfeld), the Mennonite Cemetery (Mennonitenfriedhof) on Holstenkamp
S1, S3, S31 Altona, then Bus 288 Regerstrasse (Ost)

The Hamburg borough of Altona originated in 1535 as a fishing village on the banks of the River Elbe. Lying within the Duchy of Holstein it was administered by the Counts of Holstein-Schauenburg, and from 1640 onwards by the Danish Crown. City status was conveyed in 1664 by King Frederick III (1609–1670), and Altona became one of the Danish monarchy's most important harbour towns (and the second largest city after Copenhagen). This situation changed in 1867 when war forced Denmark to cede Schleswig and Holstein to the Kingdom of Prussia (an inscribed boundary stone from this period can be found embedded in the pavement on Brigittenstrasse). Altona remained in Prussian hands until 1937, when it was finally incorporated into the Free and Hanseatic City of Hamburg by means of the Greater Hamburg Act.

Despite such vicissitudes of history, Altona has long maintained an enviable reputation for tolerance towards minorities, indeed the city's crest depicts an open gate. In the early years of the seventeenth century, for example, Sephardic and Ashkenazi Jews were welcomed and granted generous privileges. Not permitted to live in Lutheran Hamburg, due to severe restrictions on their numbers, they instead established a major Jewish community in Altona (see no. 53).

Other minorities to find a home in Altona included French Huguenots and Dutch Calvinists fleeing persecution, sects such as the Adamites and the Gichtelians, Catholics who built themselves a church on the aptly-named Große Frieheit (meaning 'great liberty'), at the border between Altona and Hamburg, and even craftsmen unaffiliated to established trade guilds. The largest influx were the 20 000 people displaced during the harsh winter of 1813–1814 as the French prepared to lay siege to Hamburg, a thousand of whom perished as recalled in a memorial on St. Petersburger Strasse (St. Pauli).

One of the most interesting minorities to leave a mark on Altona are the Mennonites, a Protestant sect founded in 1525, whose radical belief in adult baptism *(Anabaptism)* and refusal to bear arms resulted in their persecution by Catholics and Protestants alike. Industrious and sober people the Mennonites were first allowed into Altona in 1601, and permitted to live and trade on Große Freiheit. They initially

held church services in a warehouse, led by pastors who had been ordained by the Dutch religious leader Menno Simons (1496–1591), after whom the sect was named. The first Mennonite church was built on Große Freiheit in 1674 (replaced in 1915 by a new church on Mennonitenstrasse) and the first Mennonite cemetery was opened on Paul-Roosen-Strasse in 1678. Declared full in 1840 the cemetery was badly damaged during the Second World War, after which it was cleared and several of the gravestones removed to a new cemetery on Holstenkamp in the Altona district of Bahrenfeld. Dating back to 1679 and with several bearing inscriptions in Dutch the old stones can still be seen there today, in what it is officially the smallest cemetery in Hamburg.

Across the road from the Mennonite Cemetery (Mennonitenfriedhof) are several other small burial grounds, including three for Protestants along Holstenkamp and one for Jews on Bornkampsweg. Taken together this cluster of rarely-visited cemeteries is a powerful reminder of the religious tolerance for which Altona was renowned. Indeed, except for October 1938, when 800 Polish Jews were deported from Altona by the Gestapo (recalled in a memorial on Museumstrasse), Altona has retained a reputation for free-living and free-thinking.

Witness, for example, today's vibrant, multi-cultural scene at the junction of Friedensallee and Bahrenfelder Strasse, especially during the annual festival known as the Altonale. During this 14-day celebration of the performing arts Altona puts its many and varied inhabitants centre-stage, culminating in a colourful three-day street festival that is a sight to behold

59 The Smell of Hops and Malted Barley

Altona (Altona-Nord), the Holsten Brewery (Holsten-Brauerei)
at Holstenstrasse 224 (note: brewery tours in English are by
request only)
S21, S31 Holstenstrasse; Bus 3 Holstenstrasse,
Bus 180 Holstenplatz

The long history of brewing in Hamburg stretches back to the late
Middle Ages, when breweries sprang up along the River Elbe, and its
tributary the Alster. By the end of the thirteenth century there were no
fewer than 457 breweries operating in Hamburg. They used hops and
grain cultivated in the so-called Marsch- und Vierlande region to the
south-east, a fertile area which had been drained for agricultural use by
Dutch engineers during the twelfth century (see no. 45). This explains
why a Vierlande farmer's wife adorns the little fountain marking the
former site of Hamburg's Hop Market (Hopfenmarkt), alongside the
ruined Nikolaikirche on Willy-Brandt-Strasse (Altstadt).

By the fourteenth century Hamburg was second only to Berlin
as Germany's most important centre for brewing. Frisian merchants
traded German beer into the Low Countries, and the phrase "Hamburg Beer" became a generic term for all hoppy exported North German beers. It was not to last, however, and by the First World War most
breweries in Hamburg and Berlin had closed down, the German brewing crown having passed to Munich.

Little remains of Hamburg's traditional brewing industry today except for an old copper brewing kettle in front of the Hotel Hafen Hamburg, overlooking Bei den St. Pauli-Landungsbrücken. The kettle, which
dates from 1936, was once used to produce Hamburg's popular *Astra*
beer, and is a relic of the Bavaria-St. Pauli Brewery, which stood on the
aptly-named Hopfenstrasse nearby until its closure in 2003. The brewery
had been founded in 1647 in Altona by the Dutchman Peter de Voss.

Although the unmistakeable smell of fermenting beer no longer
hangs over Hopfenstrasse it can still be found elsewhere in Hamburg,
for example in the Brauhaus Joh. Albrecht at Adolphsbrücke 7 (Altstadt). This modern microbrewery overlooking the Alsterfleet brews
two notable house beers (the dark *Kupfer* and the light *Messing*),
which are available for consumption on the premises. Patrons can sit
alongside the brewery's gleaming copper kettles in which the so-called

A lofty brewing tower rises above the Holsten Brewery (Holsten-Brauerei) in Altona

'wort' (strained from mashed malted barley and water) is brought to the boil. The liquid is then cooled and hops added, converting fermentable sugars into carbon dioxide and alcohol. Very drinkable beer is the end result.

To understand the workings of a large modern brewery take a trip to Hamburg's Holsten Brewery (Holsten-Brauerei) at Holstenstrasse 224 (Altona-Nord). Founded in 1879 the brewery was taken over in 2004 by the Carlsberg Group, the fourth largest brewery in the world. Guided tours of the brewery, which take place three times daily from Monday to Friday, last two hours during which the entire brewing process is explained, from mashing and fermentation, to storage, bottling, and dispatch. The tour begins with a short audiovisual presentation followed by a walk through the brewery complex, which is laid out around an old brewing tower, topped with a weather vane in the form of the familiar Holsten Brewery logo of a knight on horseback. Although there's not as much beer to be seen in a large-scale production plant as there is in a microbrewery, since much of the process is automated and hidden away, the tour still has a few surprises. Most visitors, for example, are fascinated by the bottling plant, with its endless conveyor belts of clanking bottles. And everyone seems delighted at the end of the tour to be ushered into a cosy room decked out like a traditional tavern where they are given a glass of fresh draft Holsten Pilsener and some *Treberbrot* (bread made with residue malt from the brewing process) served with locally-cured ham. The price of admission also includes a voucher which can be redeemed in the well-stocked Holsten Shop.

Other places of interest nearby: 60, 61

60 The Story of Rote Flora

Altona (Sternschanze), Rote Flora at Achidi-John-Platz
(formerly Schulterblatt 71)
S21, S31 Sternschanze; U3 Sternschanze; Bus 15 Schulterblatt

Hamburg's smallest district, Sternschanze, occupies an area of less than half a square kilometre, squeezed in between the much larger districts of St. Pauli, Altona-Altstadt, Eimsbüttel, and Rotherbaum. It is also one of the city's newest, having been created on 1st March 2008 and incorporated into the borough of Altona. Although the name Sternschanze is an old one, recalling a star-shaped fortress erected in 1682 to provide an outlying line of defence for Hamburg, the district is best known today for its namesake neighbourhood the Schanzenviertel, which occupies roughly the same area. Long renowned for its alternative scene and left-wing activism, the spirit of the Schanzenviertel is best captured in one building: the legendary Rote Flora.

Rote Flora, a graffiti-covered, half-ruined former theatre on Achidi-John-Platz (formerly Schulterblatt 71), began life in 1888 as the Tivoli Theatre (Tivoli-Theater). Shortly after opening it was renamed the Concerthaus Flora, and eventually became the Flora-Theater, in which plays and concerts, as well as operetta, revues and even boxing matches, were staged. The original building consisted not only of the neo-Classical façade and entrance hall seen today but also a steel and glass auditorium to the rear.

The Flora-Theater was one of the very few Hamburg theatres to escape damage during the Second World War, as a result of which it stayed open until 1943 (a huge civilian air raid shelter, used today as a climbing wall, was erected immediately behind the theatre). Thereafter it was used as a storage area and in 1949 was reopened as a theatre. Times were changing, however, and between 1953 and 1964 the old theatre served as an 800-seat cinema, after which it became a branch of the discount supermarket chain 1000 Töpfe.

By the time the supermarket closed in 1987 the surrounding area had changed dramatically. From the 1970s onwards families had started moving away due to the lack of green space and the overcrowded streets. In their place arrived students, taking advantage of the close proximity of Hamburg University and cheap rents. Inspired by the area's history of political activism, stretching back to workers' opposition to National Socialism during the 1930s, the neighbourhood also became the tradi-

tional starting point for demonstrations. Those favouring the alternative scene have been in conflict ever since with those preferring to see the area re-gentrified.

The trouble started when the musical impresario Friedrich Kurz (b. 1948) came forward with a plan to convert the now-empty supermarket back into a theatre in which to stage *Phantom of the Opera*. Residents, shopkeepers, and activists alike responded negatively, fearing that such a development would change the feel of the place, and inevitably cause rents to rise. Despite continued protest the rear of the building was torn down in April 1988, resulting in several clashes between police and militant groups. The negative feedback that resulted in the local press led eventually to Kurz and his backers abandoning the project.

With the ruined theatre building now vacant it was suggested that the protestors themselves renovate and reuse it as an alternative cultural centre, and in August 1989 the City of Hamburg unexpectedly offered them a six week lease to do just that. Consequently, on 23rd September the old theatre was re-born as Rote Flora, the name reflecting the political leanings of its new proprietors. Politics soon got in the way though and the lease was declared obsolete, as a result of which the property was squatted on 1st November.

For the next two years the squatters transformed the rear of the building from a building site into a park. The City of Hamburg, on the other hand, had plans to build apartments and again the police were called in. The squatters refused to sign a new short-term lease (fear-

Graffiti changes weekly on the walls of Rote Flora

ing they might later be evicted legally) and stayed put until 2000, when once again the City of Hamburg attempted unsuccessfully to secure a signed lease. After eleven years of occupation the question of what to do with the increasingly controversial Rote Flora seemed solved when in March 2001 the building was purchased by property developer Klausmartin Kretschmer, who promised the squatters a free reign over the running of their centre. Political meetings, art events, and block parties have been staged there ever since, with the façade used as an ever-changing blank canvas for highly emotive political graffiti. It remains to be seen whether Rote Flora will bounce back once again after Kretschmer's lease expired in 2011.

Even the address of Rote Flora has controversy attached to it. Originally it was plain old Schulterblatt 71, but this was changed to Achidi-John-Platz, in memory of a young Nigerian asylum seeker and drug dealer (real name Michael Paul Nwabuisi), who died under mysterious circumstances whilst in police custody.

Other places of interest nearby: 15, 59, 61

A Legend Among Fountain Pens

Altona (Sternschanze), the former Montblanc pen factory
at Schanzenstrasse 75–77
S21, S31 Sternschanze; U3 Sternschanze

There is a longheld popular misconception that the legendary Mont-blanc fountain pen is manufactured in Switzerland. In reality, Mont-blanc has always been a German company, the story of which goes back to 1906, when the Hamburg-based entrepreneur Claus Johannes Voss joined forces with stationery expert Alfred Nehemias and engineer August Eberstein. Recently returned from America with the technical expertise required to manufacture fountain pens, the two men had already established a workshop in Berlin, and invited Voss to participate as financial backer. Relocating to Hamburg, and with further financial assistance from banker Max Koch, the four men launched the Simplo Filler Pen Company in 1908, the word 'Simplo' referring to the simple inkwell integrated into the barrel of their pens, which at the time was something completely new in Europe.

The first Simplo factory was on Caffamacherreihe (Neustadt), and it was from here that the company's first flagship model, the *Rouge et Noir*, was launched in 1909. Made of hard black rubber with a red top and gold nib the pen caused quite a sensation, the name capitalising on the current vogue for all things French. Unfortunately, despite strong sales there was trouble behind the scenes, and by 1910 both Koch and Eberstein had been replaced. Worse still was the unexpected death of Nehemias, who as he lay dying gave his partner Voss some valuable advice for the future: "Never sell cheap pens, stick with high quality".

With this in mind the restructured company moved to larger premises on Bartelsstrasse (St. Pauli) and there created the very first Mont-blanc pen. The name of the new pen is reputed to have been proposed by the industrialist Carl Schalk during a card game: "Why not call it Montblanc? After all, it's black at the bottom, white at the top and the greatest among its peers". Thereafter all pens created by the company bore the same name, it being perceived as both international and pro-nounceable in every language. As part of a publicity drive the company's new sales manager, Wilhelm Dziambor, instigated the use of the now iconic white star on the cap (the so-called 'Snowflake'), which represented the famous snow-capped mountain with its seven valleys as viewed from above. The cap went into production just prior to the First World War.

After the war the company rented further space at nearby Schanzenstrasse 75–77 (Sternschanze). Now used as a school the building still retains a pair of doorways adorned with carved Montblanc snowflakes. In 1919 an advertising department and gold nib workshop were set up here, and in the same year the first specialised Montblanc shops were opened in Hamburg. Inside the doorway at number 75 is a splendid white-tiled staircase with a *Jugendstil* balustrade rising six storeys. In the courtyard beyond, which is now used by studios and a cinema, there is a solitary Montblanc sign to remind passers-by that the company was once here.

A carved snowflake motif identifies the former Montblanc pen factory on Schanzenstrasse

Further milestones in the Montblanc story included the release of the Montblanc *Meisterstück* (Masterpiece) pen in 1924, notable for its unique lifetime warranty and the cryptic numbers 4810 inscribed on the cap (indicating the height of Mont Blanc), and in 1934 a change of company name to Montblanc-Simplo.

Bought out by Alfred Dunhill in 1977 the company made the controversial move to cease production of lower-priced pens and to broaden the use of the Montblanc name to include a range of luxury products including perfumes, jewellery and watches. Now part of the Richemont Group, Montblanc has become a successful global brand with any number of celebrity endorsements. Although serious pen collectors have felt somewhat betrayed by these developments the company tries

An old promotional sign still adorns the courtyard

to keep them happy by releasing limiting editions.

Although Montblanc products are today readily available in the company's boutique at Neuer Wall 18 (Neustadt) most collectors will want to see the early models. To do so they should visit the company's head office and factory at Hellgrundweg 100 (Eidelstadt), where the company relocated in 1986, which contains a private museum illustrating the full history of Montblanc (for factory and museum tours, which are only available to pre-booked groups during May and June, tel. +49/40/84 00 1-0 or visit www.montblanc.com). Rarities on display include pens once owned by Ernest Hemingway, Agatha Christie, and Oscar Wilde, and examples of limited editions, such as one that contains an actual piece of stone from Mont Blanc itself.

Other places of interest nearby: 15, 59, 60

62   The Emperor's Preferred Railway Station

Eimsbüttel (Rotherbaum), the Hamburg Dammtor railway station on Theodor-Heuss-Platz
S11, S21, S31 Dammtor

Hamburg's Central Station (Hamburg Hauptbahnhof), situated between Steintorwall and Kirchenallee, is everything a main station should be: bustling, noisy, and colourful. Some 450 000 passengers pass through the station daily, and piped classical music is used to soothe the anxieties of the many lost souls also drawn here for warmth and company. It is all a far cry from the city's first railway connecting Hamburg with Bergedorf, which was inaugurated on 5th May 1842, the same day the Great Fire destroyed much of the old city centre. For the next half a century this and all Hamburg's other rail connections were

serviced by a handful of rail termini, such as the Hannover Station (Hannoverscher Bahnhof) on Lohseplatz (see no. 81).

In 1900 it was decided to replace these old stations with one main passenger station, and a design competition was announced. After German Emperor William II (1888–1918) denounced the first proposal as "simply horrible" a second one was drafted, based on a hall at the Paris World Exhibition of 1889, which after approval was unveiled on 6th December 1906. Today one of the largest stations in Northern Germany, the lofty steel-and-glass vault of Hamburg Hauptbahnhof shelters eight mainline

Carved stonework makes the Dammtor railway station the most elegant in Hamburg

Jugendstil details enhance the main hall at the Dammtor railway station

tracks. They are used by four Intercity-Express lines (ICE 20, 22, 25, 28), which run to Berlin, Frankfurt-am-Main (continuing on to Stuttgart and Munich), and Bremen (continuing on to the Ruhr Area and Cologne), as well as northwards to Aarhus and Copenhagen in Denmark, and Kiel in Schleswig-Holstein. The station is also used by the A1, a regional commuter and freight service operated by AKN Eisenbahn AG, as well as the city's S-Bahn (S1, S2, S3, S11, S21, S31), which uses four of the eight mainline tracks.

A highlight for many travellers passing through Hamburg Hauptbahnhof is the so-called Wandelhalle ('promenading hall'), a shopping mall and restaurant area added to the north side of the station in 1991 (it is mirrored by a smaller gallery of shops at the opposite end of the station). The only problem in having such facilities is that they tempt travellers away from taking notice of the magnificent building itself. Even the splendid old station clock that looks down onto the Wandelallee can easily be missed in the rush to visit the fruit juice stand and the pizza stall. Therefore, for those travellers in search of a more nostalgic railway experience, one that is redolent of a more genteel age, a visit to the Hamburg Dammtor railway station on Theodor-Heuss-Platz is highly recommended.

Hamburg Dammtor was opened on July 7th 1903, as part of the general reorganisation of the city's railways. Despite being a long distance train station it is classified as a *Haltepunkt* because no trains start, end, or change directions here. The name of the station recalls a former gate through Hamburg's city walls, which stood here until the nineteenth century (see no. 20).

Hamburg Dammtor differs from Hamburg Hauptbahnhof in both scale and design. Like certain stations in Berlin it is a two-storey structure, with ticket office, waiting areas and some charming wooden-fronted shops located on the ground floor. The platforms themselves are located on the first floor, from where trains snake away on four elevated tracks designed to remove the need for disruptive level crossings on the city's busy streets.

Whereas Hamburg Hauptbahnhof looks somewhat squat from the outside, Hamburg Dammtor appears tall and elegant. The light-coloured sandstone façade rises above the ground floor in a series of piers used to support the steel-framed wooden roof that covers the platforms. The piers are suitably adorned with carved heads of the Roman god Mercury, the messenger of the gods, interspersed with winged and sunrise motifs to signify travel. Over the main entrance can be seen the *caduceus*, the symbol of Mercury comprising a herald's staff entwined with serpents and surmounted by wings.

Despite the sturdy construction of Hamburg Dammtor the overall effect is a delicate one, due primarily to the *Jugendstil* glass windows located between each pair of steel roof joists, flooding the platforms with natural light. Little wonder that when Emperor William II alighted here on his way to the Hamburg Trade Fair he is said to have remarked, "Looks rather nice". A typical Prussian understatement!

A station resembling Hamburg Dammtor (but actually called Berliner Tor) can be seen in the Miniatur Wunderland, the world's longest H0-gauge model railway, located at Kehrwieder 2–4 (Altstadt). Twin brothers Frederick and Gerrit Braun started work on the model in 2000 and it currently boasts twelve kilometres of track, 890 trains, 300 000 lights, and 200 000 tiny figures. The scenery is made from 700 kg of fake grass and 4000 kg of steel, and depicts not only Hamburg but also the fjords of Scandinavia, the Swiss Alps, and Mount Rushmore in America. By the time the layout is completed in 2020 it will be twice as long, and will encompass France, Italy and the United Kingdom. Railway fanatics wishing to experience Hamburg's full-sized railways but using vintage rolling stock should contact the Verein Verkehrsamateure und Museumsbahn e.V. (www.vvm-museumsbahn.de) and the Historische S-Bahn Hamburg e.V. (www.historische-s-bahn.de).

Other places of interest nearby: 15, 16, 53, 54

63 A Trial in the Curio House

Eimsbüttel (Rotherbaum), the Curio-Haus at Rothenbaumchaussee 11
S11, S21, S31 Dammtor ; U1 Stephansplatz; Bus 34 Museum
für Völkerkunde

There is a grand building at Rothenbaumchaussee 11 (Rothenbaum)
with a curious name – and a curious history. The so-called Curio-Haus
was built in 1911 for Johann Curio, the founder of the elaborately-
named Association of the Friends of Schooling and Education in the
Fatherland (Gesellschaft der Freunde des vaterländischen Schul- und
Erziehungswesens). This explains the presence of the sculpted Greek
god on the façade, reclining on his plinth, book in hand, accompanied
by a child with a ball. In 1946, however, the Curio-Haus played a quite
different educational role. It was here, in the building's main hall, that
a British military tribunal convened to stage a scaled-down version of
the Nuremberg Trials.

The accused during the Curio-Haus trial fell into two groups. One
comprised the SS commandants and guards responsible for adminis-
tering the concentration camps at Bergen-Belsen in Lower Saxony, Ravensbrück north of Berlin, and Neuengamme in Hamburg (see no. 51).
Of the fourteen people tried from Neuengamme, including the com-
mandant Max Pauly, eleven were sentenced to death and executed. Several of the accused were implicated in the infamous murder of children
in the school at Bullenhuser Damm (Rothenburgsort) (see no. 81). The
former football player Otto "Tull" Harder (1892–1956), a popular centre
forward during the 1920s, had served as a guard at the camp and was
sentenced to fifteen years imprisonment.

The second group of accused were businessmen from the company
Tesch & Stabenow. In 1920 the chemist Bruno Emil Tesch (1890–1946)
had become head of the German Association for Parasite Control
(Deutsche Gesellschaft für Schädlingsbekämpfung – DeGeSch). Before
the First World War he had worked with Nobel Prize Winner Fritz
Haber on the development of chemical weapons. In 1924, together with
Paul Stabenow, he founded the company Tesch & Stabenow (Testa).
Initially the company's main business was pest control and the fumiga-
tion of ships and warehouses in the Port of Hamburg.

From 1928 onwards the company was based on the first floor of
Ballin House at Meßberg 1, in the *Kontorhausviertel* (Office Quarter)
of Hamburg's Altstadt. The building, which still stands alongside the

more famous Chile-Haus, was named in honour of Albert Ballin (1857–1918), the director of the Hamburg-America shipping line HAPAG. That changed in 1938 when the name of the building was changed by the Nazis to Meßberghof because of Ballin's Jewish family origins.

Something else changed around this time, too. In 1924, DeGeSch had appointed Tesch & Stabenow as official distributor of Zyklon B, a hydrogen cyanide poison used by the army for the delousing of troops. From 1941 onwards Tesch & Stabenow commenced delivery of the poison to the concentration camps at Auschwitz, Majdanek, Neuengamme, Ravensbrück, Sachsenhausen, and Stutthof,

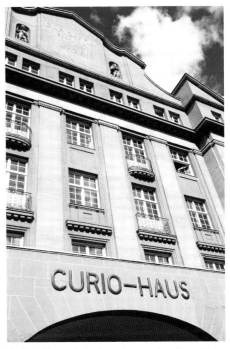

The Curio-Haus on Rothenbaumchaussee played its part in the Nuremberg trials

where it was used to murder millions in the gas chambers. Even Berlin was a Tesch & Stabenow customer, where top-ranking Nazi officials, including Hitler himself, always carried a cyanide capsule as a means of evading capture.

After the end of the war company chairman Bruno Tesch, his general manager Karl Weinbacher, and a clerk, Dr. Joachim Drosihn, were all tried before the Curio-Haus tribunal. It was established that both Tesch and Weinbacher knew about the use of Zyklon B in the concentration camps, a crime for which both were executed on 16th May 1946.

The Meßberghof today is still an office building, although one wonders if its name should revert back to the original? A plaque erected on the façade in 1997 reminds the passer-by of Tesch & Stabenow's involvement in the horrors of the death camps. The Curio-Haus also now serves as offices, and carries a plaque identifying it as the site of the first post-war trial against the SS.

Other places of interest nearby: 15, 62, 64, 65, 66

64 In a Chinese Tea House

Eimsbüttel (Rotherbaum), the Hamburg Yu Garden Chinese
Tea House (Chinesisches Teehaus) at Binderstrasse 67
U1 Hallerstrasse; Bus 34 Museum für Völkerkunde,
15 Hallerstrasse, 109 Böttgerstrasse

Hamburg in the early years of the twentieth century was home to shipping companies servicing America, Africa, India, and East Asia, trans-
forming the city into a cosmopolitan metropolis based on worldwide
trade (see nos. 29 & 64). Not only was the port used by Germans and
East Europeans departing for the New World but it also became home to
trading communities arriving into Hamburg. One of the most distinctive
of these was the Chinese community, two thousand of whom settled in
St. Pauli in the early 1920s. Most were employed in the German merchant
shipping business, with others working in laundries and restaurants.

The focus of Hamburg's Chinatown was Schmuckstrasse, although
a visit there today will prove disappointing since only two rundown
buildings (numbers 5 and 9) remain from the period. On v13ᵗʰ May
1944 the Gestapo dispersed the community, forcing many to flee to
Britain. One hundred and sixty five Chinese were arrested on suspicion
of conspiracy and sent to a forced labour camp in Wilhelmsburg, where
seventeen of them died.

Following the end of the Second World War the Chinese trickled
back very slowly into Hamburg, which they called *Hanbao*, or 'Chinese
Fort'. In 1986 a formal trading relationship was forged between Hamburg
and its sister city, Shanghai. From just three Chinese companies registered in Hamburg in 1985 there are now well over three hundred, em-
ploying more than 10 000 ethnic Chinese. By 2003 seven hundred Hamburg companies had established
commercial relations with China,
which is now the city's fourth largest foreign trade partner.

In 2008 this highly lucrative
relationship was made tangible by the unveiling of a magnificent Chinese-style building
constructed at Binderstrasse 67,
alongside Hamburg's Museum
für Völkerkunde (Ethnology Mu-

Several Hamburg street names reflect the city's trade
with Asia

The Chinese Tea House (Chinesisches Teehaus) in Rotherbaum is surrounded by a water garden

seum) (see no. 65). Dubbed the Chinese Tea House (Chinesisches Tee-haus, *Chá Lóu* in Mandarin) it is surrounded by a reduced-scale replica of the renowned Yuyuan Garden in Shanghai, featuring a classic Chinese garden landscape dotted with ponds, traversed by zigzag-shaped stone bridges. Despite the building's name only a part of the Chinese Tea House is actually given over to traditional tea ceremonies, namely the Hamburg Yu Garden Tea House; the rest is occupied by the University of Hamburg's Confucius Institute. This cultural centre is used to stage events aimed at strengthening economic ties and furthering cultural exchange between the two cities and their respective countries.

Other places of interest nearby: 15, 62, 63, 65, 66

65 Masks from the South Seas, Treasures from the Andes

Eimsbüttel (Rotherbaum), the Museum of Ethnology
(Museum für Völkerkunde) at Rothenbaumchaussee 64
U1 Hallerstrasse; Bus 34 Museum für Völkerkunde,
115 Hallerstrasse, 109 Böttgerstrasse

There is a museum in Hamburg in which it is possible to take a trip around the world without ever leaving the building. The Museum of Ethnology (Museum für Völkerkunde) at Rothenbaumchaussee 64 represents the city's superb ethnological holdings, and presents the fascinating traditional culture of peoples from all five continents. Founded in 1849 the collection grew rapidly, boasting 645 objects by 1869; ten years later the museum received the name it carries today, making 2009 the museum's official 130th birthday. Housed since 1915 on Rothenbaumchaussee this exotic collection is today considered one of the most important ethnological collections in Europe, with a total of around 600 000 artefacts, photographs, and documents.

The museum's public collection is currently spread across ten permanent exhibitions, each of which contains some unusual objects. It begins on the ground floor with an exhibition revealing a tiny part of the museum's collection of 18 000 photographs of the Near and Middle East and Africa, taken between 1864 and 1970. Called *Mit Kamel und Kamera* (With Camel and Camera) the collection is notable for the highly aesthetic quality of the images, as well as the stereotypical view of Oriental peoples as seen through the eyes of European photographers.

Next comes a small exhibition called *Ein Hauch von Ewigkeit* (A Breath of Eternity) illustrating the ever fascinating civilization of ancient Egypt. By means of several hundred artefacts, dating from between 3100 BC and 400 AD, the themes of life and death are fully explored. The most exciting is undoubtedly the mummy lurking in the basement! The exhibition dovetails neatly into the *Afrikasaal* beyond, the highlight of which has to be the frighteningly graphic advertising boards once used by a traditional healer from Togo.

The intriguing culture of the Incas of Peru is represented by the next exhibition called *Schätze der Anden* (Treasures of the Andes). The four hundred year history of this Pre-Columbian civilization is illustrated not only by means of magnificent gold and silver objects but also by

Peruvian gold in the Museum of Ethnology (Museum für Völkerkunde)

superbly modelled anthropomorphic ceramics, rare wood sculptures, and delicate textiles.

The final exhibition on the ground floor is *Indianer Nordamerikas* (The Indians of North America), which includes a Plains *teepee*, the re-construction of a *pueblo* from the Southwest, a newly-built longhouse containing sacred masks typical of the Canadian northwest coast, and a blanket-covered 'Sweat Lodge' used for spiritual purification.

The museum continues on the first floor with the *Europasaal*, in which distinctive European traditions are illustrated from Christianity to the British pub. On the other side of the vaulted foyer *(Gewölbesaal)*, itself filled with traditional canoes and outriggers, is the *Indonesiensaal* containing a shadow puppet theatre and the instruments of a *Gamelan* orchestra. The Asian theme continues with *Ein Traum von Bali* (A Dream of Bali), the centrepiece of which is an exquisitely carved princely house of the nineteenth century. All around it are objects reflecting the Hindu world of Bali, notably some terrifying witches' masks.

Masks are the focal point of the next exhibition, namely *Masken der Südsee* (Masks of the South Seas). This highly atmospheric collection from the islands of Oceania features magnificent examples dating back to the nineteenth century. Still an important part of communal living on some islands they are displayed alongside headdresses used in ritual

and ceremonial dancing, as well as plastered skulls used for cultic ancestor worship. Also on display is the striking battle outfit of a Kiribati warrior, comprising a Porcupine Fish helmet and a shell-encrusted tunic. The exhibition closes with a magnificent full-size reconstructed Maori meeting hall *(Maori-Haus)*, which it is possible to enter so long as visitors remove their shoes.

A highlight of the Museum of Ethnology is the collection of South Sea masks

The Museum of Ethnology is justifiably renowned for its extensive programme of concerts, lectures and festivals connected with its displays. Also of interest are the three annual markets it hosts, namely the Norddeutscher Ostermarkt (Easter Market) on the weekend before Palm Sunday, the Markt der Völker (People's Market) in November, and the Nordeutscher Christkindlmarkt (Christmas Market) on the first weekend of Advent. The Easter and Christmas markets especially give a good insight into the traditional life of Hamburg (for exact dates and times visit www.voelkerkundemuseum.com).

Other places of interest nearby: 15, 62, 63, 64, 66, 67

66 The Mysterous Unicorn of the Deep

Eimsbüttel (Rotherbaum), the Zoological Museum
(Zoologisches Museum) at Martin-Luther-King-Platz 3
Bus 4, 5 Grindelhof

Surely one of the most curious animals to inhabit our oceans is the Narwhal (*Monodon monoceros*), a species of whale found primarily in the Arctic coastal waters around Greenland and northern Canada. What sets the male Narwhal apart from most other whales is its distinctive single straight tusk, extending from an incisor in the upper left jaw. Perhaps not surprisingly medieval Europeans believed Narwhal tusks to be the horns of the legendary unicorn. As such they became staples of Renaissance-era 'Cabinets of Curiosities' – until their true provenance was revealed in the sixteenth century.

The name of the Narwhal is based on the Old Norse word *nár*, meaning 'corpse', in deference to the creature's mottled grey colouring, which resembles that of a drowned sailor. The Narwhal's Latin name, *Monodon monoceros*, is derived from Greek, meaning 'one tooth, one horn'. Weighing up to 1600 kilograms and very vulnerable to climate change there are thought to be approximately 75 000 Narwhals in existence today. Staying close to shore in the summer months they move into deeper offshore waters in the winter, where they make some of the deepest dives ever recorded for a marine mammal, diving to at least 800 metres over 15 times per day, with some dives reaching 1500 metres.

The most characteris-

This skull of a female two-tusked Narwhal in the Zoological Museum (Zoologisches Museum) is unique

Children are drawn to this preserved specimen of a Siberian Tiger

tic feature of the male Narwhal remains its tusk, which can grow to a length of three metres and weigh up to 10 kilograms. Zoologists are still unsure as to the exact function of the tusk, suggesting that it is most probably a secondary sexual characteristic, like the mane of a lion. The sight of male Narwhals rubbing their tusks together non-aggressively during the summer months suggests that the tusk may also be used to help determine social ranking within a group. Very occasionally the right upper incisor of a male Narwhal also grows into a tusk, as illustrated by a dozen twin-tusked skulls displayed in museums worldwide. Just such a skull can be found in Hamburg's Zoological Museum (Zoologisches Museum) at Martin-Luther-King Platz 3 but what makes the Hamburg specimen unique is that it comes from a *female* Narwhal, caught in 1684 and recorded as carrying embryos.

Only the Inuit are today allowed to hunt the Narwhal legally, relying on its flesh for important vitamins and its bones for tools and art. In Inuit legend, the Narwhal was created when a woman with a harpoon rope tied around her waist was dragged into the sea whilst out hunting. Her hair was twisted around and around in the water until it became the characteristic spiralling tusk of the Narwhal. The legend only adds to the mystique of the Narwhal, and it is little wonder that northern traders were once able to sell Narwhal tusks for their weight in gold to fascinated Europeans.

The Zoological Museum represents the public collection of the University of Hamburg (Universität Hamburg) and has its roots in the seventeenth century, when sailors returned home with zoological specimens from around the globe. Amongst the many preserved animals, birds, fishes, and plants are numerous oddities, not least of which is a huge stuffed Walrus *(Odobarus rosmarus rosmarus)* nicknamed Antje near the entrance, once a star attraction at Hagenbecks Tierpark (see no. 69). Other curiosities include specimens of *Coelocanth Latimeria*, a fish thought to have been extinct for 65 million years (until it was found alive off South Africa in 1938), the rare Siberian or Amur Tiger *(Panthera tigris altaica)*, which is on the brink of extinction in the wild, and the twisted trunk of a Strangler Fig from Cameroon. Also unusual is a collection of whale skeletons, including that of a complete Sperm Whale *(Physeter macrocephalus)*, and a display of large mammals once common in Europe, such as the Eurasian Brown Bear *(Ursus arctos arctos)*, the Elk *(Alces alces)*, and the European Bison *(Bison bonasus)*.

Even odder than the Narwhal is the so-called Hamburg Hydra. During the eighteenth century this multiple-headed sea serpent took pride of place in the natural history cabinet of a rich merchant. Whilst passing through Hamburg the twenty eight year old Swedish zoologist Carl Linnaeus (1707–1778) visited the collection, and identified the creature as a fake. So upset was the merchant, who had paid a considerable price for the object, that Linnaeus was forced to leave the city. From this time on such 'natural wonders' were viewed with increasing suspicion.

Other places of interest nearby: 15, 62, 63, 64, 65, 67

67 Amongst the Tower Blocks of Grindel

Eimsbüttel (Harvestehude), the Grindelhochäuser at
the corner of Grindelberg and Hallerstrasse
U3 Hoheluftbrücke; Bus 5 Bezirksamt Eimsbüttel

Prior to the Second World War the Jewish area known as the Grindel straddled the districts of Rotherbaum and Harvestehude, between Grindelberg-Grindelallee, Mittelweg, Klosterstern, and Dammtor (see no. 53). Most of the fine old patrician houses that once stood here were reduced to rubble during Allied air raids. Only poignant memorials recall the culture that was lost, including a large gable-end mural at Von-Melle-Park 9.

After the war, during the period of British occupation, much new housing was urgently required in the city. One of the more interesting of these housing projects took place in the former Grindel, on a rectangular plot in Harvestehude bordered by Hallerstrasse, Brahmsallee, Oberstrasse, and Grindelberg-Grindelallee. After an initial British plan for the project was used instead in Frankfurt, the Grindel project was assigned to a group of German architects, known thereafter as The Grindelberg Group (Gruppe der Grindelberg-Architekten).

Comprising Bernhard Hermkes, Rudolf Lodders, Rudolf Jäger, Albrecht Sander, Ferdinand Streb, Fritz Trautwein and Hermann Zess, the group was set the task of creating affordable and modern housing for the masses. They came up with a series of twelve elongated apartment blocks, each orientated north-south, which were constructed over the next decade. Completed in 1956 the blocks are arranged in five alternating rows of two blocks and then three. Each individual block consists of between nine and twelve storeys and contains up to

The Grindelhochäuser tower blocks stand on the site of a former Jewish district

2000 apartments. Although there are some larger penthouse-style apartments on the top floors, most of the apartments are uniformly small, occupying only about twenty square metres.

Today, the Grindelhochhäuser ('Grindel tower blocks') are considered important examples of postwar social housing and have accordingly been granted monumental protection *(Denkmal-schutz)*. Whilst the blocks might not be to everyone's taste these days, there's no denying that the architects did their best under the circumstances. The arrangement of the blocks facilitated the inclusion of pleasant green areas in the

Inside one of the tower blocks is a non-stop Paternoster elevator

spaces between, and the façades of the blocks themselves were given individuality by the use of different window styles and roof forms.

Even more individuality was brought to the project in the form of a series of large-scale sculptures, incorporated into the layout at regular intervals. Thus, visitors approaching from the southwest can't miss Barbara Haeger's bronze *Große Liegende* (1956), a reclining female nude at the corner of Grindelberg and Hallerstrasse. Other works include *Schwäne* (1958) by Karl August Ohrt, *Eselreiter* (1956) by Ursula Querner, *Großer Speerträger* (1957) by Fritz Fleer, and *Schreitende* (1956) by Hans Martin Ruwoldt (whose *Panther* can be found in the Planten un Blomen on Stephansplatz).

A final point of interest amongst the tower blocks of Grindel can be found at Grindelberg 66, which serves as the town hall *(Bezirksamt)* for the borough of Eimsbüttel. People enjoy coming here to ride on the non-stop *Paternoster* elevator that transports visitors up to the eleventh floor, from where the twelfth floor café can be reached by a normal staircase (Hamburg's oldest *Paternoster* can be found in the Sloman House shipping office at Steinhöft 11 and dates back to 1909).

Other places of interest nearby: 63, 64, 65, 66

68 Eimsbüttel's Outpost of Orthodoxy

Eimsbüttel (Stellingen), the Russian Church of St. Prokop (Russische Kirche des Heilige Prokop) at Hagenbeckstrasse 10 U2 Lutterothstrasse

One of Hamburg's least known yet most beautiful places of worship is the Russian Church of St. Prokop (Russische Kirche des Heiligen Prokop) at Hagenbeckstrasse 10 (Stellingen). Despite only having been erected in the 1960s, this fairytale church with its whitewashed walls and sky blue domes conveys the impression that it has always been there.

The church was founded by the Russian Orthodox Church Abroad (ROCOR), a semi-autonomous wing of the Russian Orthodox Church, formed in response to hostile Bolshevik religious policy in the wake of the 1917 Revolution. After Patriarch Sergius I of Moscow pledged his church's loyalty to the Bolshevik state in 1927, ROCOR separated from the Moscow Patriarchate. This schism remained in place until the two sides came together once more with the signing of the Act of Canonical Communion in 2007. The ceremony, which was attended by Russian President Vladimir Putin, was broadcast live on Russian television.

During the eighty years of division ROCOR spread its wings far and wide. Outposts of Eastern Orthodoxy were established in America, Canada, Australia, Indonesia, and, of course, Germany, which had a long political association with Russia stretching back well before the Revolution. ROCOR today boasts almost 350 parishes and more than twenty monasteries in thirty two countries, with an estimated membership of over 400 000 parishioners.

There are forty two ROCOR parishes currently in Germany – America has the most with 152 – the Church of St. Prokop representing that of Hamburg. The church was constructed between 1961 and 1965 to a plan by Alexander S. Nürnberg, the building's cruciform plan, onion-shaped domes, and belfry recalling the Russian Orthodox churches of old. On the roof of the church can be seen several distinctive Russian Orthodox crosses, made up of three horizontal bars (one of which is diagonal) crossing a vertical shaft. The upper horizontal bar recalls the inscription 'INRI' ("Jesus of Nazareth, King of the Jews"), the mocking title bestowed on Christ by the Romans in the New Testament account of the Crucifixion. The diagonal bar is a foot rest, although later

Sky blue domes adorn the Russian Church of St. Prokop (Russische Kirche des Heiligen Prokop) in Eimsbüttel

folklore holds that it refers to the two thieves hanging either side of Christ: the upwards-pointing end referring to the ultimate destiny of the repentant thief Dismas, the downwards-pointing end recalling the destiny of the unrepentant thief Gestas.

If the visitor is fortunate enough to witness a mass here – usually on Sundays at 10 am, with evening vigils on Saturdays at 5 pm – they will be rewarded with a glimpse of the building's highly atmospheric, candle-lit interior, adorned with frescoes and gilded icons. The air will be filled with the fragrance of burning incense, and the glorious unaccompanied *a capella* singing that has been the central form of worship in Russian churches for a thousand years. It is worth noting that the church's website not only has details about hours of worship but also an audio archive of orthodox prayers and hymns (visit www.prokopij.de).

Saint Prokop, incidentally, to whom the church is dedicated, was a thirteenth century merchant from Lübeck, who embraced Russian Orthodoxy as a result of trading links he made with Novgorod in northwest Russia.

Tucked away on a quiet residential street around the corner from the Russian church is another interesting place of worship. The Fazle Omar Mosque (Fazle Omar Moschee) at Wieckstrasse 24 was opened in 1957 for use by the Pakistani Ahmadiyya Muslim community. It is the second oldest mosque in Germany and was the first to be built after the Second World War (see no. 77). The mosque is easily identified by its pair of brick-built minarets.

Other places of interest nearby: 69

69

A Truly Unique Zoo

Eimsbüttel (Stellingen), Hagenbecks Tierpark at Lokstedter Grenzstrasse 2
U2 Hagenbecks Tierpark; Bus 22, 39, 181, 281, 391 Hagenbecks Tierpark

In 1848 a Hamburg fish merchant called Gottfried Clas Carl Hagenbeck exhibited six performing seals in a wooden tub on Spielbudenplatz in St. Pauli. Passers-by had never seen anything like it before and quickly asked for more. By 1874 Hagenbeck's son Carl had transformed his father's little menagerie into Hagenbecks Tierpark on Neuer Pferdemarkt, dispatching adventurers to capture exotic creatures such as giant Marco Polo Sheep *(Ovis ammon polii)* from the Pamir Mountains of Central Asia, and Przewalski's Horse (*Equus ferus przewalskii)* from Mongolia. Located since 1907 in the district of Stellingen, Hagenbeck's Zoo now offers not only 2500 animals from around the globe but also unexpected architecture, and some fascinating history, too. Despite being damaged extensively during an Allied air raid in 1943 it remains a truly unique zoo.

Entered today from Lokstedter Grenzstrasse, alongside a conveniently located U-Bahn line, Hagenbeck's Zoo was originally entered through a *Jugendstil*-style gateway on Hagenbeckallee. Bristling with sculptures of both animals and humans it is not difficult to imagine the excitement felt by those early visitors as they passed through this extraordinary portal into the magical world beyond.

Just inside the old gate can be found a bronze memorial to Carl Hagenbeck (1844–1913), which includes a lion that is said to have saved him from the ravages of a tiger. While contemplating the scene we should remember that Carl Hagenbeck was the first zoo proprietor in the world to exhibit his animals in open-air enclosures rather than in small cages. He even patented a technique to create artificial mountains across which his wild sheep could roam. His ideas would go on to revolutionise zoo design worldwide.

Rather less visionary, however, was the capture of humans during Hagenbeck's global collecting safaris, who were then exhibited as 'exotic peoples' once back in Hamburg. They included a group of Native American Sioux, Maasai warriors, a Nubian family, as well as Inuit eskimos, the latter brought back by one Captain Jacobsen from an expedition to Labrador on the northeast coast of Canada. The Inuit all succumbed to smallpox in 1881.

A splendidly ornate Jugendstil doorway at Hagenbecks Tierpark in Eimsbüttel

The human exhibits are long gone now but Hagenbeck's astounding collection of animals remains, including numerous curiosities such as dwarf Muntjack deer, Chinese Leopards, two-humped Bactrian Camels, and Zebus, the sacred cattle of the Hindus. Each species is displayed in an enclosure that approximates as far as possible the native habitat of the species, the enclosures themselves being separated by a series of beautiful botanical gardens.

Within the gardens can be found some surprising architecture and sculptures, reminding the onlooker of the many cultural contacts made both east and west by the Hagenbeck family over six generations. They include Native American totem poles of the Tlinkit people, a lion-trimmed Burmese verandah, a tiny Japanese island (reached by means of a temple gateway and planted with a trio of exotic Gingko trees), and a Thai lakeside pavilion *(Sala)*, dedicated in 2002 as a symbol of peace between Hamburg and Thailand. A 16 metre-high Nepalese pagoda was erected a year later to mark the opening of the new entrance to the

zoo on Lokstedter Grenzstrasse. Perhaps even more surprising are the life-sized plastic dinosaurs that were placed in the zoo in 1909 by the sculptor Josef Pallenberg; at the time they were a unique feature for a European zoo.

Just outside the main gate is the Lindner Park-Hotel Hagenbeck, the world's first zoo-themed hotel, fitted out in exotic colonial style with plenty of references to the history of the zoo. A humorous sculpture on the roadside by the famous German sculptor Stephan Balkenhol (b. 1957) depicts a man clinging onto the neck of a giraffe, as if trying to point the way.

Other places of interest nearby: 68

70

From the Ashes of Gomorrah

Eimsbüttel (Harvestehude), the New Main Church of
St. Nikolai (St. Nikolai Neue Hauptkirche) on Klosterstern
U1 Klosterstern; Bus 34 Klosterstern

For a couple of years in the mid-1870s the 147.3 metre-high spire of Hamburg's Church of St. Nikolai (Nikolaikirche) at Willy-Brandt-Strasse 60 (Altstadt) was the tallest building in the world (it is still the city's second highest structure after the Television Tower). One of Hamburg's five Lutheran *Hauptkirchen* (main churches) it was built between 1846 and 1863 in neo-Gothic style, to a design by the renowned English architect George Gilbert Scott (1811–1878). The building replaced an earlier church destroyed in the Great Fire of 1842, which in turn replaced a chapel erected in the twelfth century, when the Nikolaifleet was established as a harbour (the name Nikolai is a Slavic variation of Nicholas, St. Nicholas being the patron saint of sailors) (see no. 10).

The current ruinous state of the Nikolaikirche is the result of the sustained aerial bombardment of Hamburg in the Second World War, during which the clearly visible church spire acted as a convenient orientation marker for Allied pilots. Codenamed Operation Gomorrah, in reference to the sinful city destroyed by God in the Old Testament, the main campaign began on 24th July 1943 and lasted until 3rd August. Killing approximately 45000 people (including many forced labourers and children) and obliterating twenty one square kilometres of the city it was the heaviest assault in the history of aerial warfare, and one which left Germany deeply shaken.

The decision to "area bomb" residential districts of German cities – rather than attacking specific industrial targets – was taken by Prime Minister Winston Churchill in 1942. The aim was to break the morale of Germany's civilian population, which Hitler and his Luftwaffe had been trying to achieve over England since September 1940. This meant that both sides were now in flagrant denial of the Hague Aerial War Convention of 1922, which forbade air raids on civilian targets.

The man tasked with expediting Churchill's "morale bombing" was Air Chief Marshall Arthur 'Bomber' Harris (1892–1984). For Operation Gomorrah he sent a stream of bombers to Hamburg – American by day, and British by night – with instructions to bomb four areas of the city known to be densely populated by dockers and factory workers (Billbrook, Hamm, Hammerbrook, and Rothenburgsort). Wave after wave

A poignant sculpture inside the ruined Church of St. Nikolai (Nikolaikirche) in Altstadt

of Flying Fortresses dropped first Blockbuster aerial mines (to remove roofs and blow out windows), then incendiary bombs to create a sea of flames, and finally traditional high explosives. Based on flammability experiments conducted by British and American scientists the climax of Operation Gomorrah was a firestorm unleashed during the night of 27th July. Generating hurricane-force winds and temperatures reaching 1000 °F the firestorm killed 30000 people within three hours. Harris was unrepentant about his actions writing later in his memoirs that "In spite of all that happened at Hamburg, bombing proved a relatively humane method".

The 9000 tons of bombs dropped during Operation Gomorrah destroyed approximately 250000 houses and changed the face of Hamburg forever. The artificial hills in Öjendorfer Park (Billstedt) are made from some of the debris, and many buildings reconstructed after the war carry plaques bearing the date '1943'. The district of Hammerbrook was eventually rebuilt solely as a commercial area, and only a part of Rothenburgsort was ever used for housing again. On Billhorner Deich a scaled-down replica of a dockworker's house acts as an unusual memorial marking the 60th anniversary of the firestorm in Rothenburgsort (Denkmal aus Anlass des 60. Jahrestages des Hamburger Feuersturms in Rothenburgsort).

Other memorials to the victims of the firestorm include one on Heinrich-Grone-Stieg (Hammerbrook), another at the corner of Desenißstrasse and Hamburger Strasse (Uhlenhorst) (recalling the 370 people who suffocated in an air raid shelter beneath the Karstadt department store), and a mass grave between Eichen- and Kirschenallee in the Ohlsdorf Cemetery (Friedhof Ohlsdorf), laid out around a memorial hall containing a sculptural group entitled *Passage over the Styx*.

The most obvious reminder, of course, is the ruined Nikolaikirche, which has subsequently been transformed into a memorial against war, with a 51-bell *carillon* in the tower and an exhibition room in the crypt. Since the area surrounding the ruins was no longer residential it was decided in the early 1960s to build a New Main Church of St. Nikolai (St. Nikolai Neue Hauptkirche) on Klosterstern (Harvestehude). The new church contains several objects pertaining to Operation Gomorrah, including a battered statue of St. Ansgar, which once adorned the south fa-

The altar of the New Main Church of St. Nikolai (St. Nikolai Neue Hauptkirche) in Harvestehude

çade of the old church, and a so-called Coventry Crucifix, fashioned with nails from Coventry Cathedral in England, which was destroyed by the Luftwaffe in 1940. The windows of the entrance hall were in fact originally made for the old Nikolaikirche but never used because of the war, and so were used instead in the new building. A further connection between the two churches is the mosaic *Ecce Homines* by Oskar Kokoschka, the original of which adorns the new church, while a copy hangs in the ruins. Actual glass taken from the ruins has been incorporated into the apse of the Church of St. Gertrude (St. Gertrud Kirche) at Immenhof 10 (Uhlenhorst).

Other places of interest nearby: 71, 72

71

On the Trail of the
Coffee Bean

Hamburg-Nord (Hoheluft-Ost), Kaffeerösterei Burg at
Eppendorfer Weg 252
U3 Eppendorfer Baum; Bus 5 Eppendorfer Weg

From the late nineteenth century until the 1950s Hamburg was the largest European port of entry for colonial goods after London, handling exotic goods such as cocoa beans, tobacco, tea, cotton, rubber, Brazil nuts, and spices. Those days are gone now but it is still possible to recall them by following the trail of one typically exotic item: the coffee bean. Our first port of call is, of course, the Speicherstadt (Hamburg-Mitte), where the sacks of green beans would have been stored after their sea journey from Africa and South America. Part of the excellent Speicherstadtmuseum at St. Annenufer 2 is given over to the techniques of warehousing and processing coffee, as is Speicherstadt Kaffeerösterei at Kehrwieder 5 (see no. 7).

Next stop is Hamburg's former Coffee Exchange (Kaffeebörse) at Pickhuben 3. This unassuming building from the 1950s (the original exchange was destroyed in the Second World War) was once one of the hubs of world coffee trading. Unfortunately not open to the public the auction room still contains three clocks giving the current time in Hamburg, Rio and New York (the world's biggest coffee trading cities), whilst blackboards on the wall still display the prices of the last day of trading in 1958. One end of the room is taken up with a magnificent stained glass window depicting coffee plantation workers. (All Hamburg's coffee-related business is now centred on the towering International Coffee Plaza on Großer Grasbrook (HafenCity), and warehousing now takes place outside the Speicherstadt.)

From Hamburg the majority of the coffee beans would then be transported onwards to their final destination. Some, however, would remain in the city, to be used by local coffee roasters and grinders. One such customer is Kaffeerösterei Burg at Eppendorfer Weg 252 (Hoheluft-Ost), which has been in the coffee business since 1923. It is one of only six traditional coffee roasters remaining in Hamburg out of 300 that existed in the 1960s. Each morning the unmistakeable aroma of coffee wafts out of the premises as the best beans are roasted in a fifty year-old, gas powered 'Probat Spezial' roasting machine. Only by care-

This rarely-seen window is inside Hamburg's former Coffee Exchange (Kaffeebörse) on Pickhuben

fully roasting thirty kilos of beans at a time to 180 °C for up to thirty minutes can the beans be allowed to develop their full flavour, whilst also losing the acids that can make coffee bitter and disagreeable to the stomach. By comparison, some industrialised coffee roasters heat the beans to 600 °C for as little as ninety seconds. The difference in taste can be enormous.

The shop at Kaffeerösterei Burg stocks around 120 different types of coffee, which it sells not only to the public but also to other shops, hotels and cafés. Half of them are pure coffees, such as Ethiopian Sidamo and Jamaica Blue Mountain, whereas the rest are aromatized, infused with flavours such as cardamon, cinnamon, and orange. The staff, headed by owner and coffee historian Jens Burg, will gladly offer expert advice on all aspects of coffee roasting, grinding, serving, and drinking. In the back garden of the shop there can even be seen Germany's only coffee plantation, grown for educational purposes, which blooms in the summer months (in the winter the plants are stored away from the frost in the conservatory of a local hotel!).

For those with a real interest in the history of coffee a visit should be made to the Kaffeemuseum Burg at Münsterstrasse 23–25 (Eppendorf), where Jens Burg has amassed more than 2800 exhibits illustrat-

Traditional coffee roasting at Kaffeerösterei Burg in Eppendorf

ing every aspect of this fascinating trade. Guided tours and seminars are on offer, and the old packaging and advertising materials are sure to please visitors of all ages.

Hamburg can boast many cafés that serve a decent cup of coffee, some of which also offer something in addition. They include the stunning Café Paris at Rathausstrasse 4 (Altstadt), inside what was once a nineteenth century butcher's premises, the charming Cafe Mathilda at Bogenstrasse 5 (Harvestehude), with its easy chairs and books, Kaffee Stark at Wohlwillstrasse 18 (St. Pauli), which doubles as a clothes shop, and the aptly named Café Tide at Rothestrasse 53 (Ottensen), with its driftwood artworks and delicatessen.

Other places of interest nearby: 70, 72

A Visit to the Warburg Library

Eimsbüttel (Eppendorf), the Warburg Library of Cultural
Science (Kulturwissenschaftliche Bibliothek Warburg) in the
Warburg-Haus at Heilwigstrasse 116
U1, U3 Kellinghusenstrasse

There is an imposing red granite doorway at Ferdinandstrasse 75 (Altstadt) over which is inscribed the name "M. M. Warburg & Co." Although not open to the public, a peep inside the building will reveal a
splendid entrance hall clad in marble, with an imposing spiral staircase
beyond. The reason for such grandeur is that this is the private bank of
the influential Warburg family.

The bank was founded in 1798 by Marcus Moses and Gerson Warburg. Being Jewish meant that they were forbidden to join the Hamburg guilds, and so banking was one of the few ways they could make a
living. The next generation of Warburgs included five brothers, two of
whom, Paul and Felix, left Hamburg to become bankers in New York.
Paul was especially successful, being credited with the founding in 1913
of the Federal Reserve System. Both Paul and Felix remained partners
in the family bank in Hamburg, which was managed by two of their
other brothers, Max and Fritz, until the bank's 'aryanisation' under the
Nazis in 1938.

The fifth brother, Aby Warburg (1866–1929), was in some ways the
most interesting of all because he renounced a lucrative career with the
family bank in favour of becoming an art historian. In exchange for
waiving his right to become director of the bank he was given a blank
cheque with which to buy as many books as he liked. This was the
beginning of the Warburg Library of Cultural Science (Kulturwissenschaftliche Bibliothek Warburg), which Aby installed in his house at
Heilwigstrasse 114.

By the mid-1920s Aby Warburg's library had outgrown his home
and so he purchased an empty lot next door, where in 1926 he had a
new library built. Known as the Warburg-Haus, a visit there today is
a rare privilege, and one sure to engender a fondness for the man who
described himself as being "Amburghese di cuore, ebreo di sangue,
d'anima Fiorentino" (A Hamburger at heart, a Jew by birth, and Flor-
entine in spirit).

The Warburg-Haus was designed by the architect Gerhard Lang-
maack, an apprentice of Fritz Schumacher (1869–1947), director of pub-

lic works for Hamburg. The intricate brick façade, which is reminiscent of Schumacher's own style, is enhanced by a pair of Art Deco lanterns. Over the entrance can be seen the word *Mnemosyne* (Greek for memory) carved in stone. This reminds the visitor that Aby Warburg's specialist field of study was the legacy of the Classical world in Western culture, a field of academic research neglected in his day.

In the library's entrance hall there is a modest bust of Aby Warburg, together with a series of old photographs showing various internal features of the library, including a book lift and a pneumatic post system. Considered state-of-the-art at the time of construction, these novel features would be stripped out after the library's 60 000 books were shipped to London in 1933, in order to avoid

Warburg-Haus in Eppendorf was built for the art historian Aby Warburg

destruction at the hands of the Nazi regime. (The books remain to this day at the University of London).

Leading off the entrance hall there are various offices, as well as a four-storey book repository, but the highlight is yet to come. To the rear of the building there is a magnificent oval reading room, illuminated by a skylight, as well as a bay window looking out over the garden. The heart of the library, this was Aby Warburg's so-called "Arena of Scholarship", a semi-public institution that attracted many respected scholars. It was here, in conjunction with Hamburg University, that the foundations of the renowned 'Hamburg School' of art history were laid.

After the Warburg Library was emptied in 1933 the shelves were removed and the building used for commercial purposes. Fortunately in 1993 it was purchased by the City of Hamburg, and in 1995 the build-

Aby Warburg's oval reading room is once again filled with books

ing was reopened under the auspices of the Aby Warburg Foundation. Once again the reading room is stocked with books, and Aby Warburg's interest in cultural history is being pursued vigorously by a new generation of scholars.

After going into exile in 1938 the Warburg's family home at Mittelweg 17 (Rotherbaum) became a meeting place for some of Hamburg's persecuted Jews, until the building's eventual confiscation in 1941. After the war Eric Warburg, son of Max Warburg, returned to Hamburg, and in 1949 the Warburg family again became partners in the bank. The family opened their villa in Blankenese to the American Jewish Joint Distribution Committee, where Jewish children and concentration camp survivors could find refuge before emigration to Israel.

Other places of interest nearby: 70, 71

73 The Home of a Communist Hero

Hamburg-Nord (Eppendorf), the Ernst Thälmann Gedenkstätte
at Tarpenbekstrasse 66
U1, U3 Kellinghusenstrasse; Bus 34 Lokstedter Weg,
22, 39 Tarpenbekstrasse

In the Gulf of Cazones in southern Cuba there is a tiny island called
Cayo Ernesto Thaelmann. Inhabited only by iguanas it was named
by Fidel Castro in honour of Ernst Thälmann, former leader of the
Communist Party of Germany (Kommunistische Partei Deutschland –
KPD), on the occasion of a state visit to Cuba in 1972 by GDR leader
Erich Honecker (1912–1994). A bust of Thälmann, erected on the island
as a symbol of friendship between the Republic of Cuba and the GDR,
was toppled by a hurricane in 1998.

Ernst Thälmann (1886–1944) was born far away from Cuba at Alter
Wall 86 (Altstadt) in Hamburg. From an early age he worked in his
family's vegetable and haulage business and in 1903 was discharged
from military service on the grounds of being a political agitator. Instead he worked as a stoker on freighters and actively involved himself
in representing the interests of Hamburg's dock workers. At the same
time he joined the Social Democratic Party of Germany (Sozialdemokratische Partei Deutschlands – SPD), which before the First World
War was the world's most successful socialist party, and the largest
party in Germany.

In 1914 SPD members in the Reichstag voted in favour of war,
causing a rift with those members opposed to it. The latter formed
the Independent Social Democratic Party of Germany (Unabhängige
Sozialdemokratische Partei Deutschlands – USPD) instead, which
Ernst Thälmann joined in 1917, as well as the more radical Spartacist
League formed by Rosa Luxemburg (1871–1919) and Karl Liebknecht
(1871–1919). With the end of the war and the collapse of the monarchy
the Spartacist League formed the KPD in Berlin. Committed to violent
revolution the KPD attempted unsuccessfully to seize control of the
government, as a result of which both Luxemburg and Liebknecht were
executed without trial by the Freikorps, a paramilitary anti-Commu-
nist organisation formed from First World War veterans.

The USPD meanwhile was split over the question of whether or not
to join the revolutionary Moscow-based organisation Commintern.

Thälmann sided with the party's pro-Communist faction, which in November 1920 merged with the remaining membership of the KPD and abandoned the goal of immediate revolution. As a result the KPD were able to contest Reichstag elections from 1924, and in October 1925 Thälmann was made party chairman.

Memories of Ernst Thälmann at Tarpenbekstrasse 66

During the 1920s Ernst Thälmann lived at Siemssenstrasse 4 (Eppendorf) and in 1929 moved a couple of streets away to Tarpenbekstrasse 66, where he lived with his family until 1933. A little-visited memorial room (Ernst Thälmann Gedenkstätte), once visited by General Secretary of the Communist Party Leonid Brezhnev (1906–1982), is now housed in the building and contains a fascinating collection of documents, newspapers and films pertaining to Thälmann, making it the perfect location at which to finish his story.

During the years of the Weimar Republic (1919–1933) the KPD was the largest Communist party in Europe, usually polling around 10–15 % of the votes. Critics, however, accused both the KPD and the SPD of pursuing sectarian policies that prevented any possibility of forging a united front against the rising power of the Nazi Party. Thälmann's slogan at the 1932 presidential elections was "A vote for Hindenburg is a vote for Hitler; a vote for Hitler is a vote for war".

Although Hindenburg won the election he was an old man, and in January 1933 he facilitated the process whereby Adolf Hitler was able to succeed as head of state. Although the KDP was banned immediately Thälmann remained active and proposed that the KPD and SPD organise a general strike to topple Hitler. It was too little too late and on 3rd March 1933 Thälmann was arrested and imprisoned by the Gestapo. He never received a trial and after being held for eleven years in solitary confinement he was executed in Buchenwald Concentration Camp, it is said on Hitler's personal orders. The Nazi media claimed he had died during an Allied air raid. After the war Thälmann, Luxemburg and Liebknecht were all hailed in the GDR as heroes in the fight against Fascism and their remains were interred in a special Socialist Memorial (Gedenkstätte der Sozialisten) in Berlin.

Other places of interest nearby: 74, 75

74

How to Put a Ship in a Bottle

Hamburg-Nord (Eppendorf), Buddel-Bini Maritime Shop at
Lokstedter Weg 68
U1, U3 Kellinghusenstrasse, U1 Hudtwalckerstrasse;
Bus 34 Lokstedter Weg

Most children (and many adults) are fascinated by ships in bottles. How can a fully-rigged model sailing ship find its way inside a glass bottle which has such a narrow neck? To find the answer a visit must be made to the Buddel-Bini Maritime Shop at Lokstedter Weg 68 (Eppendorf).

The shop's curious name comprises two elements: 'Buddel', being North German for 'bottle', and 'Bini', being a shortening of proprietor Jochen Binikowski's own name. Jochen founded the shop in 1976 after working as an art teacher, a policeman, and having made a five-month motorcycle journey to India and back. The art of putting ships in bottles he learned as a boy from his grandfather, a former sailor. Little did he know then that what started as a hobby would eventually become a very successful business.

The Buddel-Bini story really takes off in 1980, when Jochen visited the Philippines and found not only his wife, Eda, but also a production line capable of manufacturing all of the many tools and components required for putting ships in bottles. Jochen and his wife also set about producing three charming daughters, all of whom now work in the Hamburg shop, fulfilling orders across the counter and through the Internet, as well as working in the shop's studio.

For ships in bottles visit the Buddel-Bini Maritime Shop
on Lokstedter Weg

With business increasing Jochen opened his now famous Ship-in-a-Bottle and Seashell Museum (Buddelschiff- und Muschelmuseum) in the cellar of the Ferry Station Schulau (Schulauer Fährhaus) at Parnassstrasse 29 in Wedel, just outside Hamburg's western boundary. It is here every day since 1952, between sunrise and sunset, that each passing ship registering more than 500 tonnes has been

See how a ship is put inside a bottle in the Buddel-Bini workshop

greeted by a broadcast of the national anthem of the ship's country of origin. At the same time the Hamburg flag is dropped from a 40 metre-high mast, and the respective national flag flown, which is answered by the passing ship dipping its own flag. Details of each ship are then passed by loudspeaker to onlookers gathered at the nearby Willkomm-Höft, or welcome point.

Back to the Buddel-Bini story and there were some difficult times during the 1990s, when the market was swamped with cheap, substandard ships in bottles. Jochen and his loyal staff survived by focussing on the high quality niche market, a task made easier by the arrival of the Internet and the introduction of a computerised mail order system. Today, the Buddel-Bini website (www.buddelbini.com) boasts the largest online selection of ships in bottles, with much more besides including model lighthouses, ships' clocks, flags, and sailors' hats.

As to the mystery of how a ship is placed inside a bottle, the answer will be found by visiting the workshop at Buddel-Bini (open during shop hours), where if you are lucky one of Jochen's staff will happily share the secret!

Other places of interest nearby: 73, 75

75

Adventures by Gondola
and Canoe

Hamburg-Nord (Eppendorf), the Venetian Gondola
(Die venezianische Gondel) moored at Bootshaus Barmeier
at Eppendorfer Landstrasse 180
U1 Lattenkamp; Bus 39 Eppendorfer Marktplatz

Most visitors to Hamburg will want to experience the city's waterways, perhaps by taking a whistlestop ferry tour of the harbour or else a gentle pleasure cruise across the Außenalster. Ferries can be boarded at Bei den St.-Pauli-Landungsbrücken, where any number of *faux* retired sea captains tout their tickets for Speicherstadt tours, and powerful Z-drive HADAG ferries, with their distinctively high, rear mounted wheelhouses, depart for the opposite shore. Things are a little more sedate on the Außenalster, where between the 1850s and the 1970s the lake could be explored by steamboats known as *Alsterdampfer*. One of them, the St. Georg moored at Jungfernstieg, is still in operation. The rest have now been replaced with more eco-friendly but less colourful cruisers, including some powered by solar energy and hydrogen.

A more intimate way of experiencing Hamburg's waterways is by using the manmade canals that branch off the northern reaches of the Außenalster. The Osterbekkanal, Goldbekkanal, Isebekkanal, and Uhlenhorsterkanal were once busy servicing the city's northern suburbs but are today peaceful places, flanked by the riverside gardens of charming villas. The energetic can discover this watery paradise by hiring out a canoe, rowing boat, or paddle boat from one of the many waterside rental offices *(Bootsverleih)*. Typical is the popular Bootsverleih Dornheim on the Osterbekkanal at Kaemmererufer 25 (Barmbek Süd), from where organisations including the St. Pauli Tourist Office lead roundtrips by canoe. Lasting around two and a half hours the route runs anticlockwise from the Osterbekkanal northwards along the Barmbek-Stichkanal into the Stadtparksee, then west along the Goldbekkanal to the Rondeelteich, southwards into the Außenalster and Feenteich, and then eastwards back along the Osterbekkanal.

Idiosyncratic rental offices include Bobby Reich at Fernsicht 2 (Winterhude), from whom traditionally-built wooden rowing boats are available, Bootsverleih G. Wüstenberg at Deelbögenkamp 2 (Alsterdorf), for canoe trips to the upper reaches of the Alster, and Bootshaus Silwar at Eppendorfer Landstrasse 148b (Eppendorf), located in Ham-

An exciting way to explore the Alster canals is by canoe

burg's oldest boathouse erected in 1874 (it doubles as a club for proprietor Arnim Silwar's jazz band in which he is the drummer).

Most unusual of all, however, is the Venetian Gondola (Die venezianische Gondel) moored close to Silwar at Bootshaus Barmeier at Eppendorfer Landstrasse 180. It is often said that Hamburg has more bridges than Venice and Amsterdam combined amounting to approximately 1700 in total. It therefore seems fitting that a real Venetian gondola should also have found its way to Hamburg. This happened in the late 1990s when boatbuilder and furniture designer Ina Mierig purchased a working gondola in Venice, and shipped it back to Hamburg in a glider transporter. Since then she has offered romantic one and two hour-long trips in the gondola, between April and November,

A romantic way to explore the Alster is by means of this Venetian gondola moored at Bootshaus Barmeier

either upstream through Alsterdorf or downstream into the Außen-alster (Italian antipasti and Prosecco available on request). Like most gondolas it is made from eight different types of wood, each suited to a specific task, for example oak for hull strength, pitch pine for water-proofing, durable walnut to support the beech wood oar, and cherry for the decorative carvings.

The Bootshaus Barmeier, where the gondola is based, is interesting in itself. A hundred years ago the green-and-white painted building was used as a depot from where coal was distributed inland to the northern suburbs. The boathouse today, located on a tranquil stretch of water where the Tarpenbeck joins the Alster, is used for the private storage of canoes. On the first floor there is a traditional workshop, where Ina Mierig indulges one of her other passions, namely the restoration of vintage wooden canoes. To the rear of the boathouse is a popular café.

So beloved is the Alster that it has given its name to a drink. Beer and lemonade, called *Radler* elsewhere in the German-speaking world and Shandy in England, is called *Alster-wasser* (Alster water) in Hamburg. At the southern end of the Außenalster, where it joins the Binnenalster, is the Kennedybrücke across which a line of inscribed stones mark the 10° meridian of longitude. Such lines, calculated eastwards from Greenwich, are found on all globes and atlases and are used to calculate geographical coordinates and time zones.

Other places of interest nearby: 73, 74, 76

76 Water Towers with a Difference

Hamburg-Nord (Winterhude), a tour of reused water towers
starting at the Planetarium Hamburg at Hindenburgstrasse 1b
U1 Lattenkamp; U3 Borgweg; Bus 179 Stadtpark (Planetarium)

During the late nineteenth and early twentieth centuries the public water supply of most large European cities was pressurised by first pumping the water into either a raised reservoir or a specially constructed water tower. The elevation of this body of water was precisely calculated so that gravity could be relied upon to maintain constant

hydrostatic pressure in the distribution system to which it was connected (a typical tower requires a water level of 30–40 metres above ground). In a flat city such as Hamburg the water tower was very important and more than forty once dotted the landscape.

Today, many cities have replaced their water towers with powerful, easier-to-maintain pumps, both at the water treatment plants themselves, and at subsidiary pumping stations along the way. Hamburg is no exception and only a handful of the city's historic towers are still standing, several of which have been adapted to interesting new uses.

This tour begins in the north-west corner of the Stadtpark (Winterhude), Hamburg's second largest park, where in 1915 a 64.5

The Planetarium Hamburg is built inside a former water tower in Winterhude

This former water tower in Sternschanze has been converted into a luxury hotel

metre-high red-brick water tower was constructed to a design by the renowned architect Fritz Schumacher (1869–1947) (see no. 3). The tower was one of a trio – the other two being in Sternschanze and Uhlenhorst – commissioned to ensure a reliable water supply in the rapidly developing city with its new high rise buildings. With a capacity of 3000 cubic metres it was also the last public water tower constructed in Hamburg and was only used as such until 1924, when it was deemed technologically redundant. Around the same time a planetarium was planned for the city and to keep costs down it was decided to install it inside the lower part of the water tower. One of the first planetariums in Europe it opened in 1930. During the Second World War the tower doubled as an observation post from which to direct anti-aircraft guns (the graffiti of soldiers posted here can still be seen by visitors using the viewing platform 50 metres above the ground). The Planetarium Hamburg today contains a powerful Carl Zeiss Universarium IX cosmos simulator, capable of projecting thousands of stars across the cupola of the tower, much to the delight of the planetarium's 300 000 annual visitors.

To the west of the Planetarium there are two 50 metre-high, brick-built former water towers that have been converted into unusual dwellings. The first, a splendid neo-Gothic tower at the corner of Lokstedter Steindamm and Süderfeldstrasse (Lokstedt), was built in 1911 to cater for a rapidly developing area which at the time lay outside the boundary of Hamburg. With a capacity of 5000 cubic metres it functioned mainly as a reserve tower to make up for any shortfall experienced by pumps installed over the local borehole. Much of the tower's tapering shaft is clad in copper plating, as is the tank itself and the decorative lantern placed on top. After being abandoned in the 1960s the tank area was converted into a unique single apartment with a 360° balcony running all the way around it, bringing the occupants within reach of the fire brigade's 30 metre-long ladders should the need arise.

The second tower is on Högenstrasse (Stellingen) and although rendered in a less flamboyant style it is the work of the same architects. Constructed around the same time too it also served as a reserve tower, albeit with a slightly larger capacity. Again made redundant by the introduction of powerful new pumps the Stellingen tower was abandoned in the 1970s. It has subsequently been converted into luxury apartments, a single self-contained apartment occupying each of the eleven floors.

This tour concludes at Sternschanze 6 (Sternschanze), where an octagonal water tower contemporaneous with the one in the Stadtpark was inaugurated in Schanzenpark in 1910. At the time of construction it was the biggest water tower in Europe. Abandoned in the 1950s the tower has subsequently been converted into a luxurious 17-floor, 226-room Mövenpick Hotel, replete with health spa, restaurant and terrace. It is worth noting that the hotel lobby occupies a former subterranean water reservoir built in 1863 to a design by the hydraulic engineer William Lindley and decommissioned in 1905 (see no. 36).

It is not only Hamburg's former water towers that offer magnificent views of the city. Some church spires also provide far-reaching vistas, notably the Church of St. Petri (St. Petri Kirche) at Bei der Petrikirche 2 (Altstadt), the Church of St. Nikolai (Nikolai-kirche) at Willy-Brandt-Strasse 60, and the Church of St. Michaelis (Michaelis Kirche) at Englische Planke 1 (Neustadt). Other highpoints include the University of Hamburg's 14-storey Arts Building ('Philosophenturm') on Von-Melle-Park (Rotherbaum), the Elbe-warte Restaurant on the roof of the Augustinum at Neumühlen 37 (Ottensen), and the bar at the top of the Hafen Hotel at Seewartenstrasse 9 (Neustadt). Unfortunately the viewing platform at the top of the city's highest structure, the 204 metre high Hamburg Television Tower (Heinrich-Hertz-Turm) at Lagerstrasse 2 (Sternschanze), is inaccessible to the public because of fire escape regulations.

Other places of interest nearby: 75

77

Hamburg's Most Beautiful
Mosque

Hamburg-Nord (Uhlenhorst), the Imam Ali Mosque (Imam
Ali Moschee) at Schöne Aussicht 36 (note: shoes must be
removed when visiting the prayer hall)
Bus 6 Zimmerstrasse, then walk

Standing at Schöne Aussicht 36 on the eastern shore of the Außenalster
is the magnificent Imam Ali Mosque (Imam Ali Moschee). Identified
easily by its blue dome and twin minarets, the building is the most
beautiful of more than twenty Islamic prayer halls across the Hamburg
region. One of the city's more unusual tourist attractions, a visit here
can be an enlightening experience.

The majority of Germany's more than three million Muslims are of
Turkish origin, having been invited during the 1960s as guest workers
(Gastarbeiter) to help with the country's post-war economic reconstruc-
tion. Whilst most Turkish Muslims are Sunnis a minority of Germany's
Muslims come from other countries and have built their own distinct
mosques in Hamburg. They include the Arabian Al-Muhajrin Mosque
at Kirchenallee 25 (St. Georg), and the Pakistani Ahmadiyya Fazle
Omar Mosque at Wieckstrasse 24 (Stellingen) (see no. 68). The Imam
Ali Mosque, which also contains the Islamic Centre Hamburg (Islamisches Zentrum Hamburg), serves the Shia community of Iran.

The decision to construct what is today one of the oldest and most
influential Shia centres in the West was taken in June 1953, when a
group of Iranian businessmen and émigrés met in Hamburg's Hotel
Atlantic at An der Alster 72 (St. Georg). Feeling the need to establish
a religious centre in their adopted home they sent a letter to Grand
Ayatollah Seyyed Hossein Borujerdi (1875–1961) asking for financial
assistance. The Ayatollah was keen to promote Islamic unity beyond
the borders of Iran and donated 100 000 Rials. In 1957 a plot of land was
purchased on the banks of the Alster, and on 13th February 1961 the
foundation stone was laid.

The main structure was completed in 1965 and inaugurated in
honour of the prophet Muhammad's cousin, Ali ('the exalted one'),
whom Shiites consider as the first Imam. The mosque has had several
renowned directors, the first of whom was Ayatollah Mohammad Be-
heshti (1928–1981), a cleric who was made responsible for the spiritual
well being of Iranian students in Western Europe. He actively encour-

aged them to oppose the monarchy of the Shah of Iran, contributing to the eventual success of the Iranian Cultural Revolution in the 1980s. In 1970 the renowned Iranian philosopher Mohammad Mojtahed Shabestari (b. 1936) became director at the mosque, and he was later succeeded by the future fifth president of the Islamic Republic of Iran, Seyed Mohammad Khatami (b. 1943).

The magnificent prayer hall of the Imam Ali Mosque (Imam Ali Moschee) in Uhlenhorst

Visits to the mosque by non-Muslims outside of prayer times (daily 12 am–1 pm and all day Friday) are actively encouraged, in the hope of creating a better understanding of Shia Islam in the West and of breaking down religious prejudice. The mosque's annual open days are always well attended. The building is worth visiting in its own right, especially the magnificent circular prayer hall, which is adorned with a magnificent chandelier and mosaic work inscribed with Koranic verse by tilers from the holy city of Mashhad, east of Tehran. In the early 1990s a splendid tiled *mihrab* (prayer niche indicating the direction of Mecca) was installed here, a gift from the celebrated Goharshad Mosque in Iran. Most impressive of all is the prayer room's enormous circular carpet. With a diameter of sixteen metres and covering an area of 200 square metres it is one of the largest hand-woven carpets in the world. It took twenty-two people three years to create and is said to contain approximately eighty million knots.

The Islamic Centre, which is in a separate building to the prayer hall, contains an extensive library of texts from all religions and reflects Imam Ali's own belief that "Books are the gardens of the scholars".

An increasingly popular aspect of Turkish life for non-Muslims is the *hamam*, the Middle Eastern variant of a steam bath. First encountered by Europeans through the Ottomans the Hamam was traditionally a place of social gathering, ritual cleansing, and architectural merit. Hamams such as Das Hamam at Feldstrasse 39 and Hamam Hafen at Seewartenstrasse 10, both in the Hamburg district of St. Pauli, may lack the grandeur of former times but still offer the physical benefits of a good sweat and a massage.

78

From Schoolroom to Factory Floor

Hamburg-Nord (Barmbek-Nord), the Museum of Work (Museum der Arbeit) at Wiesendamm 3
S1, S11 Barmbek; U3 Barmbek

Visiting a museum about schooling and then another about working might not be to everyone's taste, and yet there are two such museums in Hamburg, which are both more than worthy of the visitor's attention.

The Hamburg School Museum (Hamburger Schulmuseum) at Seilerstrasse 42 (St. Pauli) is suitably located inside an old school building erected in 1886. Displayed within the confines of an historical classroom, which still might jog the memory of older visitors, the collection illustrates the history of schooling in Hamburg since the time of Emperor William II (1888–1918). Wooden desks, old fashioned school uniforms, faded text books, and traditional writing equipment help convey the teaching methods and materials of yesteryear, and how they compare with those used today. Of particular interest is a reconstructed science laboratory, complete with antique equipment and examples of dissected animals, as well as a special display detailing the role of schools during the period of National Socialism. Afterwards, it is worth visiting the little museum shop where slate blackboards, lead pencils, and wooden sliding-top pencil boxes can be purchased.

The story of education in Hamburg is brought to fruition in the Museum of Work (Museum der Arbeit), which opened in 1997 at Wiesendamm 3 (Barmbek-Nord). This fascinating collection demonstrates how everday life in the workplace has changed as a result of industrialisation. A series of reconstructed workshops show the physical conditions considered normal by the manual labourer during the late nineteenth and early twentieth centuries in Hamburg. A typical example is the metalworking factory of Carl Wild, which originally stood behind a residential house in the district of Hohenfelde. Typical of the many small-scale manufacturing firms once hidden away in the backyards of Hamburg, it is here that thousands of badges, medals and brooches were produced between 1901 and 1989.

A reconstructed company office, with its formal stationery, three-tiered rack of rubber stamps, and wall maps showing various trade routes, is used to represent the administrative side of a successful Hamburg merchants' life. Meanwhile, another area of the museum repre-

One of several old printing presses in the Museum of Work (Museum der Arbeit) in Barmbek-Nord

sents the printing trade, demonstrating the dramatic transition from traditional hot metal typesetting to filmsetting and eventually digital printing. A handful of traditional printing presses are usually in operation to demonstrate the old process to visitors who have never seen it. A further area of the museum documents the cultural and social history of work, notably gender differences in the workplace and the historical evolution of women's rights.

The Museum of Work is housed in a former factory building of the New-York-Hamburger Gummi-Waaren Compagnie (NYH), a rubber company founded in 1871 on the Ostbekkanal in Barmbek. The history of the company is linked with that of the world's first synthetic material produced on an industrial scale, namely hard rubber, and three workplaces have been retained as part of the museum to convey an impression of a typical working day in the factory. Raw rubber was tapped from trees in the tropics and then shipped to Hamburg, where it was transformed into hard rubber through a chemical process known as vulcanisation (named after the Roman god of fire). Until its relocation to Harburg in 1954 the NYH factory in Barmbek manufactured mainly hair combs and jewellery.

Many factories were established in the suburbs of Hamburg during the late nineteenth and early twentieth centuries, including the Schokoladenfabrik at Wendenstrasse 130 (Borgfelde), which was founded by T. H. Speckbötel in 1908, and the Tabakfabik von Eicken at Hoheluftchaussee 95 (Hoheluft-West), which was built in 1902 for Gustav Schrader. The latter has a striking neo-Gothic façade replete with corner turret. Both have been renovated and converted for use as apartments and offices.

79

Monuments to German Colonialism

Wandsbek (Jenfeld), the Schutztruppen Memorial in
Tansania-Park at Wilsonstrasse 49
Bus 162, 262 Kuehnstrasse (Ost)

A controversial chapter in German history concerns the country's trading and colonial activities in Africa between the eighteenth and early twentieth centuries. As Germany's "Gateway to the World" the Port of Hamburg inevitably played an important part in this. A pair of little-visited monuments in the city's northeastern borough of Wandsbek illustrate two different aspects of the story, which will provoke some soul-searching in onlookers irrespective of whether they are German or otherwise.

At Schlossstrasse 78 in the district of Wandsbek itself stands the Christuskirche, built in the 1960s to replace an earlier church destroyed during the Second World War. In the old cemetery to the rear can be found the mausoleum of Count Heinrich Karl von Schimmelmann (1724–1782). Born into an aristocratic family in Holstein – at the time part of the Holy Roman Empire but administered by the King of Denmark – Schimmelmann was a landowner and industrialist whose son became finance minister to the Danish Crown. He acquired great wealth by exporting weapons and alcohol from Hamburg to Africa, and slaves from Africa to North America and the Caribbean. This lucrative triangular Atlantic trade route was completed by returning to Europe with calico and sugar cane. All Schimmelmann's slaves were branded on their chest with the letter 'S' inside a heart. A decade after his death in Copenhagen, where he owned a sugar refinery, Schimmelmann was buried in the neo-Classical mausoleum in Wandsbek together with his wife.

Fortunately, by the early nineteenth century there was no pro-slavery lobby in any German states, with Hanseatic traders from Hamburg and Bremen preferring goods such as palm oil from West Africa, from which engine lubricant, soap, and candles could be manufactured. Weapons, however, were still traded, even the most modern breech-loaders, and the trade in cheap liquor continued too, accounting for up to 60 % of Hanseatic trade on the West African coast during the 1880s. By contrast, trade on the East African coast accounted for little, where Muslim merchants had little need for Schnapps

A terracotta bust at the former Lettow-Vorbek Barracks (Lettow-Vorbeck-Kaserne) in Jenfeld

In terms of Germany's total commercial traffic, colonial business transactions were still insignificant, although Hanseatic traders were quite content. They were against permanent colonisation preferring instead to remain on the coast (preferably without being scrutinised by German civil servants), where they used intermediaries to conduct their business inland. Such Afro-German relations were egalitarian but this changed after 1871, as the newly-created German Reich extended its domain into Africa. Falling prices for African-grown products forced German businessmen to push inland (in an attempt to reduce costs by circumventing local African monopolies), where they soon established their own plantations and stores.

With Germany's gradual territorial expansion into Africa there came the need for protection, which brings us to the second monument in Wandsbek. Standing in the grounds of the former Lettow-Vorbek Barracks (Lettow-Vorbeck-Kaserne) at Wilsonstrasse 49 (Jenfeld) is the so-called Schutztruppen (Colonial Army) Memorial. It takes the form of a brick pillar topped with a Third Reich martial eagle commemorating not only German soldiers who died in Africa in both World Wars but also native *Askari* soldiers, recruited locally by the colonial powers during the scramble for Africa in the late nineteenth century. Alongside the monument are two large ceramic reliefs that once flanked the entrance to the barracks, one depicting a German soldier leading his loyal *Askari*, the other showing an *Askari* leading African porters.

Askari soldiers flank the Schutztruppen Memorial in Tansania-Park

The main concentration of *Askari* troops was in German East Africa (now Tanzania), which explains why the small garden containing the Schutztruppen Memorial is unofficially called Tansania-Park. They served under the command of Paul Emil von Lettow-Vorbeck (1870–1964), notably in Germany's fight against British supremacy during the First World War.

Despite their brutality, Germany's colonial-era soldiers were considered heroes by the Nazi regime, which is why the Wehrmacht barracks here in Jenfeld were named after Lettow-Vorbek when they were opened in 1939. The barrack buildings themselves are extensively adorned with ceramic military ornaments in the form of stick grenades, gas masks and guns, as well as busts of other colonial fighters, including Adrian Dietrich Lothar von Trotha (1848–1920), who ordered the massacre of the Herero people in German Southwest Africa in 1904 (see no. 2). The site is made even more controversial by the fact that the former barracks were until recently occupied by students of the nearby Helmut Schmidt University of the Federal Army (Helmut-Schmidt-Universität der Bundeswehr).

Not surprisingly the park and barracks are closed at present to the general public, pending a decision on how best to convey the little known and often misunderstood history represented by the site. Until that time a virtual tour of the site can be made by visiting the website of the One World Network Hamburg Association (Eine Welt Netzwerk Hamburg e.V.) (www.ewnw.de), which does much to enlighten people about Hamburg's role during the German colonial era, and its after effects.

80

An Open Air Museum

Wandsbek (Volksdorf), Museumsdorf Volksdorf at Im Alten
Dorfe 46–48
U1 Volksdorf

One of Hamburg's more remote districts is Volksdorf, lying far to the
north-east on the border with Schleswig-Holstein. Mentioned as early
as 1296 Volksdorf was one of half a dozen *Walddörfer*, or forest villages,
in this area, which were pawned to Hamburg by their founders during the Middle Ages and never returned. Despite urban development
Volksdorf's far-away feel remains tangible today, indeed it is still par-
tially separated from Hamburg by the Volksdorf Forest (Volksdorfer
Wald). This feeling is considerably enhanced by the presence of the
Museumsdorf Volksdorf at Im Alten Dorfe 46–48, a fine example of an
outdoor museum *(Freilichtmuseum)* of rural life.

The Museumsdorf Volksdorf offers children and grown-ups alike
the opportunity to experience the sights, sounds and smells (!) of a
traditional farm, without having to leave the confines of Hamburg. It
also offers the chance to learn about rural crafts and traditional building methods prevalent in the Hamburg and Holstein regions during
the seventeenth and eighteenth centuries. Except for Mondays the
museum grounds are open daily with no admission fee, and taking a
leisurely stroll here early in the morning certainly makes a change from
walking along a busy high street. Dotted about the grounds are seven
historic buildings, three of which were always here, the other four of
which have been brought in pieces from elsewhere and rebuilt. (Guided
tours of the building interiors are conducted at 3pm on Fridays, Saturdays and Sundays, but only on Sundays during the winter months.)

This tour of the museum begins with the building outside the main
gateway on the right-hand side. Constructed here in the eighteenth
century this thatched farmhouse has a ground plan of just 10 by 13 metres and was once occupied by two families, together with their cattle
and provisions. The building functions today as the Dorfkrug restaurant, offering edible delights unimagineable to its original occupants.

Immediately inside the museum gateway on the right-hand side
is the Remise, a wooden outbuilding containing a range of wagons,
threshing machines, and other agricultural machinery reflecting the
great technological advances made in farming during the nineteenth
century. Beyond lies the Harderhof, a large farmhouse that was built

Early morning at the Museumsdorf Volksdorf

here in 1757 and occupied almost continuously until 1935. After being used for several decades as a council depot it became the focal point in 1962 for the construction of the museum. The interior of the building is today comfortably furnished as if the original occupants had just stepped outside momentarily. The families living in the Dorfkrug, incidentally, would have been tenant workers of the family occupying the Harderhof. Alongside the Harderhof there is a charming stylised reconstruction of a well-stocked farmer's garden, brimming with flowers and herbs.

Continuing to the end of the narrow cobbled lane beyond the garden – watch out for the territorial geese and noisy cockerels – there is a bakehouse *(Backhaus)* of the type once found in all large farmyards. Built of brick and protected from the weather by a tiled roof it is situated away from the main buildings to reduce the risk of fire. Situated around the bakehouse are several oddities of local history, including the shattered remains of a First World War memorial, a boulder possibly used by primitive man to sharpen his axes, an Ice Age urn grave, and a venerable 300 year-old Yew tree transferred here from the town.

Backtracking and turning right reveals the Spiekerhus, another timber-framed and thatched building constructed here in 1680. The oldest building in the museum it is currently used as a meeting hall and exhibition space. Behind the Spiekerhus is the Grützmühle, a two-storied grain mill turned by a pair of horses. Together with the nearby red-tiled blacksmith's workshop *(Schmiede)* the mill is operated once a month during the museum's working days.

This tour concludes with two further seventeenth century buildings, namely a barn (Durchfahrtsscheune), and a farmhouse (Durchfahrtshaus) called the Wagnerhof, both constructed in the traditional manner with a series of rooms off a central corridor, hence 'Durchfahrt', meaning to pass through

Memorials to Human Suffering

Wandsbek (Poppenbüttel), Gedenkstätte Plattenhaus
Poppenbüttel at Kritenbarg 8
S1, S11 Poppenbüttel; Bus 8, 24, 174, 176, 178, 179, 276
Poppenbüttel

Across the seven boroughs of Hamburg there can be found today approximately sixty five memorials to those who suffered at the hands of the Nazi regime between 1933 and 1945. Taking a variety of forms, from simple wall plaques and inscribed boulders to art installations and full-blown monumental sculptures, they record for posterity the lawless violence metered out to anyone considered an enemy of the state: Jews and Jehovah's Witnesses, Roma and Sinti, prostitutes and homosexuals, Communists and Social Democrats, army deserters and resistance fighters, forced labourers and prisoners-of-war, the handicapped, jazz enthusiasts, and even children. The indiscriminate nature of these actions is best summed up by an unusual memorial at the Hanseatic Provincial High Court (Hanseatisches Oberlandesgericht) on Sievekingplatz (Neustadt). In front of the building there is a concrete slab inscribed simply "1933", the year of the beginning of Nazi rule. In stark contrast, on the other side of the slab, there is a colourful panorama of modern Hamburg fronted by row-upon-row of plant pots on iron stands. Each plant is different yet growing in harmony with its neighbour, and requiring the same attention to thrive. The message of equal rights amongst the different strata of society is unambiguous.

Some memorials gain their potency by being located exactly where the crime occurred. They include one at the former Hannover Station (Hannoverscher Bahnhof) on Lohseplatz (HafenCity), from where more than 7000 people were deported to labour and death camps in the east, and another at Lagerhaus G on Dessauer Ufer (Veddel), a former grain warehouse, which was used as a satellite camp for women from the Neuengamme Concentration Camp (Konzentrationslager Neuengamme), who were forced to work in the harbour.

Four other memorial sites where human suffering is still tangible deserve special attention here. The Gedenkstätte Plattenhaus Poppenbüttel at Kritenbarg 8 (Poppenbüttel) commemorates the predominantly Jewish women who were forced between September 1944 and April 1945 to build prefabricated houses to replace those destroyed during air raids. One of the houses, made from slabs of pre-fabricated

This prefabricated house in Poppenbüttel was built by Jewish women during the Second World War

concrete, is still standing and today contains documents relating to the women's tortured endeavours. A related site is the Gedenkstätte Zwangsarbeiterbaracke beim Flughafen Fuhlsbüttel at Wilhelm-Raabe-Weg 23 (Fuhlsbüttel), which consists of a purpose-built hut once used to house forced labourers working on the camouflaging of the neighbouring airfield. Although there were many such work camps across the Hamburg region during the Nazi era this is the only surviving accommodation hut.

The Gedenkstätte Konzentrationslager und Strafanstalten Fuhlsbüttel is a memorial inside the old gatehouse of Fuhlsbüttel Prison at Suhrenkamp 98 (Fuhlsbüttel). Opened in 1879 the prison was used from 1933 onwards as a concentration camp and Gestapo prison, in which almost 500 prisoners were murdered.

The final memorial is the most poignant of all. The Gedenkstätte Bullenhuser Damm is located in the cellars of a school at Bullenhuser Damm 92 (Rothenburgsort), where in April 1945 twenty Jewish children aged between five and twelve were injected with morphine by the SS and then hung. With British troops rapidly advancing on Hamburg the children were murdered in a futile attempt to conceal the fact that they had endured horrific medical experiments at the Neuengamme Concentration Camp. The names of the children are inscribed on stones in a small rose garden outside the school.

Other places of interest nearby: 82, 84

82 An Ideal Housing Estate?

Hamburg-Nord (Ohlsdorf), the Franksche Siedlung housing
estate between Schluchtweg and Kornweg on Wellingsbütteler
Landstrasse
S1, S11 Kornweg (Klein Borstel); U1 Klein Borstel;
Bus 179 Am Gehöckel

The waymarked riverside path between the U-Bahn station Klein Borstel and the Alstertalmuseum is enjoyed by those in search of natural
beauty within the confines of a city (see no. 84). Some of those who
use it, however, might also be interested in architecture, in which case
there is a surprise awaiting them. About half way along the path there
is a side track called Grüner Winkel, which leads up to Wellingsbütteler
Landstrasse. Here, between Schluchtweg and Kornweg, is the Franksche Siedlung, a pristine example of a German housing estate of the
1930s.

The Franksche Siedlung was built between 1935 and 1939 to a design by the architect Paul Frank (1878–1951), who spent much of the
1920s and 30s working under Fritz Schumacher (1869–1947), the director of public works for Hamburg. Whilst Schumacher was design-
ing public buildings, Frank was more concerned with the creation of
comfortable yet affordable housing for the masses. A proponent of the
pared-down New Objectivity *(Neuen Bauens)* of Bauhaus architecture,
Frank left his mark across Hamburg with a series of large-scale housing
schemes, including the so-called Jarrestadt in Winterhude. Together
with his brother Hermann he also set about improving the letting and
administration procedures of housing estates, as well as the quality of
available building materials (achievements for which the brothers were
eventually honoured with the street name Frank-Ring in Volksdorf).

The seizure of power by the National Socialists in 1933 marked a
change in housing policy in Hamburg. The massive Modernist housing schemes constructed during the time of the Weimar Republic were
now discontinued in favour of smaller, more traditional housing estates in which the inhabitants were brought closer to their natural surroundings. The Franksche Siedlung was just such an estate, reflecting
both the garden city ideals of the proto-Modernist architect Hermann
Muthesius (1861–1927), as well as the new political ideals of the Nazi
Party.

The Franksche Siedlung consists of a uniform grid of terrace

The Franksche Siedlung housing estate was built in Ohlsdorf during the 1930s

houses, strung out in a line along the side of the road. The cosy red-brick façades and pitched roofs reflect the conservative ideals of National Socialism, as does the rigorously repetitive appearance of each row, allowing little or no individual expression. Each house is identified by a row of three windows and a front door at ground level, and a further row of three windows on the first floor. Beneath the upper windows is a concrete window box supported on three projecting blocks. Despite the recent addition of front porches to some of the houses, the overall corporate identity of the estate has been retained remarkably intact. Only in the gardens behind the houses is any real individuality allowed to shine through. Generously sized to encourage occupants to grow their own food, the gardens can be seen best by walking along a narrow sandy footpath leading off Stubeheide.

An air of communal contentment hangs over the Franksche Siedlung today, indeed it seems the ideal housing estate. As such it is a fitting tribute to its architect (who incidentally was a staunch liberal before and after the Nazi era) and not the murderous regime that initiated its construction.

Other places of interest nearby: 81, 84

83 The Grave of an Arabian Princess

Hamburg-Nord (Ohlsdorf), the Ohlsdorf Cemetery
(Friedhof Ohlsdorf) at Fuhlsbüttler Strasse 756
S1, S11 Ohlsdorf; U1 Ohlsdorf; Buses 170 and 270 operate
within the cemetery

Ohlsdorf Cemetery (Friedhof Ohlsdorf) is not only Hamburg's largest cemetery but it is also recognised as the largest garden cemetery in the world, with some impressive statistics to match. Covering an area of nearly 400 hectares – equal to the city's Altstadt and Neustadt combined – the cemetery was opened to all religious denominations in 1877. Since that time approximately 1.4 million burials have taken place and at present the cemetery has 256 000 individual graves registered. The cemetery is so large that two public bus lines with twenty five bus stops are required to service the seventeen kilometres of roads.

Two million people visit the cemetery each year, drawn not only by the private graves, mass war graves, and those of soldiers from more than twenty countries, but also by the imposing mausolea, chapels, and funeral museum, all laid out against a peaceful backdrop of gardens, trees and lakes. Some visitors come particularly for the contemplative Garten der Frauen (Women's Garden) in which notable Hamburg women are buried, including the controversial prostitute Domenica Niehoff (1945–2009), who campaigned vociferously for the legalisation of her profession.

One of the most extraordinary women ever to live in Hamburg is not buried in the Women's Garden but rather in Grave U27 (78–89), between the second and third roundabouts on Kapellenstrasse, directly opposite the Grabmal-Freilicht-Museum. The gilded Arabic text on the gravestone informs the onlooker that here lies Sayyida Salme, Princess of Oman and Zanzibar (1844–1924). Exactly how an Arabian princess came to be buried in Hamburg is a fascinating tale.

Sayyida Salme was born into the family of Sayyid Said bin Sultan Al-Busaid, Sultan of Zanzibar and Oman on 30th August 1844. One of thirty six children her mother was one of the sultan's Circassian concubines. She spent her youth in the harem at the Beit el Mtoni palace on the coast of Zanzibar, where she was taught both Arabic and Swahili. In 1851 she moved into the palace of her brother, Majid bin Said, who taught her to ride and to shoot. Two years later she moved with

One of many imposing tombs in the Ohlsdorf Cemetery (Friedhof Ohlsdorf)

her mother to another palace, where she secretly taught herself to write, a skill almost unknown for Muslim women at the time.

Salme's father died in 1856, at which time her brother Majid became Sultan of Zanzibar, whilst another brother, Sayyid Thuwaini bin Said al-Said, became Sultan of Oman. Following the death of her mother in 1859 a power struggle broke out between Majid and yet another brother, Barghash bin Said. Although Salme favoured Majid, she was coerced by her sister into supporting Barghash. The dispute was eventually resolved in Majid's favour by the arrival of a British gunboat. Although Salme was eventually reconciled with Majid, Barghash never forgave her, and he eventually succeeded to the Sultancy after Majid's death in 1870.

During the 1860s Salme spent much time in Stone Town, the capital of Zanzibar, and it was there that she became acquainted with Rudolph Heinrich Ruete, a German merchant. In August 1866 she eloped with Ruete on a British ship to Aden, where she gave birth to her first son. Although the child died in infancy Salme converted to Christianity and changed her name to Emily so as to be able to marry Ruete. After their marriage on 31st May 1867 the pair moved to Hamburg, where they settled on Schöne Aussicht (Uhlenhorst) and had another son and two daughters.

Tragedy struck in 1870 when Rudolph Ruete fell beneath a horse-drawn tram and was killed, leaving his family in financial straits. To help alleviate the problem Emily Ruete wrote *Memoirs of an Arabian Princess from Zanzibar*, which was published in Germany in 1886,

Emily Ruete
Wittwe des Rudolph Heinrich Rue...
geb. 30. Aug. 1844 in Zansibar,
gest. 29. Febr. 1924 in Jena.
Der ist in tiefster Seele treu,
Wer die Heimat liebt wie du.

The Ohlsdorf Cemetery (Friedhof Ohlsdorf) contains the grave of a princess from Zanzibar

and later translated into English. The first autobiography by an Arab woman it is still in print today.

Despite having been ostracized by most of her family for renouncing her faith Emily Ruete revisited Zanzibar in 1885 and 1888, amidst speculation that German Chancellor Otto von Bismarck (1815–1898) planned to install her son as Sultan of Zanzibar. During the final visit she returned to the Beit el Mtoni palace, where she had grown up, and filled a pouch with sand from the nearby beach as a souvenir. After her death from pneumonia in Jena, Germany, at the age of 79, she was buried in her husband's grave in the Ohlsdorf Cemetery, together with the pouch of sand. An inscription on her gravestone is a reminder that she never forgot about her beloved Zanzibar: "Faithful in his innermost heart is he who loves his homeland like you".

84   Lovely Flows the Alster

Wandsbek (Wellingsbüttel), a walk along the Alstertal
beginning at the Klein Borstel U-Bahn station
U1 Klein Borstel

If the harbour is the heart of Hamburg then some would say the Alster Lake is the city's soul. Created by damming the River Alster, a tributary of the Elbe, in the thirteenth century to provide power for watermills, the lake does much to give central Hamburg its distinctive marine atmosphere. In the seventeenth century the eighteen hectare Binnenalster (Inner Alster) was separated from the one hundred and sixty hectare Außenalster (Outer Alster), and provided with three grand promenades: Ballindamm, Jungfernstieg, and Neuer Jungfernstieg. For many visitors this is as much of the Alster as they will see – but there's much more to explore.

From the northern reaches of the Außenalster the River Alster winds away north-eastwards through a handful of districts, including Alsterdorf, Ohlsdorf, Wellingsbüttel, and Poppenbüttel, before reaching its source 25 kilometres north of central Hamburg on the moors of Henstedt-Ulzburg in Schleswig-Holstein (an ornate iron grate marks the spot). As far as the U-Bahn station Klein Borstel in Ohlsdorf, where this journey begins, the Alster is canalised, but from there onwards through Wellingsbüttel the river assumes its natural course – and is all the more lovely for it.

Alighting from the train at Klein Borstel the explorer quickly leaves civilisation behind by descending into the sylvain tranquillity of the Alstertal, the river valley that stretches from here all the way to the distant district of Lemsahl-Mellingstedt. Surely this is one of the most beautiful stretches of river in Hamburg, with its idyllic combination of water, dense river forest, and swampland, providing endless adventurous opportunities for young and old alike. Little wonder that the way-marked path along the riverbank (Alsterwanderweg) is popular with everyone from joggers and cyclists to dog owners and photographers. The latter enjoy capturing images not only of the pristine natural beauty of the river but also where man has successfully enhanced it by the addition of some beautiful riverside villas, as well as an unusual 1930s housing estate (see no. 82).

After walking for a about two kilometres the riverside path passes the Langwischbrücke, beyond which there is a series of pools and a

The Alstertal has many sylvan glades

cluster of charming thatched cottages. Here, on the right-hand side, stands what must be Hamburg's most magnificently sited retirement home, the Domizil. It is located in the former grounds of the Herrenhaus, a grand mansion at Wellingsbütteler Weg 71, built in 1750 for the Kurtzrock family. Originally called Gut Wellingsbüttel the mansion was constructed in brick and then re-worked during the late nineteenth century in a combination of neo-Classical and neo-Rococo styles. Today the building contains the smart Café im Herrenhaus, which caters for all tastes, from those wishing to enjoy a candlelit gourmet dinner to the weary walker desiring nothing more than a cold drink and a comfortable seat on the beautiful terrace.

On the banks of the Alster stands this picturesque gatehouse

This walk finishes opposite the Herrenhaus in the so-called Torhaus, a timber-framed red-brick gatehouse built for the same family in 1757. One wing of the gatehouse contains the Alstertalmuseum, which documents the history of Hamburg's north-eastern districts. Subjects include the prehistory of the area, the development of agriculture, shipping on the Außenalster, as well as the narrow gauge electric railway, which between 1904 and 1961 connected Wohldorf-Ohlstedt, Volksdorf, and Alt Rahlstedt (the tiny Kleinbahnmuseum Wohldorf is housed inside the former Wohldorf-Ohlstedt railway station at Schleusenredder 10, making it the most northerly museum in Hamburg).

Other places of interest nearby: 81, 82

***

Standing in Wellingsbüttel, on the banks of the gently-flowing Alster, is perhaps the ideal place to finish this odyssey during which some of the more unusual and unsung corners of Hamburg have been explored. Looking back downstream, along the river which together with the Elbe accounted for the founding of the city over a thousand years ago, gives the satisfied explorer the chance to reflect on the myriad cultures and characters that continue to shape this maritime powerhouse in the north of Germany.

Opening times

for museums and other places of interest (after each name is the borough, followed by the district in brackets)
Correct at time of going to press but may be subject to change.

Alstertalmuseum, Wandsbek (Wellingsbüttel), Wellingsbütteler Weg 75a, Sat & Sun 11am–1pm, 3–5pm

Alt-Hamburger Aalspeicher, Hamburg-Mitte (Altstadt), Deichstrasse 43, daily 12am–11pm

Altona Jewish Cemetery (Jüdischer Friedhof Altona), Altona (Altona-Altstadt), Königstrasse 10a, Oct–Mar Tue, Thu & Sun 2–5pm, Apr–Sep Tue & Thu 3–6pm, Sun 2–5pm; guided tours in German each Sun at 12am; closed for Jewish holidays; men must wear a *kippah* available at the gate

Altona and North German State Museum (Altonaer Museum – Norddeuteches Landesmuseum), Altona (Ottensen), Museumstrasse 23, Tue–Sun 10am–5pm

Archaeological Museum Hamburg (Archäologisches Museum Hamburg), Harburg, Harburger Rathausplatz 5, Tue–Sun 10am–5pm

Arts and Crafts Museum (Museum für Kunst und Gewerbe), Hamburg-Mitte (St. Georg), Steintorplatz, Tue, Wed, Fri, Sat & Sun 10am–6pm, Wed & Thu 10am–9pm

BallinStadt Emigration City, Hamburg-Mitte (Veddel), Veddeler Bogen 2, Apr-Oct daily 10am–6pm, Nov-Mar daily 10am-4.30pm

Benjamin Klemann Schumacherei, Hamburg-Mitte (Neustadt), Poolstrasse 9, Mon–Sat 9am–5pm

Bergedorf and Vierlande Museum (Museum für Bergedorf und die Vierlande), Bergedorf (Bergedorf), Schloss Bergedorf, Bergedorfer Schlossstrasse 4, Apr–Oct Tue–Thu 11am–6pm, Sat & Sun 11am-6pm, Nov–Mar Tue–Thu 12am-4pm, Sat & Sun 11am–5pm

Bonscheladen, Altona (Ottensen), Friedensallee 12, Tue–Fri 11am–6.30pm (demonstration 4.15pm), Sat 11am–4pm (demonstration 2.30pm)

Botanischer Sondergarten Wandsbek, Wandsbek (Wandsbek), Walddörferstrasse 273, daily 7am–dusk

Brauhaus Joh. Albrecht, Hamburg-Mitte (Altstadt), Adolphsbrücke 7, daily 11am–12pm

Buddel-Bini, Hamburg-Nord (Eppendorf), Lokstedter Weg 68, Mon–Fri 10am–8pm, Sat 10am–2pm

Bunkermuseum, Hamburg-Mitte (Hamm), Wichernsweg 16, Thu 10–12am, 3–6pm

Café im Herrenhaus, Wandsbek (Wellingsbüttel), Wellingsbütteler Weg 71, Wed–Sun 10am–6pm

Café Mathilda, Eimsbüttel (Harvestehude), Bogenstrasse 5, Mon–Fri 11.30am–12pm, Sat 12am–10pm, Sun 12am–11pm

Café Paris, Hamburg-Mitte (Altstadt), Rathausstrasse 4, Mon–Fri 9am–11.30pm, Sat & Sun 9.30am–11.30pm

Café Tide, Altona (Ottensen), Rothestrasse 53, Mon–Fri 8am–6pm, Sat 10am–6pm

Chinese Hamburg Yu Garden Tea House (Chinesisches Teehaus), Eimsbüttel (Rotherbaum), Binderstrasse 67, daily 11am–7.30pm

Church of St. Gertrude (St. Gertrud Kirche), Harburg (Altenwerder), Altenwerder Kirchweg, for monthly opening times visit www.kirche-suederelbe.de

Church of St. Gertrude (St. Gertrud Kirche), Hamburg-Nord (Uhlenhorst), Immenhof 10, Mon, Tue, Thu & Fri 10–12am (Tue 4–6pm)

Church of St. James (Jacobikirche), Hamburg-Mitte (Altstadt), Jakobikirchhof 22, Apr–Sep Mon–Sat 10am–5pm, Oct–Mar Mon–Sat 11am–5pm

Church of St. Michaelis (St. Michaelis Kirche), Hamburg-Mitte (Neustadt), Englische Planke 1, May–Oct daily 9am-7.30pm, Nov–Apr daily 10am–5.30pm

Church of St. Nikolai (Nikolaikirche), Hamburg-Mitte (Altstadt), Willy-Brandt-Strasse 60, documentation centre and panorama lift daily May–Sep 10am–8pm, Oct–Apr 10am–6pm

Church of St. Pankratius (St. Pankratius Kirche), Harburg (Neuenfelde), Organistenweg, off Arp-Schnitger-Stieg, daily 9am–6pm

Church of St. Petri (St. Petri Kirche), Hamburg-Mitte (Altstadt), Bei der Petrikirche 2, Mon, Tue, Thu & Fri 10am–6.30pm, Wed 10am–7pm, Sat 10am–5pm, Sun 9am–8pm

Church of St. Severin (St. Severini zu Kirchwerder), Bergedorf (Kirchwerder), Kirchenheerweg 12, Sun mass 9.30am

Das Feuerschiff, Hamburg-Mitte (Altstadt), Vorsetzen, Mon–Sat 11am–1pm, Sun 9am–11pm

Das Hamam, Hamburg-Mitte (St. Pauli), Feldstrasse 39, Mon–Wed & Fri 10am–10pm, Sat & Sun 11am–9pm; women only Mon, Fri & each second Sun, mixed Tue, Wed, Sat & each second Sun

Deichgraf, Hamburg-Mitte (Altstadt), Deichstrasse 23, Mon–Fri 12am–3pm, Sat 12am–10pm, Sun (Summer) 12am–9pm

Denkmal aus Anlass des 60. Jahrestages des Hamburger Feuersturms in Rothenburgsort, Hamburg-Mitte (Rothenburgsort), Billhorner Deich, first and third Sun each month 2–4pm

Der Treppenkraemer, Altona (Blankenese), Hans-Lange-Strasse 23, Fri 12am–6pm, Sat & Sun 9am–6pm

Die Kleine Fischkiste, Cuxhaven, Halle X, Niedersachsenstrasse, Mon–Fri 7am–6pm, Sat 7am–4pm, Sun 8am–4pm

Elbewarte Restaurant, Altona (Ottensen), Augustinum, Neumühlen 37, Tue, Thu, Sat & Sun 3–6pm

Ernst Thälmann Gedenkstätte, Hamburg-Nord (Eppendorf), Tarpenbekstrasse 66, Tue 10am–1pm, 5–8pm, Wed & Thu 10am–1pm, Fri 10am–5pm, Sat 10am–1pm

FahnenFleck, Hamburg-Mitte (Altstadt), Neuer Wall 57, Mon–Fri 10am–7pm, Sat 10am–6pm

Fischereihafen, Hamburg-Mitte (St. Pauli), Gross Elbstrasse 143, Mon–Thu, Sun 11.30am–10pm, Fri & Sat 11.30am–10.30pm

Fischerhaus, Hamburg-Mitte (St. Pauli), St. Pauli Fischmarkt 14, daily 11am–11pm

Fish Auction Hall (Fischauktionshalle), Altona (Altona-Altstadt), Grosse Elbstrasse 9, Apr–Sep Sun 5.30–12am, Oct–Mar Sun 6–12am; Fish Market (Fischmarkt), Sun 5–10am, Oct–Mar 7–10am

Floating Church (Flussschifferkirche), Hamburg-Mitte (Altstadt), Kehrwiedersteig, mass most Sundays at 3pm

Freiheit & Roosen, Hamburg-Mitte (St. Pauli), Paul-Roosen-Strasse 41, Mon–Fri 12am–8pm, Sat 12am–6pm

Friesenkeller, Hamburg-Mitte (Altstadt), Neuer Wall 9, daily 11.30am–10.30pm

Gedenkstätte Bullenhuser Damm und Rosengarten für die Kinder vom Bullenhuser Damm, Hamburg-Mitte (Rothenburgsort), Bullenhuser Damm 92, Sun 10am–5pm

Gedenkstätte Konzentrationslager und Strafanstalten Fuhlsbüttel, Hamburg-Nord (Fuhlsbüttel), Suhrenkamp 98, Sun 10am–5pm

Gedenkstätte Plattenhaus Poppenbüttel, Wandsbek (Poppenbüttel), Kritenbarg 8, Sun 10am–5pm

Gedenkstätte Zwangsarbeiterbaracke beim Flughafen Fuhlsbüttel, Hamburg-Nord (Fühlsbüttel), Wilhelm-Raabe-Weg 23, Apr–Nov first sunday in the month 2–4pm

Geology and Palaeontology Museum (Geologisch-Paläontologisches Museum), Eimsbüttel (Rotherbaum), Bundesstrasse 55, Mon–Fri 9am–6pm

German Customs Museum (Deutsches Zollmuseum), Hamburg-Mitte (Altstadt), Alter Wandrahm 16, Tue–Sun 10am–5pm

German Electron Synchrotron (Deutsches Elektronen-Synchrotron) (DESY), Altona (Bahrenfeld), Notkestrasse 85, guided tours on the first Saturday of the month at 10am; meeting point at Building 01 inside the main entrance; tours in English only by special request www.desy.de

German Painters' and Varnishers' Museum (Deutsches Maler- und Lackierer Museum), Bergedorf (Billwerder), Glockenhaus, Billwerder Billdeich 72, Feb–Nov Sat & Sun 2–5pm

Gröninger Brauereikeller, Hamburg-Mitte (Altstadt), Willy-Brandt-Strasse 47, Mon–Fri 11am–12pm, Sat 5–12pm, Sun 3–10pm

Grossrohrpost, for tour times and tickets (German only; English by request) see Hamburg Underworlds Association (Hamburger Unterwelten e.V.)

Hagenbecks Tierpark, Eimsbüttel (Stellingen), Lokstedter Grenzstrasse 2, Mar–Jun & Sep–Oct 9am–6pm, Jul–Aug 9am–7pm, Nov–Feb 9am–4.30pm

Hamam Hafen, Hamburg-Mitte (St. Pauli), Seewartenstrasse 10 (Haus 2), mixed Thu–Mon 10am–10pm, Sat & Sun 11am–9pm, women only Tue & Wed 10am–10pm

Hamburg Harbour Museum (Hafenmuseum Hamburg), Hamburg-Mitte (Kleiner Grasbrook), Australiastrasse 50a, Easter–Oct Tue–Sun 10am–6pm

Hamburg Museum (Museum für Hamburgische Geschichte), Hamburg-Mitte (Neustadt), Holstenwall 24, Tue–Sat 10am–5pm, Sun 10am–6pm

Hamburg Observatory (Hamburger Sternwarte), Bergedorf (Bergedorf), Gojenbergsweg 112, tours by appointment only www.hs.uni-hamburg.de

Hamburg School Museum (Hamburger Schulmuseum), Hamburg-Mitte (St. Pauli) Seilerstrasse 42, Mon–Fri 8am–4.30pm, first Sun in the month 12am–5pm

Hamburg Underworlds Association (Hamburger Unterwelten e.V.), www.hamburgerunterwelten.com

Harry's Hamburger Hafenbasar, Hamburg-Mitte (Altstadt), GREIF Floating Crane, Sandtorhafen, Tue–Sun 11am–5pm

Hatari Pfälzer Stube, Hamburg-Mitte (St. Pauli), Schanzenstrasse 4, Mon–Sat from 12am, Sun from 4pm

Hilfskrankenhaus Wedel, for tour times and tickets (German only; English by request) see Hamburg Underworlds Association (Hamburger Unterwelten e.V.)

Hindu Temple (Hindu Tempel), Hamburg-Mitte (Rothenburgsort), Billstrasse 77, Mon–Sat 11am–6pm, Sun 11am–5pm

Holsten Brewery (Holsten-Brauerei), Altona (Altona-Nord), Holstenstrasse 224, guided tours in German (English by request) Mon–Fri 9am, 11.15am, 1.30pm, advance booking necessary www.holsten-brauwelt.de; Holsten Shop Mon–Thu 8.30am–5pm, Fri 8.30am–3.30pm

HSV-Museum, Altona (Bahrenfeld), HSH Nordbank Arena, Sylvesterallee 7, daily 10am–6pm

Imam Ali Mosque (Imam Ali Moschee), Hamburg-Nord (Uhlenhorst), Schöne Aussicht 36, Sat–Thu 9–12am, 1–8pm; for prayer times www.izhamburg.de

International Maritime Museum Hamburg (Internationales Maritimes Museum Hamburg), Hamburg-Mitte (HafenCity), Koreastrasse 1, Kaispeicher B, Tue–Sun 10am–6pm; Meerwein Restaurant and Oyster Bar, Tue–Sun from 11.30am

Jenisch-Haus, Altona (Othmarschen), Jenischpark, Baron-Voght-Strasse 50, Tue–Sun 11am–6pm

Joachim Lührs Kunstantiquariat, Hamburg-Mitte (Neustadt), Michaelisbrücke 3, Mon–Fri 11am–6.30pm, Sat 11am–5pm

Kaffee Stark, Hamburg-Mitte (St. Pauli), Wohlwillstrasse 18, daily 10am–12pm

Kaffeemuseum Burg, Hamburg-Nord (Eppendorf), Münsterstrasse 23 -25, Mon–Fri 8am–2pm

Kaffeerösterei Burg, Hamburg-Nord (Hoheluft-Ost), Eppendorfer Weg 252, Mon–Fri 8am–2pm

Kajüte SB12, Altona (Blankenese), Strandweg 79, Mar–Sep daily 11am–11pm

Käppn Lührs Museum & Oevelgönner Seekiste, Altona (Othmarschen), Övelgönne 61, Fri & Sat 3–7pm, Sun 10am–1pm, 3–7pm by appointment only for groups of four or more, www.museum-seekiste.de

Kiekeberg Open Air Museum (Freilichtmuseum am Kiekeberg), Rosengarten-Ehestorf, Am Kiekeberg 1, Apr–Oct Tue–Sun 10am–6pm, Nov–Mar Tue–Sun 10am–4pm

Kleinbahnmuseum Wohldorf, Wandsbek (Wohldorf-Ohlstedt), Schleusenredder 10, Sun 1–4pm

Knut Harms Friseur, Hamburg-Mitte (Altstadt), Kleine Johannisstrasse 6, Mon–Fri 9am–6pm

Kramer-Witwen-Wohnung, Hamburg-Mitte (Neustadt), Krayenkamp 10, Tue–Sun 10am–5pm; in winter Sat & Sun only

Ladage & Oelke, Hamburg-Mitte (Altstadt), Neuer Wall 11, Mon–Fri 10am–7pm, Sat 10am–6pm

Mineralogical Museum (Mineralogisches Museum), Eimsbüttel (Rotherbaum), Grindelallee 48, Wed 3–6pm, Sun 10am–5pm

Miniatur Wunderland, Hamburg-Mitte (Altstadt), Kehrwieder 2–4, Mon, Wed, Thu 9.30am–6pm, Tue 9.30am–9pm, Fri 9.30am–7pm, Sat 8am–9pm, Sun 8.30am–8pm

Montblanc Boutique, Hamburg-Mitte (Neustadt), Neuer Wall 18, Mon–Fri 10am–7pm, Sat 10.30am–6pm

Montblanc Museum, Eimsbüttel (Eidelstadt), Hellgrundweg 100, by appointment only tel. +49/40/84 00 1-0, www.montblanc.com

Museum Elbinsel Wilhelmsburg, Hamburg-Mitte (Wilhelmsburg), Kirchdorfer Strasse 163, Apr–Oct Sun 2–5pm

Museum of Ethnology (Museum für Völkerkunde), Eimsbüttel (Rotherbaum), Rothenbaumchaussee 64, Tue–Sun 10am–6pm, Thu until 9pm

Museum of Work (Museum der Arbeit), Hamburg-Nord (Barmbek-Nord), Wiesendamm 3, Mon 1–9pm, Tue–Sat 10am–5pm, Sun 10am–6pm

Museumsdorf Volksdorf, Wandsbek (Volksdorf), Im Alten Dorfe 46–48, grounds daily Tue–Sun 9am–5pm; buildings only with a guided tour Apr–Oct Fri, Sat & Sun 3pm, Nov–Mar Sun 3pm

Museum Ship Cap San Diego (Museumsschiff Cap San Diego), Hamburg-Mitte (Neustadt), Vorsetzen, Überseebrücke, daily 10am–6pm

Museum Ship Rickmer Rickmers (Museumsschiff Rickmer Rickmers), Hamburg-Mitte (Neustadt), Bei den St. Pauli-Landungsbrücken, Pontoon 1a, daily 10am–6pm

Neuengamme Former Concentration Camp (KZ-Gedenkstätte Neuengamme), Bergedorf (Neuengamme), Jean-Dolidier-Weg 75, Mon–Fri 9.30am–4pm, Apr–Sep Sat & Sun 12am–7pm, Oct–Mar Sat & Sun 12am–5pm

New Botanical Gardens (Neuer Botanischer Garten), Altona (Gross Flottbek), Hesten 10, daily 9am until an hour and a half before sundown; Loki Schmidt Haus Mar–Oct Tue–Sat 1–5pm, Sun 10am–5pm (Nov until 4pm)

New Main Church of St. Nikolai
(St. Nikolai Neue Hauptkirche), Eimsbüttel (Harvestehude), Klosterstern, Mon–Fri 8am–6pm, Sun Mass 6pm

Oberhafen-Kantine, Hamburg-Mitte (HafenCity), Stockmeyerstrasse 39, Mon–Sat 12am–10pm, Sun 12am–6pm

Ohlsdorf Cemetery (Friedhof Ohlsdorf), Hamburg-Nord (Ohlsdorf), Fuhlsbüttler Strasse 756, Apr–Oct 8am–9pm, Nov–Mar 8am–6pm

Old Commercial Room, Hamburg-Mitte (Neustadt), Englische Planke 10, 12am–11.30pm

Old Elbe Tunnel (Alter Elbtunnel), Hamburg-Mitte (St. Pauli), Bei den St. Pauli-Landungsbrücken, cars Mon–Fri 5.30am–8pm, pedestrians only Sat & Sun

One World Network Hamburg Association (Eine Welt Netzwerk Hamburg e.V.), www.ewnw.de

Otto Hatje, Altona (Altona-Altstadt), Alte Königstrasse 5, Tue–Fri 10am–6.30pm, Sat 10am–2pm

Planetarium Hamburg, (Winterhude), Stadtpark, Hindenburgstrasse 1b, ticket office Mon & Tue 10am–5pm, Wed & Thu 10am–9pm, Fri 10am–10pm, Sat 12am–10pm, Sun 10am–8pm; viewing platform Thu–Sun 9am–5pm

Planten un Blomen, Hamburg-Mitte (St. Pauli), Stephansplatz, Oct–Mar 7am–8pm, Apr 7am–10pm, May–Sep 7am–11pm; Japanese Tea House May–Sep Tue–Sat 3–6pm

Puppenmuseum Falkenstein, Altona (Blankenese), Grotiusweg 79, Tue–Sun 11am–5pm

Rahimi Handel, Maburg-Mitte (Altstadt), Am Sandtorkai 32, Mon–Fri 10am–5pm, Sat 12am–5pm by appointment only

Rieck Haus Open Air Museum (Freilichtmuseum Rieckhaus), Bergedorf (Curslack), Curslacker Deich 284, Apr–Sep Tue–Sun 10am–5pm, Oct–Mar Tue–Sun 10am–4pm

Riepenburger Windmill (Windmühle Riepenburger Mühle), Bergedorf (Kirchwerder), Kirchwerder Mühlendamm 75a, Apr–Oct Tue & Thu 12am–4pm, first and third Sun 1–5pm

Russian Church of St. Prokop (Russische Kirche des Heiligen Prokop), Eimsbüttel (Stellingen), Hagenbeckstrasse 10, vigil Sat 5pm, Sun Mass 10am, www.prokopij.de

Ship-in-a-Bottle and Seashell Museum (Buddelschiff- und Muschelmuseum), Schulauer Fährhaus, Wedel, Parnassstrasse 29, Mar–Oct 10am–6pm, Nov–Feb Sat & Sun 10am–6pm

Speicherstadt Kaffeerösterei, Hamburg-Mitte (Altstadt), Kehrwieder 5, daily 10am–7pm

Speicherstadtmuseum, Hamburg-Mitte (Altstadt), St. Annenufer 2, Apr–Oct Mon–Fri 10am–5pm, Sat & Sun 10am–6pm, Nov–Mar Tue–Sun 10am–5pm

Spicy's Gewürzmuseum, Hamburg-Mitte (Altstadt), Am Sandtorkai 32, Tue–Sun 10am–5pm

St. Pauli Tourist Office, Hamburg-Mitte (St. Pauli), Beim Grünen Jäger 7–8, Mon–Sat 10am–7pm

Stüdemann's Tea Shop, Hamburg-Mitte (St. Pauli), Schulterblatt 57, Mon–Fri 9am–7pm, Sat 9am–5pm

Swedish Gustav-Adolf Church (Schwedische Gustav-Adolfskirche), Hamburg-Mitte (Neustadt), Ditmar-Koel-Strasse 36, Wed–Sat 2–5pm, Sun Mass 11am

Tiefbunker Steintorwall, for tour times and tickets (German only; English by request) see Hamburg Underworlds Association (Hamburger Unterwelten e.V.)

Tropen Brendler, Hamburg-Mitte (Altstadt), Grosse Johannisstrasse 15, Mon–Wed 9.30am–6pm, Thu & Fri 9.30am–6.30pm, Sat 9.30am–4pm

Turm Bar, Rotherbaum (Eimsbüttel), Rothenbaumchaussee 2, Mon–Fri 6pm–1am, Sat & Sun 6pm–4am

U-Bootmuseum Hamburg, Hamburg-Mitte (HafenCity), Versmannstrasse 24, Mon–Sat 9am–8pm, Sun 11am–8pm

Under Hamburg Association (unterhamburg e.V.), www.unterhamburg.de

Marine motif on a former sailors' school in Finkenwerder (see no. 28)

Venetian Gondola (Die venezianische Gondel), Hamburg-Nord (Eppendorf), Bootshaus Barmeier, Eppendorfer Landstrasse 180, Apr–Nov, www.diegondel.de

Walther Eisenburg der Mützenmacher, Hamburg-Mitte (Altstadt), Steinstrasse 21, Mon–Fri 9am–6pm, Sat 10am–1pm

Warburg Library of Cultural Science (Kulturwissenschaftliche Bibliothek Warburg), Eimsbüttel (Eppendorf), Warburg-Haus, Heilwigstrasse 116, by appointment only www.warburg-haus.de

Windmill 'Johanna' (Windmühle Johanna), Hamburg-Mitte (Wilhelmsburg), Schönenfelder Strasse 99a, first Sun in the month 2–6pm; closed Jul & Aug

Witthüs Teehaus, Altona (Nienstedten), Elbchaussee 499a, Tue–Sat 2–11pm, Sun 10am–11pm

Zoological Museum (Zoologisches Museum), Eimsbüttel (Rotherbaum), Martin-Luther-King-Platz 3, Tue–Sun 10am–5pm

Bibliography

GUIDEBOOKS

Hamburg (Martina Beuting), Michael Müller Verlag, 2008

Spaziergänge Hamburg (Anna Brenken & Egbert Kossak), Ellert & Richter Verlag, 2000

Hamburg Vis-à-Vis (Gerhard Bruschke), Dorling Kindersley, 2008

PastFinder Hamburg – City and Travel Guide (Andrea Dimitriadis, Maik Kopleck & Sindith Küster), PastFinder Ltd, 2008

Beatles Guide Hamburg (Ulf Kruger & Astrid Kirchherr), Europa Verlag 2001

City Spots Hamburg (Paul Murphy), Thomas Cook Publishing, 2008

Hamburg von Unten – Entdeckungsreisen in die Stadt unter der Stadt (Lou A. Probsthayn), L&H Verlag, 2004

Literarisches Hamburg – 99 Autoren und ihre Orte in der Stadt (Kai-Uwe Scholz), Jena Verlag, 2002

Zu Fuß durch Hamburg – 21 Stadtteilrundgänge durch Geschichte und Gegenwart (Werner Skrentny), Europäische Verlagsanstalt, 2007

Hamburg Baedecker Allianz Reiseführer (Various), Mair DuMont 2009

Kulturverführer Hamburg (Various), Metz, 2008

Wallpaper City Guide Hamburg (Various), Phaidon, 2008

Hamburgs Attraktionen am Hafen (Michael Zapf), Murmann Verlag, 2007

HIDDEN HAMBURG

Stille Winkel in Hamburg (Anna Brenken), Ellert & Richter, 2007

Das Unbekannte Hamburg – Entdecken Sie die Schönheiten und Geheimnisse der Stadt (Joachim Buttler), Ellert & Richter Verlag, 2009

Hamburgs dunkle Welten – Der geheimnisvolle Untergrund der Hansestadt (Ulrich Alexis Christiansen), Ch.Links Verlag, 2008

Hamburg Geheim – Die unbekannten Seiten der Stadt (Lou A. Probsthayn), Boyens Buchverlag, 2008

ILLUSTRATED BOOKS

Eine Kulinarische Entdeckungsreise durch Hamburg und das Alte Land (Katrin Lipka), Neuer Umschau Verlag, 2007

Speicherstadt und HafenCity (Egbert Kossak), Ellert & Richter Verlag, 2004

Hamburg City Panoramas 360° (Helga Neubauer, Thorsten Tiedeke & Wolfgang Vorbeck), New Zealand Visitor Publications, 2006

Kleine Könige – Über Leute und ihre Läden (Ernestine Stadler & Frank Taubenheim), Hamburger Abendblatt, 2002

ARCHITECTURE AND MONUMENTS

Hamburg (Architecture & Design Guides) (ed. By Christian Datz), teNeues, 2005

The Flak Towers in Berlin, Hamburg and Vienna 1940–1950 (Michael Foedrowitz), Schiffer Publishing, 2005

Gedenkstätten in Hamburg: Ein Wegweiser zu den Stätten der Erinnerung an die Jahre 1933–1945 (Detlef Grabe & Kerstin Klingel), Landeszentrale für politische Bildung, 2008

Boote unter Beton: Die Hamburger U-Boot-Bunker (Jan Haitmann), Elbe-Spree-Verlag, 2007

Der Ohlsdorfer Friedhof – Ein Handbuch von A–Z (Helmut Schoenfeld), Edition Temmen, 2006

HISTORY

'Aryanisation' in Hamburg – The Economic Exclusion of Jews and the Confiscation of their Property in Nazi Germany (Frank Bajohr & George Wilkes), Berghahn Books, 2002

Paper and Iron – Hamburg Business and German Politics in the Era of Inflation 1897–1927 (Niall Ferguson), Cambridge University Press, 2002

The Emigrants – From Hamburg to the New World (Gerhard Fuchs), Fuchs Verlag, 2000

Travels in the North of Germany (Thomas Hodgskin), Archibald Constable, 1820

Patriots and Paupers – Hamburg 1712–1830 (Mary Lindemann), Oxford University Press USA, 1990

Inferno – The Devastation of Hamburg 1943 (Keith Lowe), Viking, 2007

Branntwein, Bibeln und Bananen. Der deutsche Kolonialismus – eine Spurensuche in Hamburg (Heiko Möhle), Verlag Libertäre Assoziation, 1999

The End – Hamburg 1943 (H. E. Nossack), Chicago University Press, 2007

Hamburg – Eine kleine Stadtgeschichte (Christian Schnee), Sutton Verlag, 2003

WEBSITES

www.hamburg-tourism.de (Hamburg Tourist Board)

www.hamburg.de (Official City Portal)

www.kulturkarte.de (extensive culture listings with maps)

www.hamburgerunterwelten.de (Hamburg Underworlds Association)

www.unter-hamburg.de (Under Hamburg Association)

www.stattreisen-hamburg. de (thematic walking tours of Hamburg)

www.alternative-stadtrundfahrten.de (tours of sites where Nazi persecution and civil resistance occurred in Hamburg)

www.hojobeck.de (comprehensive survey of wartime bunkers and shelters in Hamburg)

www.spottedbylocals.com/hamburg (useful and entertaining city Blog)

www.hvv.de (Hamburg Public Transport)

www.lostplaces.de (unusual and little-known architectural locations in Germany)

www.germany-tourism.co.uk (German Tourist Board)

www.germany.travel (German Tourist Board)

An old sign at the Hafenmuseum (see no. 7)

Acknowledgments

First and foremost I would like to thank my Viennese publisher, Christian Brandstätter Verlag, for realising the first edition of this book, especially Elisabeth Stein (commissioning editor), Else Rieger (editowr), Ekke Wolf (design), Brigitte Hilzensauer (German translation), and Helmut Maurer (maps).

For kind permission to take photographs, as well as for arranging access and the provision of information, the following people are most gratefully acknowledged:

Bettina Beermann (Museum für Hamburgische Geschichte); Beatlemania Hamburg; Jochen Binikowski & Ida Schneider (Buddel-Bini); Henrik Bodin (Schwedische Gustav-Adolfskirche); Gereon Boos (Harry's Hamburger Hafenbasar); Henning Bunte (St. Pauli Tourist Office); Jens Burg, Magusch Matthiesen & Annette Simbolon (Kaffeerösterei Burg); Prem Chand & Narinder Kumar Goswami (Hindu Temple); Martina Fähnemann, Peter Maass & Klaus Pidde (Hapag-Lloyd AG); Nicky Gardner & Susanne Kries (Hidden Europe); Heiko Gebertshan (Deutsches Maler- und Lackierer Museum); Michael Grube (Hamburger Unterwelten e.V.); Jan Haack (Museum der Arbeit); Jane Hale; David Hanowski (Hamburg Beatles Tour); Rahlf Hansen (Planetarium Hamburg); Hanni Heinrich; Vanessa Hirsch & Karin Funk (Altona Museum); Rainer Huke (Traditionsschiffhafen); Imam Ali Mosque and Islamisches Zentrum Hamburg; Internationales Maritimes Museum Hamburg; Irina von Jagow, Inka Lê-Hûu & Lina Nikou (Jüdischer Friedhof Altona); Käpt'n Schwarz Große Hafenrundfahrt; Thomas Kahlbom (Museum für Kommunikation); Marie Koehler & Ulrike Mann (Hotel Louis C. Jacob); Lars Küntzel (Walther Eisenburg der Mützenmacher); Uschi Lewen (Oevelgönner Seekiste); Cornelia Löw; Kerstin Maksen & Barjalai Nek Mohamad Pirzad (Afghan Museum); Michael Merkel & Karen Sczakeal (Helms-Museum); Kai Merten & Kathrin Blum; Petra Meyer (Spicy's Gewürzmeusem); Ina Mierig (Die venezianische Gondel); Heiko Möhle (Eine Welt Netzwerk Hamburg e.V.); Claudia Nast (Diekmann Restaurants/Restaurant Austernbar im Maritimen Museum Hamburg); Karl Niendorf (Montblanc); Ingrid & Rolf Osthues (Tropen Brendler); Kerstin Paatz (Helms Museum); Marianne Pieper & Marita Podczuck (Warburg-Haus/Aby-Warburg-Stiftung); Marek Pryjomko; Susanne Rölfer (Altonale); Reinhard P. Rauch (Old Commercial Room); Bernard Rausch (Hafenmuseum); Karin Rosenberg (Harry's Hamburger Hafenbasar); Uwe Scheer (Ernst Thälmann Gedenkstätte); Miriam Solomon (Jüdische Gemeinde in Hamburg); Speicherstadtmuseum; Uwe Sponnagel (Bonscheladen); Wattwagenfahrten Werner Stelling & Strand-Bazar (Cuxhaven-Sahlenburg); Navid Taghizadeh (Turm Bar); Kristin Teuchtmann; Ludger Trautmann; Heike Treffan (Schloss Bergedorf); Anne Volkmann (Rahimi Handel); Gunnar Wulf (Stadtteilarchiv Hamm); and Daniela Zeunig (Oberhafen-Kantine).

For accommodation, the staff at the Michaelis Hof and Hotel Bremer Hof.

For invaluable website support, Richard Tinkler, and for assistance in selecting the photographs, Bob Barber, Andreas Eberhart, and Simon Laffoley.

Thanks also to my great cousin James Dickinson for support, newspaper cuttings and bringing my work to a wider audience – his boundless enthusiasm has been both inspirational and infectious.

Finally, very special thanks to my father Trevor for inspiring me to track down unusual locations in the first place – thanks Dad for making it all such fun!

Hamburger Susanne Rölfer dressed up for the Altonale (see no. 58)

2ⁿᵈ Revised Edition published by The Urban Explorer, 2014
A division of Duncan J. D. Smith
contact@duncanjdsmith.com
www.onlyinguides.com
www.duncanjdsmith.com

First published by Christian Brandstätter Verlag, 2010

Graphic design: Stefan Fuhrer
Typesetting and picture editing: Ekke Wolf
Revision typesetting and picture editing: Franz Hanns
Maps: APA, Vienna
Printed and bound by GraphyCems, Spain

ISBN 978-3-9503662-1-1

Fresh herring at Altona's Sunday fish market (Fischmarkt)
(see no. 54)